LIBRARY IN A BOOK

TERRORISM

Harry Henderson

Facts On File, Inc.

TERRORISM

Facts On File, Inc.
11 Penn Plaza
New York, NY 10001

Library of Congress Cataloging-in-Publication Data
Henderson, Harry,
Terrorism / Harry Henderson.
p. cm.—(Library in a book)
Includes index.
ISBN 0-8160-4259-4
1. Terrorism—Research. I. Title. II. Series.
HV6431 H43 2001
303.6'25—dc21 00-059315

Facts On File books are available at special discounts when purchased in bulk quantities for businesses, associations, institutions or sales promotions. Please call our Special Sales Department in New York at 212/967-8800 or 800/322-8755.

You can find Facts On File on the World Wide Web at http://www.factsonfile.com.

Text design by Ron Monteleone
Illustrations by Dale Williams

Printed in the United States of America.

MP Hermitage 10 9 8 7 6 5 4 3 2 1

This book is printed on acid-free paper.

CONTENTS

PART III
APPENDICES

PART I

OVERVIEW OF THE TOPIC

CHAPTER 1

INTRODUCTION TO TERRORISM

Compared to many nations, particularly in the developing world, the United States suffers very little from terrorist attacks from either domestic or foreign sources. In the past decade a handful of major bombings have occurred, including the bombing of the World Trade Center in New York in 1993, the horrific attack on the federal building in Oklahoma City that took 168 lives in 1995, and a bombing in Atlanta during the 1996 Summer Olympics. Abroad, U.S. embassies in Kenya and Tanzania were bombed in 1998, killing 700 people (few of them U.S. citizens), and a U.S. Marine Corps barracks in Lebanon and other facilities have also been attacked. U.S. vulnerability to terrorism was further underscored by the October 12, 2000 attack that killed 17 sailors aboard the navy destroyer U.S.S. *Cole* in Aden Harbor.

While each of these attacks was a tragedy for the victims and their families, the annual toll taken by terrorism on U.S. citizens is typically measured in ones or dozens, not hundreds or thousands. And unless one is engaged in slightly riskier activity (such as diplomacy or high-profile business travel), the risk of any U.S. citizen being killed or kidnapped by a terrorist is much less than the risk of being killed by lightning.

Why, then, does terrorism create so much fear and anxiety in the United States? In part, it is because that is precisely what terrorism is designed to do. By striking without warning with bombs or by armed ambush, the terrorist is telling societies around the world that he or she has the power and ability to impose a state of fear at any time. Given enough terrorist attacks, fear turns into chronic insecurity and a loss of faith in one's government and institutions. In some parts of the world, such as Northern Ireland, the Middle East, and parts of Latin America, terrorism is not the sporadic action of possibly deranged individuals but part of a long-term strategy used by some groups in an attempt to force political change.

Military experts use the term "force multiplier" to refer to a factor (such as new weapons or improved communications) that increases the power and effectiveness of a military unit. Fear of terrorism has grown because of the possibility that terrorists may be acquiring force multipliers in the form of weapons of mass destruction, whether chemical, biological, or nuclear. Thus, although the overall rate of terrorist attacks declined through the 1990s, anxiety about terrorism remains high.

Coping with terrorism requires an understanding not only of terrorists' motivations and methods, but also of the relationship between terrorism and other forms of violence and of political change. This quest for understanding begins with an attempt to define just what one means by terrorism.

DEFINING TERRORISM

As with pornography, one's first impulse may be to say, "I may not be able to define it, but I know it when I see it." If a suicide bomb demolishes a city bus in Israel, an airliner is hijacked by people armed with machine pistols, or a cult releases deadly nerve gas into the Tokyo subway, virtually all observers will agree that a terrorist act has occurred.

In order to make laws about terrorism, one needs a legal definition. Here is the one used by the United States government:

> *The term "terrorism" means premeditated, politically motivated violence perpetrated against noncombatant targets by subnational groups or clandestine agents, usually intended to influence an audience.*
>
> *The term "international terrorism" means terrorism involving citizens or the territory of more than one country.*
>
> *The term "terrorist group" means any group practicing, or that has significant subgroups that practice, international terrorism.*[1]

The key parts of this definition are that the violence is motivated by political considerations, that it targets noncombatants (not soldiers engaged in military action), and that its perpetrators are not themselves part of a government.

Political analyst, security counselor, and White House adviser Brian Jenkins gives a somewhat expanded version of this definition of terrorism, noting that

> *All terrorist acts are crimes. Many would also be violations of the rules of war, if a state of war existed. All involve violence or the threat of violence, often coupled with specific demands. The targets are mainly civilians. The motives are political. The actions generally are designed to achieve maximum publicity. The perpetrators are usually members of an organized group, and unlike other criminals, they often claim credit for the act. (This is a true hall-*

> *mark of terrorism.) And, finally, it is intrinsic to a terrorist act that it is usually intended to produce psychological effects far beyond the immediate physical damage. One person's terrorist is everyone's terrorist.*[2]

The problem with these definitions is not that they are inaccurate, as far as they go, but that they are not complete enough to explain how terrorism relates to other forms of violence or to violent action by government itself. Although governments (which consider themselves to have a monopoly on legitimate force) never define their own actions as terrorism, many analysts speak also of "state terrorism" in describing, for example, the use of death squads by authoritarian Latin American governments to eliminate the political opposition. As noted by linguist and activist Noam Chomsky:

> *The term terrorism has come to be applied mainly to "retail terrorism" by individuals or groups. Whereas the term was once applied to Emperors who molest their own subjects and the world, now it is restricted to thieves who molest the powerful. Extricating ourselves from the system of indoctrination, we will use the term 'terrorism' to refer to the threat or use of violence to intimidate or coerce (generally for political ends), whether it is the wholesale terrorism of the Emperor or the retail terrorism of the thief.*[3]

The discussion of terrorism, then, must encompass not only political violence initiated by groups fighting against governments, but also terroristic actions taken by governments themselves. That is because while the focus of this and most books on terrorism is on the acts of terrorist groups, the context for understanding these acts must include the response of the target government and in turn, the effects of that response on the political climate of the society.

Terrorism versus War

If war has been described as politics by other means, is terrorism simply war by other means? Or can terrorism be distinguished from war? Both war and terrorism, after all, can create innocent victims. As Brian Jenkins notes: "Although we may make moral distinctions between dropping bombs on a city from 20,000 feet and car bombs driven into embassies by suicidal terrorists, the world may not share that fine distinction."[4]

Some argue that the only difference between war and terrorism is that war kills a lot more people, and wars are fought by governments. This seems simplistic, however. In the international legal system that has developed in the past century, wars are supposed to be fought according to certain rules. One expert in the field states the following:

> *The fundamental principle underlying the whole structure of the international humanitarian law applicable in armed conflicts is that belligerents shall not inflict on their adversaries harm out of proportion to the legitimate goals of warfare . . . for instance, that belligerents shall not kill their prisoners for, having captured them, they have to that extent weakened the military forces of the enemy, and killing them would add nothing to this result. [this implies that]*
> *(1) distinction shall be made at all times between belligerents and civilian populations; (2) the civilian population, as well as objects of civilian character, shall not be made the object of deliberate attacks; (3) in attacking military objectives, any unreasonable damage to the civilian population and objects of civilian character shall be avoided; (4) no weapons or other means and methods of warfare shall be used which are calculated to cause unnecessary or otherwise excessive suffering.*[5]

These laws are clearly not observed by terrorists. It can be argued that terrorist violence is not "out of proportion" to its goals, because the goals of terrorism are different from those of warfare. Both the terrorists and the military want to force their opponents to submit to certain demands. The military accomplishes this by destroying the opponents' ability to resist or by making it clear that the costs to the enemy of continuing to resist are worse than those of accepting the terms offered for surrender. The terrorist, however, does not have the means to destroy the government's ability to resist, but only, perhaps, to destroy the people's willingness to back the government by creating a demoralizing fear. Thus most militaries do not want to kill prisoners, not only because doing so is felt to be dishonorable and it does not further weaken the enemy force, but also because one wants one's own soldiers not to be killed after they are captured. The terrorist, on the other hand, may choose to kill because doing so heightens the fear effect that he or she is trying to achieve.

Attacking civilians or causing unnecessary damage is supposed to be avoided in war. Many militaries, including that of the United States, have *generally* avoided deliberately attacking civilians, but even here there have been exceptions, such as the massacre at My Lai during the Vietnam War. But despite the claims made for "smart weapons," which can supposedly distinguish between civilian and military buildings, in cases such as the U.S. bombing of Serbia in 1999, deciding to conduct such attacks implies willingness to accept some amount of "collateral damage" (damage to other areas than the intended target) and killing of civilians.

Therefore, the difference between war and terrorism is not always one of effect, but of goals and purposes. The killing of civilians may be an accidental outcome of war, but it is often viewed as necessary by the terrorist.

TERRORISM AND REVOLUTION

Terrorists and revolutionaries are both seeking radical political change. While some revolutions target mainly the government they are trying to overthrow and its facilities and military forces, others are less discriminating. (Indeed, even the American Revolution, which is often looked upon as a relatively chivalrous battle between redcoats and bluecoats, included considerable terrorism against British loyalists on the part of colonists who supported the revolt.)

Further, doctrines of revolution such as those that spring from Marxism-Leninism actually see a role for terror as part of the revolutionary process. Leon Trotsky noted the following:

> *A victorious war, generally speaking, destroys only an insignificant part of the conquered army, intimidating the remainder and breaking their will. The revolution works in the same way: it kills individuals, and intimidates thousands. In this sense, the Red Terror is not distinguishable from the armed insurrection of which it is the direct continuation.*[6]

There are, however, some distinctions that can be made between terrorism and revolution. Revolution generally implies an activity that is more focused, broader based, and more systematic than terrorism. A revolution (as distinguished from a mere coup) implies some base of support and some ability to create a new government to replace the old. However, an earlier terrorist campaign may create the conditions for revolution (which is indeed the hope of most terrorists), and a revolution may be accompanied by terrorist acts, either incidentally or by policy.

TERRORISM AND GUERRILLA WARFARE

If the relationship of terrorism to revolutions seems difficult to pin down, the distinction between terrorism and guerrilla (or "unconventional") warfare is even more problematic. According to the U.S. military, this type of warfare consists of the following:

> *A broad spectrum of military and paramilitary operations conducted in enemy-held, enemy-controlled, or politically sensitive territory. Unconventional warfare includes, but is not limited to, the interrelated fields of guerrilla warfare, evasion and escape, subversion, sabotage, and other operations of a low visibility, covert or clandestine nature. These interrelated aspects of unconventional warfare may be prosecuted singly or collectively by predominately indigenous personnel, usually supported and directed by (an) external source(s) during all conditions of war or peace.*[7]

In the latter part of the 20th century, guerrilla operations aimed at established governments were common, particularly in Latin America and Africa. These conflicts have frequently included such actions as the burning of villages, assassinations of government officials such as local mayors, and even wholesale massacres. Viewed in themselves, these are certainly terrorist acts. According to an expert on guerrilla warfare:

> *To claim that guerrilla [warfare] is necessarily coupled with terrorism is certainly grossly inaccurate. A number of important guerrilla movements steadily refused to resort to terrorism . . . And yet . . . The fact is that most of the contemporary guerrilla movements either habitually, or at various stages of their activities, use terrorism, at least as a form of revolutionary tactics.*[8]

Nevertheless, while guerrillas often use terrorism (and governments, in turn, use terroristic tactics against guerrillas and the people who may be supporting them), guerrilla organizations are different from typical terrorist groups. While guerrillas generally conduct raids rather than seek pitched battles, they are equipped similarly to regular light military units, and they usually have military weapons such as mortars, rocket launchers, heavy machine guns, or even light artillery. They view themselves as soldiers under military-style discipline. Guerrilla forces may number from hundreds to thousands, and to be successful, they must be supported by a significant number of people who provide supplies and often concealment, whether because they share the guerrillas' objectives or because they fear retaliation. Although guerrillas frequently also depend on outside help (particularly for heavy weapons and military advisers), they have ties to the indigenous community.

In conducting their war, guerrillas sometimes do observe at least an approximation of the laws of war that are supposed to govern conventional armies. They can take and exchange prisoners or negotiate with enemy commanders.

Terrorist groups, on the other hand, are typically small (tens or at most, hundreds). Their typical actions are bombings, ambushes, assassinations, hijackings, and kidnappings. Their weapons of choice are the homemade bomb and the automatic pistol. Many terrorist groups have little support from or interaction with the surrounding population. They are not organized along military lines, but typically in small cells. (See "How Terrorist Groups Work" for an explanation of cells.) Their demands and negotiations are for things like ransoms, safe passage, or the freeing of imprisoned comrades.

These distinctions appear in sharp relief when one compares, for example, the Vietcong of the 1960s or the Afghani resistance fighters of the early 1980s with a group like the Weathermen of the early 1970s or even the German Red Army Faction of about the same period. But as noted above, guerrillas sometimes use terrorist tactics, and it becomes rather pointless to try to determine whether a group such as Peru's Shining Path is a terrorist or a guerrilla organization.

STATE TERRORISM

As we have noted, governments themselves have often used terrorist-style tactics against their opponents, including killing, torture, or kidnapping followed by "disappearance." The most devastating state terror comes when an ideological faction controls a totalitarian state and targets its political enemies for virtual extermination. For example, the Chinese Cultural Revolution under Mao Zedong beginning in the mid-1960s and the regime of Cambodian dictator Pol Pot starting in the mid-1970s represented radical attempts to reshape society by any means necessary. Millions of real or suspected political enemies were killed, "reeducated," or dispossessed. Eventually such movements end because they destroy the ability of society to sustain itself, or provoke reactions such as the Vietnamese invasion of Cambodia in 1979.

State terrorism can be more subtle when it is part of an ongoing struggle between a regime and insurgent forces. It is frequently a "chicken-and-egg" question whether state terrorism is a response to provocation by insurgent terrorists or guerrillas, or a basic policy that itself creates the conditions for insurgency.

One thing is clear: the state terrorism of the 20th century, from Hitler, Stalin, and Mao to the death squads of Argentina and Guatemala, has killed many more people than nongovernmental terrorist groups have. Of course, this does not justify the latter terror, but is part of the context needed to understand it.

THE DEVELOPMENT OF MODERN TERRORISM

The use of terror is evident as far back as history has been recorded. The massacre of the inhabitants of a captured city was a common feature of warfare until the last few centuries. A would-be conqueror could expedite conquest by proclaiming that cities that refused to yield immediately would be razed and their inhabitants killed. In battle, most casualties were inflicted only after one side broke and ran. The conduct of politics via assassinations was also commonplace and resulted, for example, in the short terms of office of many later Roman emperors.

Nongovernmental groups also practiced early forms of terrorism. The word *assassin,* for example, derives from the name of a 13th-century Islamic sect that is said to have partaken of hashish before carrying out stabbing attacks on its political enemies. Other cultures, too, have had groups of stealthy killers, such as Japan's ninjas.

REVOLUTION AND STATE

While terror may have been common in the ancient and medieval world, the idea of terrorism as a political tactic can be traced to the late 18th century, the beginning of the modern age of revolutions, when terror was systematically linked to political philosophies. French revolutionaries such as Robespierre embraced terror as a tool for political transformation as part of a total revolution in society.

> *One of the original justifications for terror was that man would be totally reconstructed; one didn't have to worry about the kinds of means one was using because the reconstruction itself would be total and there would be no lingering after-effects. . . . [Modern] terrorism was initiated by people who had millennial expectations, who expected the world to be utterly transformed.*[9]

To assert, as the American colonists and then the French did, that the individual has "inalienable" rights is to suggest that extreme means may be necessary to secure or preserve those rights. Insurgents who felt themselves sufficiently justified could view terror as a means to attaining the transcendent value of liberty. States such as revolutionary France (and in the 20th century, revolutionary Russia) could also embrace terror, claiming that it was necessary in order to preserve the revolution. As early as 1790, a British conservative, Edmund Burke, referred to the new French government as "the reign of terror."

TERRORISM AND ANARCHY

During the 19th century, several forces led to the development of terrorist groups in Europe (particularly Russia) and to a lesser extent, in the United States. The ideas of political democracy and liberalism were spreading. But at the same time, industrialization was displacing large masses of people from the rural economy to the factory, where harsh and exploitative working conditions were typical. When workers tried to organize to demand better conditions, the response was often brutal suppression by the government, the employer's private police, or both.

One response to this situation was Karl Marx's development of the idea of socialism. In socialism, the people would own and benefit from the means of production. Marx saw an inherent struggle between workers and capitalists that could only be resolved by a gradual process of revolution. He did not advocate individual acts of terrorism, but rather thought in terms of a mass movement.

Another group known as anarchists sought more immediate and radical change. Anarchists focused not on the mass but on the individual. They did not trust any government. Some anarchists believed in using only peaceful means. Others, such as the Russian Peter Kropotkin, promoted universal anarchist revolution carried out through violence. He also proclaimed a key idea of modern terrorism, the "propaganda of the deed." This meant that rather than just issuing proclamations that could be ignored by opponents and the general public, the revolutionary would do things that could not be ignored—such as setting off bombs. Kropotkin also recognized, as modern terrorists do, that the media is an extremely necessary and useful tool, because it disseminates news about the terrorists' deeds and hence amplifies their terrifying effect. The early terrorists also knew that some stories would be bigger than others. Thus the German-American anarchist Johan Most observed as early as the 1880s that "Everyone now knows, for example, that the more highly placed the one shot or blown up, and the more perfectly executed the attempt, the greater the propagandistic effect."[10]

Another anarchist, Karl Heinzen, a German, was even more explicit in his tactics. When the European revolutions of 1848 failed to dislodge conservative governments, he concluded that revolutionaries could not successfully confront the government directly. Instead, they had to create chaotic, confused conditions that would paralyze authorities. The method he recommended for achieving this goal was widespread, indiscriminate use of bombs. In Russia, bombing and assassination became a persistent tactic of anarchists seeking to overthrow the czar.

Awakening Nationalism

The early 20th century saw the awakening of many nationalist impulses. For example, many Jews began to embrace Zionism and its vision of a Jewish state in Palestine. Many of the Arab peoples in the Middle East developed a stronger sense of their own nationhood. Both sides began to rebel against British colonialism. Some of that rebellion began to take the form of terrorism. Similarly, ethnic minorities that had been kept in a second-class position in their own land, such as Irish Catholics, began to develop revolutionary or terrorist organizations. Meanwhile, the Soviet Union began to organize a network of communist parties in many countries, which all sought a "proletarian revolution."

POSTCOLONIALISM AND THE COLD WAR

Following World War II, Britain and France, while part of the victorious alliance, had been seriously weakened economically. They did not have the strength both to rebuild and to vigorously defend their overseas colonies. Indigenous populations throughout what became known as the Third World were desperately poor, while European elites controlled most of the countries' wealth and resources. A combination of instability, desperation, and democratic ideals led to the emergence of popular uprisings, often taking forms ranging from sporadic terrorism to large-scale guerrilla warfare. For example, the Islamic population in France's colony of Algeria began a bloody struggle for independence in the 1950s.

In Latin America, where most nations were already independent, the struggle took a different form. From Mexico south to Chile, most countries were ruled by some form of oligarchy in which an elite of established families and wealthy industrialists controlled most of the national wealth. There too, guerrilla groups, usually inspired by communist or socialist ideas, took up arms against the governments.

The Cold War between the United States and the western democracies on one side and the Soviet Union and the communist bloc on the other inevitably became bound up in the postcolonial struggles. Communism offered an appealing alternative to the desperately poor. To contain it, the United States tended to support the oligarchs who promised to keep order and protect the investments of U.S. and other foreign corporations. In the 1970s, Noam Chomsky told U.S. citizens the following:

> *The military juntas of Latin America and Asia are our juntas. Many of them were directly installed by us or are the beneficiaries of our direct intervention, and most of the others came into existence with our tacit support, using military equipment and training supplied by the United States. . . . Terror in these states is functional, improving the "investment climate," at least in the short run, and U.S. aid to terror-prone states . . . is positively related to terror and improvement of investment climate and negatively related to human rights.*[11]

Meanwhile, the Soviet Union offered weapons, training, and advisers to the rebel groups. (After the reunification of Germany in 1990, it was revealed that the East German intelligence service had secretly funded many of the leftist terrorist groups in western Europe.) In the Western Hemisphere, the overthrow of the Cuban government by Fidel Castro in 1960 offered the Soviets a base from which to encourage leftist revolutions and guerrilla wars throughout Central and South America.

The "proxy war" of terrorism and rebellion offered practical advantages to leaders on both sides of the Iron Curtain. As one observer has noted, "the truth is, at a time when it is difficult to mobilize great masses of people without provoking a global conflict with irreparable damage, terrorism tends to become more and more a substitute for war."[12]

According to terrorism expert Walter Laqueur, the Cold War created a crescendo of terrorism around the world:

> *Multinational terrorism reached its climax in the early 1970s, involving close cooperation between small terrorist groups in many countries, with the Libyans, the Algerians, the North Koreans and the Cubans acting as paymasters, suppliers of weapons and other equipment as well as coordinators. . . . The Soviet Union supported a number of terrorist movements such as some Palestinians and African groups and the exile Croats; mostly such assistance would be given through intermediaries so that its origins would be difficult to prove and any charges of complicity could be indignantly denied."*[13]

Two of the world's most persistent hotbeds of terrorism can also be described as legacies of colonialism. In the Middle East, contradictory British colonial policies begun during World War I had set Jews and Palestinians on a collision with each others' interests. After Israel had repeatedly demonstrated its military strength, Islamic extremists turned to terrorism as a weapon against the Jewish state and its American and European allies. Northern Ireland, too, was essentially a colony created by British policy since the 16th century. Some members of the Catholic population, frustrated by their lack of rights and economic opportunity, turned to terrorism and the Irish Republican Army (IRA) in the 1970s.

Often joined with ideology, nationalism and ethnicity can provide a powerful bond that can sustain terrorist activity by denying ambiguity or the possible humanity of the opponent. As an Irish observer, Ed Cairns of the University of Ulster, has noted:

> *The practice of dividing people into "us" and "them" is so deeply ingrained that it's almost unconscious. It's as if there's a computer in the back of the head of every person who lives in Northern Ireland that's programmed to work out what side another person is on.*[14]

Thus the wellsprings of later 20th century terrorism are complex, deriving from the struggle against colonialism, the inspiration of communist or socialist ideology, and the bonds of nationalism, ethnicity, and religion. Often these factors are mixed together in the same movement. The IRA, for example, sometimes used marxist rhetoric, yet represented an ethnic group that was defined in part by religion.

TERRORISM IN THE WESTERN DEMOCRACIES

Terrorist and revolutionary activity were not confined to the developing nations (Third World), however. The 1960s also saw a leftist movement, mostly on the part of intellectuals and students, in both Western Europe and the United States. In France, the movement also spread to the working class, while in the United States, despite the efforts of activists, it remained confined mainly to the student antiwar effort, the civil rights movements, and black and brown power movements.

Groups such as Germany's Red Army Faction, France's Action Directe, and Italy's Red Brigades based their ideology on Marxism-Leninism, emphasizing action against the government and capitalists in urban population centers. From roughly 1970 to the mid-1980s, they carried on extensive bombing campaigns as well as some shootings and kidnappings. In the United States, groups such as the Weathermen and New World Liberation Front carried on similar activities, but on a smaller scale.

From the mid-1980s through the 1990s, the focus of terrorism in the western democracies seemed to shift from the Left to the Right. As Walter Laqueur observes:

> *Left-wing ideology was virtually all-pervasive in the 1970s, and this was reflected in the propaganda of nationalist groups such as the IRA, the Basque separatist group ETA, and the Palestinian terrorists—for example in anti-imperialist slogans and calls for working-class solidarity, and so on. . . .*
>
> *During the 1980s, left-wing terrorism petered out, a trend that coincided with the collapse of the Soviet bloc, though it was not caused by the collapse. Instead, the terrorist initiative in Western countries such as the United States, and also Germany and Turkey, moved to the extreme right. Yesterday's theories about the progressive character of terrorism ceased to make sense and became, in fact, embarrassing. The burning of a hostel housing foreign guest workers in Germany could hardly be described any longer as a liberating act. Neither could the bombing of the World Trade Center in New York or the bombing of a government building in Oklahoma City be interpreted as a prologue to a revolution that would help the masses. The old wisdom about one person's terrorist being another person's freedom fighter was no longer heard.*[15]

In the future, terrorism may come from both the Right and Left in response to economic globalism. The Left opposes the control of the world's economic resources by multinational corporations and decries what it sees as the inability of democratic governments to hold the economic behemoths accountable. The Right views globalism in the form of the United Nations and other institutions as a threat to the sovereignty of countries, regions, and localities. Extremists on both sides have shown their willingness to use violence in order to be heard.

WHO IS THE TERRORIST?

Although the ideologies and motives that inspire terrorism and the role of terrorism in particular conflicts differ considerably, scholars have tried to identify some more or less universal characteristics of terrorists and the structure and operation of terrorist groups.

As David Rapoport notes, the terrorist is someone who has made decisions about issues that trouble us and confronts us with more than just the fact of violence:

> *The terrorist acts in an environment where the society has a good deal of ambivalence about the cause the terrorist is concerned with. Society is unwilling to come to grips with the cause the terrorist is proposing, but will ignore the cause unless it finds it cannot do so. What the terrorist does is indicate that he is willing to die or sacrifice himself for the cause. . . . One problem with contemporary definitions of terrorism, because they focus on the killing, is that they really can't see why somebody like the IRA, for example, would engage in hunger strikes; how that really performs the same functions, and even performs it better than killing does sometimes. . . . Whether the violence is inflicted on oneself or on others, it's the striking character of the act which, first of all, calls attention and secondly . . . galvanizes latent emotions.*[16]

Most people who are not pure pacifists can visualize some conditions under which they would use force to resist or change what they consider to be intolerable conditions. As Douglas Pike has concluded:

> *What seems more to the point is not language but thought pattern, world view, philosophy of politics . . . what are the limits of force, irrational violence, terror, in that ascending order, in bringing about social change? All of us fall somewhere along this force-violence-terror continuum. Toward one end are those who believe that less rather than more is justified; toward the other are those who advocate more on grounds of imperative need or as principle . . .*[17]

However, where terrorists have chosen to place themselves on the continuum of violence is a product of personality and psychology as well as commitment to ideology. According to political sociologist I. L. Horowitz's study of the biographies of terrorists, one can draw some general conclusions about the attitudes of people who engage in terrorism, and the beliefs or expectations they have about the results of their actions:

1. *A terrorist is a person engaged in politics who makes little if any distinction between strategy and tactics on one hand, and principles on the other. . . .*
2. *A terrorist is a person prepared to surrender his own life for a cause considered transcendent in value. . . .*
3. *A terrorist is a person who possesses both a self-fulfilling prophetic element and a self-destructive element*
4. *A terrorist is a person for whom all events are volatile and none are determined. . . .*
5. *A terrorist is a person who is (a) young; (b) most often of middle class family background; (c) usually male; and (d) economically marginal. . . .*
6. *A terrorist performs his duties as an avocation. . . .*
7. *The terrorist distinguishes himself from the casual homicide in several crucial respects: he murders systematically rather than at random; he is symbolic rather than passionate . . . and his actions are usually well planned rather than spontaneous. Terrorism is thus primarily a sociological phenomenon; whereas homicide can be more easily interpreted in psychological terms. . . .*
8. *The terrorist by definition is a person who does not distinguish between coercion and terrorism because he lacks access to the coercive mechanisms of the state.*
9. *A terrorist is a person who, through the act of violence, advertises and dramatizes a wider discontent. . . .*
10. *A terrorist believes that the act of violence will encourage the uncommitted public to withdraw support from a regime or institution, and hence make wider revolutionary acts possible by weakening the resolve of the opposition.*
11. *A terrorist may direct his activities against the leadership of the opposition by assassinating presidents and power holders. . . . Other terrorists may direct their activities against the symbols of establishment and agencies. . . .*
12. *A terrorist does not have a particularly well-defined ideological persuasion.*[18]

An important part of a terrorist's psychology is the attitude toward the group. As is well known, being in a group can add a dimension of intensity to any activity. In speaking of revolutionary groups, Arthur Koestler makes an observation that is equally applicable to terrorists:

> *The total identification of the individual with the group makes him unselfish in more than one sense. . . . It makes him perform comradely, altruistic,*

heroic actions—to the point of self-sacrifice—and at the same time behave with ruthless cruelty toward the enemy or victim of the group. In other words, the self-assertive behavior of the group is based on the self-transcending behavior of its members, which often entails sacrifice of personal interests and even of life in the interest of the group. To put it simply: the egotism of the group feeds on the altruism of its members.[19]

HOW TERRORIST GROUPS WORK

The terrorist group may offer psychological reinforcement to the individual, but it also serves more immediately practical purposes. Although individuals (such as Theodore Kaczynski, the Unabomber, or Oklahoma City bombers Timothy McVeigh and Terry Nichols) can strike grievous blows, a sustained terrorist campaign requires organization and resources.

According to counterterrorism specialist James Fraser, a terrorist group is organized something like a pyramid. At the very top are a few leaders who make the overall policy and plans. Below them is a somewhat larger group of terrorists who actually carry out attacks. This is called the *active cadre.* Members of the active cadre often specialize in particular activities, such as intelligence or surveillance, bomb-making, or communications. The next lower and broader level of the pyramid is composed of the "active supporters." These people are crucial for the sustained operation of the terrorist campaign, because they provide intelligence and warning, weapons and supplies, communications, transportation, and safe houses. Finally, there is a diffuse group of "passive supporters" who agree with the goals of the terrorist group, help spread their ideas, and provide money and other support.

The neatness of this organizational scheme is somewhat misleading, however. Most terrorist groups are small, with fewer than 50 members. The same individuals may play several roles or shift rapidly from one role to another. Most terrorist groups receive little public support, and so don't have access to the resources needed to mount a major campaign.

Terrorist groups face very difficult challenges. First of all, they have to keep their members' identity and/or whereabouts secret. After all, the police or army generally have more than enough force to overwhelm any terrorists they can locate. Since the 19th century, terrorists have used a specialized structure that seeks to preserve secrecy. The active terrorists are divided into groups of about five people, called cells. Each cell is usually organized for a particular role, such as tactical assault or intelligence. Generally the members of a cell do not know anyone outside the cell. Communications are maintained by the cell leader, who might communicate with only one other cell leader. When an operation is planned, leaders can link several cells together operationally into a "column," so that intelligence, support, and combat functions can be brought to bear.

The cell system seeks to preserve secrecy by limiting the amount of information authorities can learn. If a cell member is captured and interrogated, he or she ideally knows only the identities of other people in the same cell. But the same compartmentalization that serves secrecy also makes communication within, and coordination of, the group very difficult. If something in an operation starts to go wrong, or the police mount a raid or sweep, it may be hard to alert the group members to abort or change the operation or to evacuate and go into hiding.

Especially in a large group such as the Provisional Irish Republican Army, because most members lack direct access to the leadership, they cannot always verify the authenticity of orders or give feedback to the leaders. It is fairly easy for one or a few leaders and the chain of command that reports to them to splinter or split off, creating a new faction.

Compared to soldiers in a conventional military unit, members of a terrorist group may individually have high morale (indeed, the impetus of fanaticism can go beyond normal morale). But the terrorist group usually lacks the systematic discipline and training of a military unit, even if it calls itself an army and adopts military nomenclature.

TERRORISM AS COMMUNICATION

Given the importance to terrorists that their actions "send a message" that will compel opponents to respond, students of communications theory can usefully examine terrorism from the perspective of the problems with successful communication. Thus Philip A. Karber suggests the following:

> *As a symbolic act, terrorism can be analyzed much like other mediums of communication, consisting of four basic components: transmitter (terrorist), intended recipient (target), message (bombing, ambush) and feed-back (reaction of target). The terrorist's message of violence necessitates a victim, whether personal or institutional, but the target or intended recipient of the communication may not be the victim. . . . Terrorism is subject to many of the same pathologies and disruptions suffered by more conventional forms of communication. These include lack of fidelity in the medium of transmission (the choice of victim conveys wrong message to target), background noise (competing events obscure the message), target distortion (recipient misinterprets the meaning of the one signal and fails to regulate output to changing circumstances or target feedback). . . .*
>
> *However, if terrorism is to be conceived of as "propaganda of the deed," we must devise a content analysis of symbolic violence.*[20]

The relationship between terrorism and the media is complex, of course. The media is not simply a mirror or even a passive amplifier; it both reflects and shapes the public response. The public response to terror is usually begins with shock and rage and continues with a demand that something be done to prevent future attacks. Thus following the 1995 Oklahoma City bombing, public anxiety and outrage were translated in a year or so into the passage by Congress of an antiterrorism act that gave the government new legal tools and correspondingly diminished civil liberties. And while a venerable strategy of terrorists is to provoke the government into repressive measures in the hope that this in turn will cause unrest or revolt, this strategy has more often than not backfired, resulting in the destruction of the terrorists themselves.

COUNTERTERRORISM

Counterterrorism can be defined as the attempt to prevent terrorism or at least reduce its frequency and severity. Understanding the terrorist's psychology, motivations, and goals is an important part of this effort. Another part is the use of intelligence, including surveillance, eavesdropping, informers, and devices to detect bombs and weapons, such as those in airports.

The counterterrorist must face the fact that our modern society provides the terrorist with both new methods of operation and new vulnerabilities to exploit. To give some examples:

- Cell phones free the terrorist from the need to use a pay phone or a possibly tapped land line.
- Using readily available encryption programs, terrorist communications can be given the protection once only available to the Central Intelligence Agency (CIA) and the KGB, the Soviet secret police.
- As terrorists discovered in the 1960s, the modern airliner is a flying can full of potential hostages who are isolated from immediate help, and it's also a potential getaway vehicle for the terrorists.
- Modern society is vitally dependent on infrastructure: Everything from water supply and power to transportation, communication, and information systems. A properly placed plastic explosive—or a computer virus—can cause damage far greater than the effort expended.

INTELLIGENCE

The first line of defense against terrorists is the attempt to find out who they are and what they are up to. This can be done through eavesdropping or monitoring telephone or computer communication, giving rewards for information, sending undercover agents to infiltrate terrorist groups, or using paid informants. Controls on financial transactions can be used to discourage money laundering or illicit funds transfers.

These tactics are sometimes effective. The larger a terrorist group becomes, the less secrecy it can preserve, the less effectively it can screen potential recruits, and thus the easier it is to infiltrate. However, the most deadly terrorist groups are often the small ones that become widely known only after they have blown up something. Correspondingly, many of the groups the FBI infiltrated in the 1970s were not terrorists but radical political groups. The routine monitoring of political groups without a legal warrant based on evidence of a specific crime raises serious First Amendment and privacy issues. So does the use of routine surveillance or monitoring of communications by government supercomputers. The attempt of the Clinton administration to seriously restrict the use of publicly available computer encryption programs during the mid-1990s (which ultimately failed), pitted the ability to uncover evidence of terrorist activity against the right of privacy. (See Chapter 3 for more about civil liberties issues involved with terrorism.)

The issues that arise in counterterrorism often seem to be technical or limited in application. But, as Secretary of Defense William Cohen noted, if U.S. citizens decide they need and want more security against terrorism:

> *your liberty suddenly starts to get infringed upon. And this is the real challenge for a free society: How do you reconcile the threats that are likely to come in the future with the inherent and the constitutional protections that we have as far as the right of privacy? Right now, we have yet to contend with this. We haven't faced up to it.*[21]

Cohen went on to argue that thinking through the restrictions we can live with and implementing them today might prevent a future terrorist disaster that could panic U.S. citizens into giving up their liberties wholesale. But libertarians believe that there will always be crises and further demands, and that each time a freedom is given up it sets a precedent that can be extended elsewhere.

HARDENING THE TARGET

If the government's intelligence services cannot uncover a pending attack, perhaps the target can be made difficult for the terrorist to penetrate. This generally means the installation of detection or screening systems. But what do you protect, and how much? Counterterrorists (and the governments they work for) don't have unlimited resources. Spending money to guard against one thing means not having it to use against something else.

The issue of airport security is a classic example of this dilemma. The 1988 bombing of an airliner over Lockerbie, Scotland, triggered widespread calls for the strengthening of security measures designed to stop terrorists from bringing bombs or weapons aboard planes. In tests conducted by the U.S. Federal Aviation Administration (FAA) in 1993 and 1996, the proportion of undercover testers who were able to breach airport security had declined from 75 percent to 40 percent. While that shows some improvement, it also suggests that U.S. airports are still rather vulnerable to determined terrorists. The explosion aboard TWA flight 800 off Long Island, New York, in 1996 led to a new wave of demands and proposals for heightened security—even though investigators eventually concluded that the plane had probably been destroyed by a design flaw in its center fuel tank.

Strengthening security could take the form of improved training for airport personnel, in addition to the deployment of new technology. For example, a scanning device called the CTX 5000, deployed in some airports in the late 1990s, uses the same three-dimensional imaging technique as a hospital CAT scan, making it much easier to identify weapons or other suspicious objects. Other devices under development will be able to chemically "sniff" for vapors given off by explosives.

However, there are prices to be paid for such new advances in both cost and convenience. The new detectors are still very expensive. Another proposal, requiring that every bag be matched to verify that its owner is on board, would deter those terrorists who are not suicidal but could cause substantial delays. In many airports in Europe and the Middle East, passengers go through not one or two screenings but a dozen or more. It is unlikely that U.S. travelers, who place such a premium on convenience and speed, would accept such a situation.

The practice of using "profiles" (sets of characteristics that correlate with a "typical" terrorist) raises important questions. While the specific criteria used are kept secret, some obvious examples might include origin, destination, and method of payment (cash payment considered suspicious). However, representatives of ethnic groups frequently associated in the public mind with terrorism (such as Arab-Americans) have suggested that ethnicity is being used implicitly as a criterion, although authorities deny this.

DETERRENCE

It is also possible that even if some terrorist attacks can neither be detected nor physically stopped, the consequences to the terrorists can be made sufficiently unpleasant to discourage future attacks. Cooperation with other nations to investigate, arrest, and extradite suspected terrorists can make terrorism a riskier activity, but it can be difficult for nations to agree on just who should be considered a terrorist and who a possible political refugee.

Another way to deter terrorism is to strike at the nations that sponsor it. The United States has done this on a number of occasions. In 1999, for example, President Bill Clinton ordered cruise missile attacks against a pharmaceutical factory in Sudan said to be involved with chemical weapons production and against Osama bin Laden's terrorist base camps in Afghanistan. But such military responses are often of limited effectiveness because individual terrorists can spread out into the countryside. Intelligence about targets can be wrong: the factory in Sudan appears to have been making only pharmaceuticals, after all. The killing of innocent people in such attacks can also arouse the very anger against the United States that motivates terrorism.

TERRORISM AND FOREIGN POLICY

At the beginning of the 21st century, U.S. leaders began to refer to the country as "the world's only superpower." Can the United States reduce terrorism by working to change social conditions that create the despair that leads to desperate deeds? This would seem to make sense, but the world's economic, social, and demographic imbalances are not easy to fix. Others suggest that if the United States wants to get out of the terrorist crosshairs, it should disengage from the world:

> *The best way to lessen the chances of an attack that could cause hundreds of thousands or even millions of casualties is to eliminate the motive for such an attack. Terrorists attack U.S. targets because they perceive that the United States is a hegemonic superpower that often intervenes in the affairs of other nations and groups. Both President Clinton and the Defense Science Board admit that there is a correlation between U.S. involvement in international situations and acts of terrorism directed against the United States. The board also noted that the spread of WMD [weapons of mass destruction] technology and the increased willingness of terrorists to inflict mass casualties have made such an attack more likely.*[22]

While it may be true that the United States would experience less terrorism if it "minded its own business," others would say that the benefits of peacekeeping operations outweigh the risks.

THE NEW TERRORISM?

Statistically, the news about terrorism improved during the 1990s. Indeed, one expert noted in 1997 that "Terrorist incidents, both domestic and international, have fallen to levels not seen since the 1970s. Whether measured by the number of incidents, the number of fatalities, or the number of groups, raw statistics demonstrate that the level of terrorist violence has declined since the mid-1980s."[23]

However, the disturbing possibility exists that while terrorist attacks may be fewer in the future, they may also be both less predictable and more deadly. Walter Laqueur points to what he calls a "new terrorism" that is distinguished from traditional terrorism in both motives and methods. (Other writers call it "superterrorism.") According to Laqueur:

> *Traditional terrorism, whether of the separatist or the ideological (left or right) variety, had political and social aims, such as gaining independence, getting rid of foreigners, or establishing a new social order. Such terrorist groups aimed at forcing concessions, sometimes far-reaching concessions, from their antagonists. The new terrorism is different in character, aiming not at clearly defined political demands but at the destruction of society and the elimination of large sections of the population. In its most extreme form, this new terrorism intends to liquidate all satanic forces, which may include the majority of a country or of mankind, as a precondition for the growth of another, better, and in any case different breed of human. In its maddest, most extreme form it may aim at the destruction of all life on earth, as the ultimate punishment for mankind's crimes.*[24]

While fears that terrorists motivated by religious fanaticism would seek to bring about an apocalypse or Armageddon at the millennium proved unfounded, groups such as Japan's Aum Shinri Kyo cult show that the potential exists. And the same fanaticism that cults such as the Branch Davidians or Heaven's Gate brought to their self-immolation could be as easily turned to the destruction of others.

The Terrorism of Mass Destruction

The new terrorism of fanatics poses difficult problems for counterterrorism. Because such groups are not interested in political gains or such things as money or the freedom of prisoners, negotiation with them can be fruitless. And according to Canadian strategic analyst Ron Purver,

> *What makes these groups especially dangerous is that they may not be constrained by some of the political disincentives—fear of alienating potential supporters or of unleashing massive government retribution, etc.—that may have operated in the past in the case of more traditional terrorist groups.*[25]

The other problem is the potential availability of weapons of mass destruction—chemical, biological, or even nuclear. With such weapons any terrorist attack can be an unprecedented disaster. The decline in the number of attacks would be of little comfort in such a case.

Chemical weapons are clearly available to terrorist groups, either through "homebrew" means or rogue states. In Japan, Aum Shinri Kyo deliberately focused on recruiting people with the necessary technical skills for its 1995 poison gas attack on the Tokyo subway, and it explored a range of chemical, biological, and even radiological options. It is reported that Hezbollah terrorists are compiling information on how to produce chemical agents as well as stockpiling protective gear.

The story is much the same with biological agents. Until recently, it has been fairly easy for terrorists to order pathogens (disease microbes) simply by posing as medical researchers. In 1995, Larry Wayne Harris, a white supremacist, was convicted of having obtained three vials of bubonic plague bacteria using a fake letterhead. (He claimed to have been doing counterterrorism research to forestall an attack of "super germ-carrying rats" from Iraq.) Later, four militia members in Minnesota were convicted of planning to use a biological toxin to assassinate federal agents.

Since then, control procedures have been tightened considerably. Yet, according to Robert Blitzer, head of the terrorism investigation unit of the Federal Bureau of Investigation (FBI), "The consensus of people in the law enforcement and intelligence communities is that it's not a matter of if it's going to happen, it's when. We are very concerned."[26]

Biological attack need not be particularly high tech. In 1984, members of the Rajneesh cult in Oregon faced the prospect of a local vote to restrict the use of the land on their commune. Two of the cultists decided to sidetrack the voters from the polls. They cultured a batch of *Salmonella* (bacteria that can cause serious food poisoning), and then spread the material into salad bars and coffee creamers at 10 local restaurants and in supermarket produce bins. More than 750 people became ill, though no one died.

The number of incidents involving chemical, biological, or (occasionally) radioactive materials seems to be rising. In 1997, the FBI opened 74 investigations of such terrorism, and in 1998 it opened 181. However, about 80 percent of the cases have turned out to be hoaxes. The remainder were either only threats, very small-scale attacks (such as pouring a noxious chemical in the doorway of an abortion clinic), or attempted attacks that failed. By the end of the century there had been no U.S. attacks comparable to the Tokyo subway attack, and nothing further overseas.

Compared to a traditional bomb, a chemical or biological weapon (CBW) may be potentially more deadly, but it can also be more dangerous to the user and less reliable. People untrained in the safe handling of such materials may well kill themselves before they have the opportunity to kill others. The delivery of chemical and biological weapons requires that they be dispersed in such a way that many people will be exposed. A rocket or bomb with a CBW warhead may be ineffective because the explosion of the warhead destroys the toxic agent, disperses it prematurely, or unfavorable winds intervene.

Because terrorists may try to avoid these problems by introducing toxic agents directly into a city water supply or a building's air supply, guarding these points of entry can provide some security against attack.

The Clinton administration proposed spending $1.4 billion in fiscal year 2000 on programs designed to detect, prevent, or deal with the effects of chemical or biological terrorism, more than doubling the amount spent in 1999. Clearly the threat is being taken seriously. But terrorism experts disagree on the extent of the risk and the appropriateness of devoting so much money and resources on what might be a nebulous threat. Daniel S. Greenberg, a science policy analyst, believes that there has been

> *a whiff of hysteria-fanning and budget opportunism in the scary scenarios of the saviors who have stepped forward against the menace of bioterrorism. . . . While a gullible press echoes [their] frightening warnings, there are no independent assessments of the potential for terrorist attacks or the practicality of the proposed responses.*[27]

Jonathan B. Tucker and Amy Sands, two researchers at the Center for Nonproliferation Studies at the Monterey Institute of International Studies in Monterey, California, believe that the relatively small number of chemical and biological attacks, mostly outside the U.S., may be because

> *Historically, traditional terrorist organizations have eschewed chemical or biological agents for several reasons, including unfamiliarity with the relevant technologies, the hazards and unpredictability of toxic agents, moral constraints, concern that indiscriminate casualties could alienate current or future supporters, and fear that a mass-casualty attack could bring down the full repressive power of the affected government on their heads.*[28]

This implies that the future risk of terrorist attacks with weapons of mass destruction may be dependent on whether the nature of terrorists and their motives is indeed changing as Walter Laqueur suggested. Brian Jenkins believes that there are

> *two kinds of situations that lead entities that use violence to abandon the constraints of moral and political order that stop them from using weapons of*

mass destruction. The first is connected with ethnic or racial conflicts where the goal is genocide. The second happens when these entities put themselves on the fringe of the political and social systems and enter into religious fanaticism, believing sincerely that they have the mandate of God.[29]

On a practical level, the U.S. government has stepped up the coordination of intelligence-gathering efforts that focus on chemical, biological, and nuclear weapons. With federal assistance, in 1997 more than 20 cities staged mock attacks in order to assess and improve the responses of their emergency services. Experts in emergency medicine write articles on the training of "first responders" in mass attack situations. As Seattle, Washington, fire chief A. D. Vickery notes:

The public safety first responder needs to be taught and provided necessary equipment to manage a situation (such as in a weapons of mass destruction incident that could involve biological or chemical weapons). This includes confining and isolating an incident; detecting, decontaminating and treating large numbers of people on the scene; organizing regional capabilities; and having initial capabilities within the city or town for about 24 hours until federal assistance can arrive.[30]

In 2000, the Centers for Disease Control and Prevention, the top U.S. agency for tracking epidemics, began to study bioterrorism.

Terrorists have traditionally favored attacks on discrete, highly visible, symbolic targets, such as public buildings or officials. They have generally sought to kill or maim people directly. However, a "new terrorist" or an unfriendly foreign power that seeks to strike a truly crippling blow against a nation may well target its basic infrastructure instead. As Thomas W. Franzier, president of GenCon, a conference dealing with genetics and biological resources notes:

The U.S. has around a five-day supply of foods for the table. If food shipments were interrupted, it would be only a matter of a few days until many kinds of foods become unavailable. Hoarding would occur with an effective attack on a critical infrastructure such as the national power grid or telephone grid. And introducing a deadly zoonotic [animal-affecting] pathogen into a large number of meat animals could destroy domestic and foreign markets for that species. Attacking critical infrastructures with biological agents is quite feasible today.[31]

Nuclear terrorism remains the biggest nightmare for many people. A nuclear explosion, after all, would fulfill the new terrorist's apocalyptic desires in the most visible possible way. But nuclear weapons are even more difficult for terrorists to handle. The possible obtaining of a ready-made warhead (perhaps from the former Soviet arsenal) through purchase or theft is a nightmare to any security agency, but warheads have complex safety interlocks, and it has been proposed that the weapons be fitted with devices that would allow them to be remotely destroyed or disabled if terrorists obtain them. Closer coordination between U.S. and former Soviet scientists and engineers is also a goal of U.S. agencies, and, to a lesser extent, Russian agencies.

Building a nuclear weapon from stolen fissionable material would require considerable training. Refining the fissionable material from uranium is possible, given the resources of a rogue state such as Iraq or Libya.

Nuclear weapons are less likely to be of interest to traditional political terrorists, except perhaps as a deterrent to attack by government forces. With a nuclear weapon, it is essentially all or nothing—the terrorists cannot try to use varying degrees of force in negotiations as with the killing of passengers on a hijacked jet.

CYBERTERRORISM

Perhaps the least tangible terrorist attack is one that targets information systems. Computer users have become familiar in recent years with computer viruses such as Melissa and the Love Bug that can spread like wildfire through networks and hamper computer operations or even destroy data. The Internet has also proven to be vulnerable not only to hackers or crackers who can steal sensitive financial or other information, but to a simple brute force approach called a "denial of service attack." In February 2000, major commercial web sites such as Amazon.com, Yahoo!, and eBay were bombarded by a flood of information requests that had been launched from programs that had been spread earlier via a virus. The information flood made it difficult or impossible for users to buy things on the web, and thus cost the online merchants at least some short-term cash flow.

While not being able to buy a product online is only an inconvenience, attacks on the computers that control critical functions such as power and air traffic control could cause more direct economic damage and even loss of life. On the other hand, these critical computers tend to be more closely guarded and isolated from direct access via the Internet.

A variety of computer security measures have been proposed and are being implemented to varying degrees:

- Improving national monitoring centers that give early warning of attacks
- Increasing the number of highly trained computer security experts and investigators

- Training system administrators and users in how to recognize hacker attacks and the "social engineering" techniques hackers often use to trick people into revealing their passwords
- Possibly creating software that can act as a cyber "immune system," automatically adapting to, targeting, and neutralizing viruses

Another aspect of cyberterrorism is the use of computer systems and the Internet by terrorists themselves. Many of the groups certified as terrorists by the U.S. Department of State have their own web sites, which they use to spread their message. Freely available encryption programs offer terrorists the opportunity to coordinate their operations using e-mail that is difficult for the government or any outsider to read. The National Security Agency (NSA) is rumored to be using massive quantities of supercomputing power to crack codes being used on the web. An international surveillance program called Echelon was recently revealed by civil libertarians. Echelon apparently has the capability to process and screen massive amounts of communications including satellite transmissions, cell phone calls, and computer messages.

The federal government fought an unsuccessful battle in the mid-1990s to restrict the export and use of the most secure encryption systems. As a practical matter, there is no way to prevent the spread of either information or software on the worldwide, decentralized Internet. Further, businesses demand high-quality encryption to protect their data. Another government proposal, the Clipper Chip, would have offered such encryption built into the PC itself, but at a price—the government would have a key that it could use to unlock any message, presumably after having obtained a court order. But civil libertarians have waged a major campaign against this proposal, and a related proposal to require that encryption users provide a copy of their code key in a "key escrow" from which the government could retrieve it. Libertarians believe that potential for government abuse of such snooping abilities is simply too great to permit their use.

TERRORISM IN THE 21ST CENTURY

To sum up, what does the situation with regard to terrorism look like at the beginning of the new century? Based on the writings of experts, it seems fair to say that

- The rate of conventional terrorist attacks has been declining in the United States and throughout much of the world.
- Some of the traditional trouble spots, notably Northern Ireland, Israel/Palestine, and North and South Korea seem to be approaching a peaceful resolution, but the peace process remains fragile and uncertain.

- There remains the potential for conventional terrorism to flare up if economic conditions in the developing nations become worse, or if the tensions created by economic globalization are not resolved.
- Weapons of mass destruction are becoming more accessible to terrorists. They appeal most to "new terrorists" who seek total destruction for symbolic reasons.
- Information systems are vulnerable to terrorist attack, although security is gradually being improved.
- Many counterterrorism measures impose costs in money, convenience, or liberty.
- People demand both security and freedom, and there is no simple way to provide one while guaranteeing the other.

---

[1] 22 U.S.C. 2656f(d).

[2] Brian Jenkins, quoted in Jacob W. F. Sundberg, "Introduction to International Terrorism—The Tactics and Strategy of International Terrorism," in Magnus D. Sandbu and Peter Nordbeck, eds. *International Terrorism: Report from a Seminar Arranged by The European Law Students Association 1987.* [Lund]: Juristförlaget i Lund: Distribution, Akademibokhandeln i Lund, 1989.

[3] Noam Chomsky, quoted in Jay M. Shafritz, et al. *Almanac of Modern Terrorism,* New York: Facts On File, 1991, p. 264.

[4] Brian Jenkins, quoted in Jay M. Shafritz, et al. *Almanac of Modern Terrorism,* p. 256.

[5] Frits Kalshoven. *The Law of Warfare: A Summary of Its Recent History and Trends in Development.* Leiden: A. W. Sijthoff, 1973, pp. 27–29.

[6] Leon Trotsky. *Against Individual Terrorism.* New York: Pathfinder Press, 1974, pp. 3–4.

[7] U.S. Dept. of Defense, Joint Chiefs of Staff. *Dictionary of Military and Associated Terms (Incorporating the NATO and IADB Dictionaries).* Washington, D.C., 1 April 1984, p. 164.

[8] Edward Kossoy. *Living with Guerrilla: Guerrilla as a Legal Problem and a Political Fact.* Geneva: Librarie, Droz, 1976, p. 328.

[9] Interview with David Rapoport, cited in Alex P. Schmid and Albert J. Jongman, et al. *Political Terrorism.* Rev. ed. New York: North-Holland, 1988, p. 22.

[10] Johan Most. *Freiheit,* September 13, 1884. Reprinted in W. Laqueur, ed. *The Terrorism Reader.* New York: New American Library, 1978, p. 100.

[11] Noam Chomsky and E. S. Herman. *The Political Economy of Human Rights,* vol. 1, *The Washington Connection and Third World Fascism.* Nottingham: Spokesman, 1979, pp. 16–17.

[12] Robert Thompson, *Revolutionary War in World Strategy 1945–1969*. London: Secker & Warburg, 1970, p. 4.

[13] Walter Laqueur. *Terrorism*. London: Weidenfeld and Nicolson, 1977, p. 53.

[14] Quoted in Annie Murphy Paul, "Dispatch from Derry," *Psychology Today*, vol. 31, Nov.–Dec. 1998, p. 28ff.

[15] Walter Laqueur. *The New Terrorism*, pp. 106–107.

[16] Also in: Interview with David Rapoport, cited in Schmid and Jongman, p. 22.

[17] Douglas Pike, "The Viet-Cong Strategy of Terror," cited in Schmid and J. Jongman, p. 16.

[18] I. L. Horowitz, "Political Terrorism and State Power," *Journal of Political and Military Sociology I* (1973), pp. 147–157.

[19] Arthur Koestler, *The Ghost in the Machine*. London: Hutchinson, 1967, pp. 243, 251.

[20] Philip A. Karber, "Urban Terrorism" Baseline Data and a Conceptual Framework," *Social Science Quarterly 52* (December 1971), pp. 527–533.

[21] Secretary of Defense William Cohen, remarks before World Affairs Council, Los Angeles, June 1998. Quoted in Ivan Eland, "Preserving civil liberties in an age of terrorism." *Issues in Science and Technology*, vol. 15 (Fall 1998) p. 23ff.

[22] Ivan Eland, "Preserving civil liberties in an age of terrorism." *Issues in Science and Technology*, vol. 15 (Fall 1998) p. 23ff.

[23] Larry C. Johnson, "The Threat of Terrorism is Overstated," in Laura K. Egendorf, ed. *Terrorism: Opposing Viewpoints*. San Diego, Calif.: Greenhaven Press, 2000, p. 27.

[24] Walter Laqueur. *The New Terrorism: Fanaticism and the Arms of Mass Destruction*. New York: Oxford University Press, 1999, p. 81.

[25] Quoted in Jose Vegar, "Terrorism's New Breed," *Bulletin of the Atomic Scientists*, vol. 54, March–April 1998, p. 50ff.

[26] David E. Kaplan, "Terrorism's Next Wave: Nerve Gas and Germs are the New Weapons of Choice," *U.S. News & World Report*, vol. 123, November 17, 1997, p. 26ff.

[27] Daniel S. Greenberg, "The Bioterrorism Panic," *Washington Post*, March 16, 1999, p. A21.

[28] Jonathan B. Tucker and Amy Sands, "An Unlikely Threat," *Bulletin of the Atomic Scientists*, vol. 55, July 1999, p. 46.

[29] Vegar, Jose, "Terrorism's New Breed," p. 50ff.

[30] Juan Otero and Deborah Rigsby, "NLC Explains Local Role, Need for 'First Response' to Terrorism." *Nation's Cities Weekly*, vol. 21, September 7, 1998, p. 1ff.

[31] James P. Lucier, "We Are What We Eat—and That Makes the United States Vulnerable." *Insight on the News*, vol. 14, November 16, 1998, p. 6.

CHAPTER 2

SURVEY OF INTERNATIONAL TERRORISM

This chapter presents a regional overview of terrorism in Northern Ireland, Europe, the Middle East, Africa, Asia, Latin America, and the United States. Each section begins with a brief description of the region's major conflicts and developments as they have related to terrorist activity since the 1960s. This is followed by an alphabetical listing of terrorist groups that play (or have played) a significant role in terrorist activities in that region.

NORTHERN IRELAND

The roots of what came to be called the "Troubles" in Northern Ireland began in the 16th century when Henry VIII, king of England, established the Protestant Church of England as the official state church, and Catholics were persecuted and often deprived of civil rights. When Henry tried to establish Protestantism in Ireland, the Catholic population rebelled. The situation was exacerbated when Henry's daughter Elizabeth I encouraged the settlement of English Protestants in a large section of Northern Ireland. Many of the Irish living in what became known as the Plantation of Ulster were displaced. Because the newcomers (mainly Scottish and English) were also ethnically different from the Irish, the bitter conflict that ensued combined two of humankind's most thorny issues—religion and ethnicity.

During the 17th century, things got steadily worse. Expansion of the English settlement continued, and the Irish revolted. The revolt was put down by Oliver Cromwell, whose forces massacred thousands of Irish Catholics. In 1688, when the Catholic James II was forced off the British throne by William of Orange after a short three-year reign, James II used Ireland as a base for his attempt to retake the throne. The Protestant supporters of William defended the town of Derry from the Catholic forces until the English army could break the siege. In 1690, William finally defeated James at the battle of the Boyne river. About a hundred years later, the Protestants began to call themselves "Orangemen," after William, and have celebrated their victory at the Boyne with an annual parade.

GROWTH OF IRISH NATIONALISM

The 18th century ended with a revolt by the Irish nationalist Thomas Wolfe Tone, who tried to unite both Protestants and Catholics against the foreign rule of Britain. Although the revolt failed, it strengthened Irish nationalism. In the 19th century, Irish nationalists resisted British attempts to unite all of Ireland with what had become Great Britain, and the people of Ireland suffered the terrible potato famine of 1845–48, which disproportionately killed Irish Catholics, who were generally poor, and forced many others to emigrate, many to the United States. Meanwhile, the Protestants consolidated their power in Northern Ireland. Called Unionists, they believed that only uniting Ireland with Britain could give the island a successful economy. They were opposed by the Republicans, who sought an independent Irish state.

By the late 19th century, an organization called the Irish Republican Brotherhood (originally formed by Irish immigrants in New York City) was waging a campaign of bombing and assassination against the British, not unlike that of the modern Irish Republican Army (IRA). During World War I, the British, in part to keep the Irish from aiding Germany, promised "home rule" to Ireland. But some Republicans either did not believe the British or did not want to wait, while Unionists wanted no part of any Irish Republic dominated by the Catholics of the south. On Easter Monday in 1916, a full-scale Republican rebellion, today known as the Easter Rebellion or Easter Rising, broke out in Dublin, led by several thousand armed followers of Patrick Pearse and James Connolly. However, the lightly armed rebels were no match for a British force that arrived with artillery and forced the rebels to surrender. But Pearse created from the rebellion a force whose name would later become ominous: the Irish Republican Army. When the British reacted to the rebellion with a wave of executions and imprisonments, the IRA vowed to carry on the struggle.

REPUBLICANS AND THE IRA

By a 1921 treaty, the British tried for a compromise: Southern Ireland became an independent state, while predominately Protestant Northern Ireland continued to be ruled and protected by Britain until some future time when it could be peacefully joined to the Irish Republic. Of course, most Unionists did not want to be part of the south and demanded continued

British protection. Meanwhile, although many moderates accepted the division of Ireland at least temporarily, the extreme Republicans represented by the IRA did not. The IRA fought the new Irish government, demanding that the Republic fight for a united, independent Ireland. However, the Republican movement was split in 1932 when one of its main leaders, Eamon de Valera, took over the Irish government. As the IRA began to wane in the south, the Unionists in the north and the British were locked into a tight embrace, with the British allowing the Unionists some measure of self-rule and the ability to keep themselves firmly separate from the south.

By the 1930s, what was left of the IRA had split in two. A moderate wing, following the agenda of the Sinn Féin political party, sought to persuade the north to unite with the south on socialist principles. The other wing, however, held to the old Republican demand to drive the British out of Northern Ireland, creating an Irish Republic on nationalist principles. This more militant faction formed the Provisional Wing of the IRA, which by the 1950s was carrying out small-scale terrorist activities in the north.

The "Troubles" Begin

By the 1960s, the Catholics in Northern Ireland had become frustrated; for decades they had been denied access to economic opportunities and fair treatment by authorities. A new movement emerged that focused not so much on republicanism as on civil rights. At first the violent wing of the IRA, having engaged in sporadic terrorism earlier in the decade, played only a marginal role in the new struggle. But when Catholics marched for civil rights, better housing, and education, they were viciously attacked by the Protestant-controlled police (the Royal Ulster Constabulary, or RUC) and by police reservists (called B-Specials) who functioned as a sort of Protestant paramilitary group.

During the summer of 1969, Catholic civil rights demonstrators trying to march from Londonderry to Belfast were tear-gassed and beaten by the RUC and the B-Specials. Then, on August 15, the Protestants added insult to injury by holding their traditional "Apprentice Boys" or Orangemen parade. Many of the police openly joined the parade, and the Protestants armed themselves with sticks, rocks, and Molotov cocktails. Belfast and Londonderry (Derry for short) were swept by fires and rioting. When the British army arrived to quell the disturbances, it made matters worse by openly siding with what many of the soldiers viewed as Protestant English countrymen. This bitterly disappointed Catholics who had hoped the army would play a neutral, peacekeeping role and perhaps even protect them from abuses by the RUC and B-Specials. Increasingly, they saw the IRA as their only alternative.

Temporarily patching up its internal differences, the IRA declared war on the British Army, vowing to drive it out of Northern Ireland through waves of bombings, assassinations, and other violent actions. In response to the renewed terrorism, in 1973 Britain enacted the Emergency Powers Act, which, while supposedly reforming the existing Special Powers Act, still allowed the police to arrest persons and hold them without trial and to conduct secret trials and trials without a jury. Such measures were viewed by the British as necessary to prevent terrorists from intimidating witnesses. Supporters believed the measures were necessary for dealing with the emergency created by the Provisional IRA terrorists (who by 1969 had split from the moderate wing of the IRA), while opponents saw them as just another way to institutionalize the oppression of the Catholics.

Besides supporting the police, British military (including the elite Special Air Service and intelligence units) played an independent role in fighting the IRA. Gradually, however, British frustration with the seemingly intractable situation led to a policy under Prime Minister Margaret Thatcher of "Ulsterization"—increasingly, letting the Irish solve their own problems, replacing British forces with an expanded RUC without the B-Specials and other ties to Protestant groups. During the 1980s, effective intelligence and the use of secret testimony by Irish informants (called "supergrasses" for "snakes in the grass") led to the imprisonment of many IRA activists and to protests by human rights groups.

QUEST FOR PEACE

Despite its bomb and gun attacks, the mainstream IRA increasingly concluded that it could not defeat the British. Meanwhile, ordinary Irish people in both the Catholic and Protestant communities exerted pressure for a peace settlement.

During the 1990s, peace seemed tantalizingly close. On August 31, 1994, the official IRA announced a cease-fire and said it was ready to join peace negotiations. Some smaller extremist factions (such as one calling itself the Real IRA) continued their attacks. On April 10, 1998, voters in both Northern Ireland and the Irish Republic approved a new legislative council for Northern Ireland that included both Catholics and Protestants. Authorities in the north and south also cooperated in making regional policies in areas such as transportation and the environment. On August 15, however, an IRA splinter group set off a car bomb in Omagh, killing 28 people. In 1999, the peace process seemed to falter when the IRA and Protestant groups bickered about disarmament or the "decommissioning" of weapons. Nevertheless, large-scale terror attacks had not resumed by early 2000.

GROUPS IN NORTHERN IRELAND

Irish Republican Army (IRA) The principal militant organization dedicated to the removal of the British-run Northern Ireland government and the unification of Northern Ireland with the Irish Republic in the south. The IRA emerged from the Easter Rising of 1916, and the pressure IRA guerrillas exerted against the British helped encourage the formation of the Irish Free State that became the current state of Ireland. However, Irish Republicans split between those willing to accept a divided Ireland (with the Irish Free State in the south and the north remaining British) and those insisting on a republic encompassing all of Ireland. The IRA sided with the latter group during the Irish civil war of 1921–23, but were defeated by former IRA leader Michael Collins, who led the Free State forces. The IRA began a new bombing campaign against the British in both Northern Ireland and southern Ireland in the 1930s. In 1939 the organization was banned by the Irish Free State, which became the Republic of Ireland in 1949. The IRA then focused on Northern Ireland. Following the failure of military actions against the British up to the early 1960s, the IRA turned for a time to civil disobedience and nonviolent action. More militant members objected to this moderate approach and formed the Provisional Irish Republican Army (see that entry for more details). The political wing of the modern IRA is known as Sinn Féin. See the entry on Sinn Féin for more details.

Loyalist Volunteer Force (LVF) Formed in 1996 as an extremist offshoot of the Ulster Volunteer Force, the LVF has launched vicious attacks on both Catholic and Protestant leaders who support the Northern Ireland peace process. However, the group declared a cease-fire and gave up some of its weapons in 1998.

Provisional Irish Republican Army (PIRA) This organization, also called the Provisional Wing of the Irish Republican Army, was formed in 1969 when the IRA split into two groups. By 1972, the "official" IRA had renounced terrorism, and the Provisional Wing became the main vehicle for those who wanted to carry on a violent struggle against British rule in Northern Ireland. Gradually the older members of the PIRA, motivated by Republican nationalism, gave way to a younger generation that looked toward leftist ideology that emphasized political action over terrorism. The "Provos" carried on a protracted campaign of violence into the early 1990s, seeking to keep world attention focused on Northern Ireland while sapping the will of the British people to maintain their rule in the province. Most PIRA attacks have taken place in Northern Ireland, against British security forces and officials, using well-honed techniques of bombing and ambush. The British, in turn, have kept up relentless pressure on the PIRA through the use of investigators and informants. (Informants discovered by the PIRA are often brutally tortured and killed.) The PIRA has been sustained by widespread nationalist sentiment among the Catholic population of Northern Ireland and by support raised through robberies, donations from sympathizers in the United States, and weapons and other help from Libya. The PIRA and the Basque group ETA have also developed a long-standing cooperation.

Real IRA A small, violent wing of the radical Republican 32-County Sovereignty Movement, the Real IRA seeks to remove all British forces from Northern Ireland and unite it with the Irish Republic. The group bitterly opposes the Northern Ireland peace process, including the adoption by Sinn Féin in September 1997 of the Mitchell Principles of democracy and nonviolence. The group claimed responsibility for the car bomb attack in Omagh, Northern Ireland, on August 15, 1998, which killed 29 persons and injured 220. The group later issued a cease-fire.

Sinn Féin ("We, Ourselves") Founded in 1900 by Irish nationalist Arthur Griffith, Sinn Féin began as a movement to promote Gaelic culture in the face of British influence. Following the British suppression of the Easter Rebellion (a failed insurrectional attempt to end British rule in Ireland that was held on Easter Monday, 1916) during World War I, Sinn Féin became the rallying point for political organization by Irish nationalists. Following election victories in 1918, Sinn Féin set up an Irish parliament known as the Dáil Éirann, which declared Irish independence, a status recognized by the British with the establishment of the Irish Free State in southern Ireland. When republican leader Eamon de Valera entered the Irish parliament in 1927 and most Irish seemed to be reconciled to the permanent division of the island, Sinn Féin essentially disbanded. However, with the resurgence of the Irish Republican Army in the 1960s, Sinn Féin reemerged as the political wing of the IRA. When the IRA split into "official" and provisional wings, Sinn Féin mirrored this split, with Gerry Adams becoming leader of the radical provisional wing of Sinn Féin in 1983. During the years of rampant terrorism, Sinn Féin, although not recognized by the British as a legitimate political party, provided a means for the more peacefully inclined to support Irish nationalism, a conduit for support for the IRA, and a way for the British to communicate indirectly with the IRA. During the peace process of the late 1990s, Sinn Féin won representation in a democratically elected assembly intended to share ruling power between Catholics and Protestants in Northern Ireland.

Ulster Defense Association (UDA) An outlawed Protestant paramilitary and vigilante organization in Northern Ireland, the UDA was formed in the early 1970s and has tens of thousands of members. The group is the most powerful Protestant group in the violent conflict in Northern Ireland and has unofficial ties with the Royal Ulster Constabulary. The group has been implicated in many beatings, killings, and kidnappings of Catholics.

Ulster Volunteer Force (UVF) A group of armed Protestant nationalists in Ulster, Northern Ireland, formed in 1966. The UVF took its name from a popular home-rule organization in existence earlier in the century. The UVF violently attacked the Irish Republican Army and its suspected sympathizers in the early 1970s, conducting numerous bombings. In 1976 the organization claimed to renounce violence.

EUROPE

Europe has seen both ideology-based terrorism (both Left and Right) and terrorism based on nationalism or ethnicity. Since the fall of the Soviet Union and the end of the cold war, the predominant source of terrorism has changed from ideology to nationalism.

LEFTIST TERRORISM

Since the 19th century, European anarchists, socialists, or communists have sometimes carried on a violent struggle against the capitalist system, particularly in times when workers suffered harsh economic and social conditions. The student movements that erupted in the late 1960s in most of the western world included a considerable component of marxist thought and combined the traditional appeal to the working class with a new struggle against American imperialism as typified by the war in Vietnam. Inevitably, for a relatively small number of extremists, protests and politics were not enough—especially when the political gains were limited.

A number of leftist terrorist groups were formed in the late 1960s and early 1970s, including Germany's Red Army Faction (RAF), France's Action Directe, and Italy's Red Brigades. Some of the extremists, such as the Baader-Meinhof gang, the forerunner of the RAF, combined criminal motivations with leftist ideology. (The gang decided that bank robbery would make a satisfactory funding source. While Ulrike Meinhof showed dedication to her communist principles, her partner in crime, Andreas Baader, lived an upscale lifestyle with some of the robbery proceeds.)

In many ways the RAF's fate was typical of that of other European leftist terrorists. During the 1970s the RAF engaged in a series of bombings, robberies, and murders. As German police arrested and jailed RAF leaders, other members tried to use terrorism to gain their freedom. A series of murders, including the killing of the pilot of a hijacked airliner in October 1977, caused even many committed leftists to reject the group. While the RAF tried to gain exposure by participating in the anti-NATO agitation of the 1980s, it never regained its earlier prominence. The fall of the Berlin Wall and the reunification of Germany removed the communist East German government that had secretly supported many leftist European terrorists and that offered sanctuary when things became too hot. Similarly, changing politics undermined support for the Red Brigades in Italy, despite the group's effective organization, which combined the advantages of decentralized cells with the ability to launch coordinated attacks.

RIGHT-WING TERRORISM

If the 1970s was the decade of the Left in Europe, the 1980s saw right-wing terrorism predominate. Europe's generally strong economic growth diminished the appeal of leftist ideology. While the economic trends culminating in the 1990s with the European Union and its single currency seemed to be bringing about the triumph of globalism over nationalism, fear of a loss of national identity amid a growing influx of immigrants from countries such as Turkey, as well as the stress caused by the need to integrate millions of former East Germans, fueled a modest resurgence of German nationalism and, in more extreme form, neofascism or neo-Nazism. During the early 1990s, German neo-Nazis, who had started by fighting in the streets against leftists, switched their focus to beating immigrants, tourists, and Jews.

Meanwhile in France, the moderate right wing took control of parliament in 1986 and a coalition government was formed under Jacques Chirac. In the 1988 election, the more radical right-wing candidate Jean-Marie Le Pen, whose National Front party ran on an anti-immigration platform, did surprisingly well in the first round of voting. Austria, too, saw a right-wing resurgence in 1999 when Jorg Haider's Freedom Party scored electoral victories and forced its inclusion in the ruling coalition.

Although more extreme forms of the sentiments that have led to right-wing gains have sometimes been expressed in terrorist activity, large-scale, organized right-wing terrorism comparable to the leftist terrorism of the 1980s did not emerge in Europe during the 1990s.

ETHNIC-BASED TERRORISM

Besides ideological conflicts, long-standing grievances of ethnic minorities have also been a source of European terrorism. In Spain since the 1950s, the Basques, a unique ethnicity completely separate from the dominant Spanish, have sought an independent homeland within Spain. The Basque Nation and Liberty party (ETA) evolved from a political group into a terrorist group when Basque aspirations were brutally repressed by Francisco Franco's regime in the early 1960s. The ETA and its more militant offshoot (ETA-M) carried on a terror campaign that reached its peak in the late 1970s. During the 1980s, however, more liberal Spanish policies allowed Basque nationalists to express their views more openly through the political process, and support for the ETA declined. Increasingly, the ETA began to be seen as a marginal group by even the Basques themselves.

Another ethnic-based terrorist group is found in Turkey. The Kurds, too, form a distinct ethnic minority. The Kurdish Workers' Party (PKK) had a Marxist-Leninist ideological base, but later appealed to the more popular sentiment of nationalism. PKK leaders went to Lebanon, where they trained with experienced Islamic terrorists. Returning to Turkey and backed by Syria, the PKK waged guerrilla war, massacring thousands of Turkish villagers. During the 1990s, however, the PKK announced it was seeking a peaceful political solution in negotiation with the Muslim government that had come to power in Turkey. However, the kidnapping of PKK leader Abdullah Ocalan by Turkish agents in February 1999 and his subsequent trial and death sentence (with execution suspended as of early 2000) cast doubt on the future of the peace process.

GROUPS IN EUROPE

Action Directe (AD) A French marxist terrorist organization founded in 1979, the group specialized in bombing banks, businesses, and other targets that it associated with capitalism and imperialism. In August 1985, however, the group turned its attention to military targets and claimed joint responsibility with Germany's Red Army Faction for a bombing at the U.S. Air Force base in Rhein-Main, West Germany, that killed two American soldiers. Action Directe then became part of an umbrella group called the Anti-Imperialist Armed Front (AIAF), which called upon international workers to combat the "Americanization of Europe." In 1985, Action Directe terrorists assassinated French General Rene Audran and the next year they killed Georges Besse, chairman of the Renault automobile company. Following these actions, however, an intensive police investigation led to the arrest of many of Action Directe's key leaders, and the group faded away.

Euzkadita Azkatasuna (ETA; Basque for "Basque Fatherland and Liberty") ETA is a radical Basque separatist organization. Originally an offshoot of a Basque nationalist party during the 1950s, by the early 1960s ETA had given up on peaceful politics and begun terrorist actions against the Spanish government. Many ETA supporters looked to the Marxist-based insurgents in the Third World for inspiration, and a more militant faction called ETA-M (for "military") emerged in the 1970s and carried out some of the worst Basque terrorist attacks of that and the following decade. In 1968, the ETA assassinated Meliton Manzanas, police chief in the city of San Sebastian. In 1973, ETA assassinated Luis Carrero Blanco, the prime minister of Spain. In a steady stream of shootings and bombings during the 1970s and 1980s more than 800 people died. Meanwhile, the more moderate political faction renounced violence. ETA is believed to have forged links with other terrorist organizations, such as the Irish Republican Army, as well as the governments of Libya and Cuba. Despite a decline in influence after the 1980s, the ETA's ability to tap into a broad base of Basque nationalist sentiment has enabled the group to survive punishing blows from Spanish authorities. In September 1998 the ETA declared a "unilateral cease-fire," but by 2000 the group was again staging large-scale attacks.

Grupo de Resistencia Antifascista, Primero de Octubre (GRAPO; Spanish for "Antifascist Resistance Group, October 1") This small Spanish Maoist group was formed in 1975 with a focus on removing U.S. and NATO facilities from Spain and creating a communist state. The group was secretive, though it was believed to have ties to Action Directe in France and the Red Brigades in Italy. GRAPO was active through the 1980s, bombing U.S. cultural and military facilities and shooting police officials. Its attacks culminated in 1990 with the bombing of the Madrid Stock Exchange, the Constitutional Court, and the Economic Ministry. However, police sweeps resulted in the arrest of most of the group's leadership, rendering it inactive for the rest of the 1990s.

Kurdistan Workers' Party (PKK) A Kurdish insurgent group in Turkey, based on Marxist-Leninist ideology, the PKK began in 1984 as a rural guerrilla group but then expanded into urban areas. In 1993, in response to severe government repression of the Kurdish minority, the PKK began to expand its attacks on government facilities to include Turkish diplomats and businesses throughout Western Europe, as well as attacking Turkey's tourist industry by targeting foreign tourists. In 1995, the Turkish army began a military campaign against PKK bases in northern Iraq, and in 1999 Turkish authorities captured PKK leader Abdullah Ocalan, who was sentenced to death (this sentence was suspended as of 2000). These events severely weakened the PKK's power.

P2 This shadowy group has been linked to right-wing, neofascist, and Masonic groups in Italy. It may have been implicated together with the Red Brigades and the Mafia in the kidnapping of former Italian prime minister Aldo Moro in 1978. In 1980 the uncovering of a P2 membership list that included many prominent Italian military, government, and police officials led to the downfall of the Italian government and severely strained relations between Italy and NATO.

Popular Forces of April 25 (FP-25; in Portuguese, "Forças Populares do 25 Abril") This Portuguese leftist group sought to overthrow the Portuguese government and replace it with a marxist state. More immediately, it sought to break all ties between Portugal and the United States and NATO. During the mid-1980s the group enacted bombings, rocket attacks, and assassination attempts, including attacks on the U.S. embassy in Portugal and a NATO headquarters outside Lisbon. In 1986 the group appeared under a new name, "Armed Revolutionary Organization."

Red Army Faction (RAF; in German, "Rote Armee Faktion") One of the largest European leftist terrorist organizations, the RAF emerged out of the widespread radical student movements of the late 1960s. Dominated in its early years by the mercurial terrorists Andreas Baader, Ulrike Meinhof, and Gudrun Ensslin, the group was also known as the Baader-Meinhof Gang. The group began in 1968 with attacks on West German corporate facilities. During the 1970s, the RAF forged links in an emerging international terror network that included the major Palestinian groups, who provided the RAF with training. In turn, RAF members carried out operations on behalf of the Palestinians, including the 1975 seizure of the OPEC ministers in Vienna. In 1977, however, a failed hijacking led to the suicide of Baader, Ensslin, and another jailed member. The group then turned its attention back to domestic targets including businesses and NATO facilities. Despite frequent arrests of key leaders, the RAF's well-educated, trained, and highly motivated core membership kept the organization effective into the 1990s. Another reason for the group's robustness emerged in 1990 when records of the former East German intelligence service revealed that the RAF had been trained and closely supervised by the East German interior ministry.

Red Brigades (BR, in Italian, "Brigate Rosse") Like many European leftist terrorist groups, the Red Brigades emerged from the radical student activism of the late 1960s. It was founded in 1970 by a small group of young Italian communists. In the mid-1970s, the group began a brutal campaign of kidnapping and violent attacks, including "kneecapping" victims (breaking or shooting their kneecaps, thus crippling them). The main targets were people considered to be important figures in the establishment or ruling class, including judges and other officials, police, and the military. During the 1980s the group began to target NATO officials, kidnapping and then releasing U.S. deputy commander of NATO Brigadier General James Dozier. The group also expressed its solidarity and cooperation with the major Palestinian terrorist groups. In the late 1970s and early 1980s (and again in 1987), Italian police managed to sweep up many BR leaders and their extensive weapons caches. Combined with an internal split in 1984, these events rendered the group virtually defunct.

Revolutionary Cells (RZ; in German, "Revolutionaere Zellen") A left-wing German terrorist group formed in 1973, its leaders vowed to strike fear into the heart of the ruling class through shooting, bombing, and taking hostages. The group bases its organization and methods on urban guerrilla tactics, with small cells operating independently against local targets. Its ability to disguise its members as ordinary citizens and its skill with time-delayed bombs and other weapons made the Revolutionary Cells a difficult problem for West German authorities in the late 1980s.

Revolutionary Organization 17 November (in Greek, "Epanastatiki Organosi 17 Noemvri") This small, Marxist Greek radical group, active mainly during the 1970s, was named to commemorate the killing of a demonstrator in Athens in 1973. The group's terrorist attacks (typically, shootings from ambush) targeted U.S. and NATO officials and Greeks associated with them. The group called for the severing of all ties between Greece and NATO.

Terra Lliure (in English, "Free Land") This group sought the establishment of an independent Catalan state in Spain's Catalonia region. Formed in the 1970s, Terra Lliure undertook a terror campaign in the early 1980s, mainly targeting banks and tourism-related businesses such as travel agencies with small bombs. In 1987 the group claimed credit for bombings of the U.S. consulate general's office in Barcelona as well as a United Service Organizations (USO) club.

MIDDLE EAST

Along with Northern Ireland, the Middle East is the region most often associated with terrorism. At the crossroads of Europe, Africa, and Asia and endowed with a plentiful supply of the modern world's most vital resource, oil, it seems inevitable that this area would be the focus of a variety of conflicts.

The modern situation in the Middle East is the result of several developments. Following World War I, the remnants of the Turkish Ottoman Empire that had ruled the area for hundreds of years were displaced by British and French forces that sought to control the area. Meanwhile, European Jews had developed a strong movement called Zionism, with the goal of reestablishing of the biblical Jewish state in what was now Palestine. Just as the British had tried to pacify the Irish during World War I by promising them home rule, in the Balfour Declaration of November 2, 1917, they promised the Jews who had begun to settle in Palestine in increasing numbers that they could have their state. At the same time, the British sought to retain their alliance with Arab nations against Germany's ally, Turkey, by promising Arabs that they too could have self-determination after the war. Meanwhile, in the Sykes-Picot agreement of 1916, both the British and the French agreed to carve out spheres of influence in the Middle East and proposed to share Iran with Russia. There would be no way to fulfill all three of these agendas.

Following the war, the British drew boundaries to create what would eventually become the modern Arab nations of Syria, Jordan, Egypt, Saudi Arabia, Iraq, Iran, and Libya. They then chose rulers for the new states from the traditional ruling families in the Arab world. The British kept a close eye on these clients rulers and while the Islamic world did develop a pan-Arabist movement, the attempt at unification made little headway amid the long-standing rivalries among many of the ruling families. In 1922, the British received a mandate from the League of Nations to rule the Protectorate of Trans-Jordan, which included Palestine with its predominately Arab population and a significant minority of Jewish settlers.

In the three-cornered conflict that erupted just before World War II, both the Arabs and the Jews wanted independence from British rule, but neither was willing to join the other in an independent Palestine. The Arabs revolted against the British, and they and the Jews also fought each other.

By the end of World War II, it was clear that the British had little enthusiasm or resources for continuing their role as protector of Palestine. Thousands of Jews, refugees of the Holocaust, began to smuggle themselves into Palestine past the British authorities. Seeing the influx as threatening to their future self-determination, Palestinian Arabs began to arm themselves and prepare for full-scale fighting against the Jews as soon as the British pulled out. In turn, a Jewish terrorist group, the Irgun, attacked British soldiers and Palestinians. The dual objectives of the Irgun were to make it too painful for the British to remain and to intimidate and drive out Palestinian Arabs.

One obvious possibility for settlement was a partition of Palestine into separate Jewish and Palestinian states. The British liked this idea, and the United Nations agreed and proclaimed the partition on May 15, 1948. Amid great rejoicing, the Jews declared the establishment of the new state of Israel on their side of the partition line. Palestinian and neighboring Arab forces immediately invaded the new Jewish state, which defended itself and prevailed in the fighting.

While the struggle between Arabs and Jews in Palestine remained the fulcrum of unrest in the Middle East, the Arab world itself was being pulled in different directions. All of Israel's Arab neighbors proclaimed their willingness to join together to "drive Israel into the sea." In 1967, however,

Israel's armed forces struck crushing blows at both Egypt and Syria in the Six-Day War. In October 1973, Egypt under President Anwar Sadat and Syria made a surprise attack on Israel during the Jewish Yom Kippur holiday. They achieved remarkable success at first, with Egyptian forces driving the Israelis deep into the Sinai while Syria, attacking from the Golan Heights, almost made it to Jerusalem.

This near-victory helped change alignments in the Arab world. Because the success of his forces had restored Arab self-respect, Sadat was powerful enough to seek better relations with both Israel and the United States (earlier, he had been aligned with the Soviets). Israel, under Prime Minister Menachem Begin, wanted peace but also insisted on controlling enough territory to allow the nation to defend itself in some depth from any future attacks. In the Camp David Peace Accords, mediated by U.S. president Jimmy Carter, Israel agreed to give up the Sinai in exchange for peace with Egypt.

Egypt, Saudi Arabia, and Jordan tacitly agreed that Israel was there to stay and decided to focus on their own economic development. But "rejectionists" in the Arab world, such as Syria and Iran, refused to accept any accommodation of Israel. (Extreme rejectionists were responsible for Sadat's assassination in 1981.)

The Palestinians were caught in the middle of the Arab-Israeli struggle. Many of them had fled during Israel's wartime expansion, and were living in squalid refugee camps, stuck in a political limbo without civil rights or hope for the future.

Some joined or supported the Palestine Liberation Organization (PLO), led by Yasir Arafat and founded in 1964. But the PLO suffered setbacks. In 1970, forces of Jordan's King Hussein, who was pursuing a moderate policy toward Israel, expelled the PLO. The more militant wing of the PLO killed 11 Israeli athletes at the 1972 Olympic Games in Munich, Germany—marking the growing international reach of terrorist activities.

Meanwhile, the PLO shifted its guerrilla operations to Lebanon, who together with other radical Islamic groups launched constant rocket bombardments and raids across the Israeli border, accompanied by suicide bombings and assassinations. They also began to attack targets in Israel, Lebanon, and even western Europe that were associated with Israel or the United States. In 1982, however, Israel invaded Lebanon, destroying much of the PLO infrastructure but also becoming embroiled in an endless battle between armed militias and other groups—a conflict that left much of the once beautiful city of Beirut in rubble.

Yasir Arafat's position as PLO leader was challenged from two directions in the late 1980s. Relocating in Tunis, he concluded that terrorism would never bring about a Palestinian state. In 1988, Arafat implicitly recognized Israel's right to exist, renounced terrorism, and sought to reinvent himself as a peacemaker and political spokesperson for the Palestinian people in the international community. While militant PLO members rejected Arafat and formed an organization called Hamas, in 1987 Palestinian youths began a remarkable movement that became known as the Intifada. They demonstrated throughout the Israeli-occupied territories, demanding self-government, and despite frequent clashes between rock-throwing youths and Israeli troops shooting rubber bullets, Israel could not suppress the uprising. Arafat, equally caught by surprise, could not co-opt it for his own purposes.

As world opinion began to swing in favor of the Intifada, Arafat emerged as the only Palestinian leader who had the international stature to negotiate with Israel and to seek American help. By 1994, the Israelis were willing to take the first steps toward Palestinian autonomy, and a quasi-national Palestine Authority was empowered to handle domestic affairs in the Palestinian territories.

As in Northern Ireland, the road to peace remained rocky and uncertain. Arab extremists continued to make terrorist attacks, while right-wing Israelis resisted the peace process. In 1995, Israeli prime minister Yitzhak Rabin was assassinated by an Orthodox Jewish fanatic. Some Israeli settlers in the occupied territories have said they would violently resist their areas coming under Palestinian control.

By fall 2000 growing Palestinian frustration at the slowness of progress toward statehood and reaction to Israeli right-wing leader Ariel Sharon's visit to the Temple Mount (Haram ash Sharif) had triggered large-scale clashes that lead to more than 170 deaths, mostly among Palestinians. Although the violence had subsided somewhat by November, the future of the entire peace process was called into question.

The Palestinian conflict is not the only source of Middle East terrorism. In 1979, a fundamentalist Shi'ite Muslim government inspired by Ayatollah Khomeini overthrew the American-backed Shah in Iran. Emphasizing a relatively minor element of Islam, the *jihad* or holy war, the Iranians and other Shi'ite fundamentalists attacked not only Israel but also the United States, whose globe-girdling secular culture threatened to undermine what they saw as the purity of their faith. But the fundamentalists have had an equally significant agenda of seeking to overthrow moderate Islamic or secularist governments and replace them with a system of strict religious law (*Sharia*).

Elsewhere in the Islamic world, Iraq's ruler, Saddam Hussein, remains a persistent thorn in the side of the West. Many believe he is still pursuing the development of weapons of mass destruction despite his defeat by a coalition of Western and moderate Arab military forces in the Persian Gulf War of 1990–91. Still, the overall trend at the end of the 1990s was toward moderation in the Islamic world, underscored by the surprising victory of liberal, secularist parties in Iranian elections in 2000.

Terrorism

GROUPS IN THE MIDDLE EAST

Abu Nidal Organization (ANO) A loose coalition of organizations founded and operated by terrorist leader Sabri al-Banna (Abu Nidal), who broke with the Palestine Liberation Organization in 1974. (The ANO designation is used by the U.S. State Department, not the terrorists themselves.) The organization has operated under other names such as the Arab Revolutionary Council, Fatah Revolutionary Council, and Black September. Since the 1980s, organizations under this umbrella have conducted more than 100 terrorist actions in more than 20 countries, killing about 900 people. Actions include attacks on passengers in airports in Vienna and Rome in December 1985 and the massacre of worshippers at an Istanbul synagogue in 1986. In 1993, six members of the organization were arrested, convicted, and given long prison terms. The organization was dormant during the remainder of the decade, and by early 2000 there were conflicting reports about Abu Nidal's health and whereabouts.

Arab National Youth Organization for the Liberation of Palestine (ANYOLP) The ANYOLP was a radical offshoot that broke away from the Popular Front for the Liberation of Palestine in 1972. The group engaged in hijackings and violent attacks, such as one on an Israeli diplomat in Cyprus in April 1973. Israel's retaliatory raid on Beirut led to the death of several PLO leaders and the breakup of the ANYOLP.

Armed Islamic Group (GIA; in French, "Groupe Islamic Armée") An Algerian Islamic extremist group, the GIA seeks to replace the secular Algerian regime with an Islamic state. When the Algerian government refused to recognize the election victory of the Islamic Salvation Front in 1992, the GIA began a campaign of terrorist attacks, often massacring village inhabitants. In September 1993, the GIA began to target foreigners in Algeria and had killed more than 100 by early 2000. In 1994, the GIA hijacked an Air France flight to Algiers, and it has also been linked to 1995 bombings in France.

Black September A terrorist organization founded primarily to seek revenge for the expulsion of militant Palestinian groups by the Jordanian army in 1970, Black September assassinated Wasfi al-tal, the prime minister of Jordan, in 1971. In 1972, the group claimed credit for the massacre of Israeli athletes at the Munich Olympics. According to observers, Black September, rather than being a true independent group, served as a vehicle for Abu Nidal and other al-Fatah leaders to carry out terrorist acts without taking direct responsibility for them.

Democratic Front for the Liberation of Palestine (DFLP) A Marxist-Leninist Palestinian group founded in 1968, the DFLP opposed the efforts of the Palestine Liberation Organization as being too moderate and lacking "class consciousness." The DFLP specialized in attacking Israelis, both within Israel and in the occupied territories. In May 1974, DFLP terrorists disguised as Israeli soldiers killed 27 Israelis and wounded 134 in a school in Ma'alot, Israel. During the later 1970s and 1980s they conducted minor bombings and unsuccessful hostage-taking attempts.

al-Fatah (Harakat al-Tahrir al Filistini, or Palestine Liberation Movement) Founded in 1957, al-Fatah is the largest organization in the umbrella group PLO (Palestine Liberation Organization). Al-Fatah has been led since 1964 by Yasir Arafat. However, in the 1990s Arafat renounced violence and moved into mainstream politics as leader of the Palestine Authority and the nascent Palestinian state. During the 1960s al-Fatah mounted guerrilla raids into Israel from bases in Jordan. In September 1970, Jordan's King Hussein attacked and expelled al-Fatah from the country, and the group established new bases in Lebanon and Syria. The expulsion also resulted in the more militant Black September faction splitting off from al-Fatah; the split also proved to be useful to Arafat, who could support terrorism at arm's length through al-Fatah while preserving deniability by claiming the PLO was not responsible. During the 1970s, al-Fatah expanded its terrorist activities to western Europe and also provided a sort of international training school for terrorists. In 1982, Israel invaded Lebanon, forcing al-Fatah to abandon its bases there. The group dispersed to Tunisia, Algeria, South Yemen, and other countries, but in the late 1980s it began to infiltrate into Lebanon again.

Fatah Revolutionary Council See above under Abu Nidal Organization.

Hamas (also called the Islamic Resistance Movement; in English, "Courage") Hamas emerged in 1987 as a radical offshoot of the Palestinian branch of the Muslim Brotherhood. Its growth coincided with that of the Intifada, or Palestinian uprising against the Israeli occupation. Hamas demands not only a Palestinian state, but one "from the Mediterranean Sea to the Jordan river," which would of course eliminate Israel. The group engages in both political and terrorist activities, with its main base of operations in the Gaza Strip and portions of the West Bank. Its specialty is suicide bomb attacks against military and civilian targets in Israel, but it has also attacked Palestinians it views as Israeli collaborators. In fall 2000, the group claimed responsibility for a Jerusalem car bombing amid renewed clashes between Israelis and Palestinians.

Hezbollah (in English, "The Party of God") A radical Shi'ite organization founded in 1978, Hezbollah is dedicated to the establishment of fundamentalist Islamic rule in Lebanon and elsewhere. Hezbollah drew most of its inspiration and much of its backing from the fundamentalist revolution and regime in Iran, starting in 1979. Most of the group's terrorist activity targets U.S. and Israeli interests, including actions carried out under the rubric of "Islamic Jihad." Hezbollah terrorists bombed the

U.S. embassy and Marine barracks in Lebanon in October 1983 and the U.S. embassy annex in Beirut in September 1984. They also held foreign hostages in Lebanon during the 1980s. By 2000 the group had apparently stepped up efforts to train Palestinians in guerrilla tactics.

Irgun (Irgun Zvai Leumi; in English, "National Military Organization") An Israeli terrorist group founded in 1938, Irgun conducted terrorist attacks against the Palestinians and the British occupation authorities. The group's two most devastating attacks were the bombing of the King David Hotel (which housed British offices) on July 22, 1946, which killed 90 people—many not involved with the British, and the massacre of Arab villagers at Deir Yassin on April 9, 1948, an action conducted with the Stern Gang. Irgun leader Menachem Begin later became prime minister of Israel.

Islamic Group (IG; in Arabic, Al Gama'at al-Islamaya) A large, militant Islamic organization based in Egypt since the late 1970s, IG's spiritual leader is Sheikh Omar Abdel Rahman, who was convicted and imprisoned in the United States in connection with the 1993 World Trade Center bombing and various assassination plots. Starting in 1992, the Islamic Group began to attack foreign tourists in Egypt, hoping to hurt the nation's economy and destabilize the secularist government of Hosni Mubarak. The group also claimed credit for a 1995 assassination attempt against the Egyptian leader. In November 1997, terrorists from the group killed 58 tourists at Luxor, Egypt.

Islamic Jihad The actual nature of this group has been hard to determine. Its name has surfaced mainly in connection with certain terrorist actions such as the April 1983 bombing of the U.S. embassy in Beirut and the bombings later that year of the U.S. Marine Corps barracks in Beirut and the barracks for the French peacekeepers. However, "Islamic Jihad" may simply be an umbrella term used by radical Shi'ite organizations such as Hezbollah when they feel it is safer to not claim direct responsibility for an action.

Jewish Defense League (JDL) This militant Jewish group was founded in Brooklyn, New York, in 1968, by Rabbi Meir Kahane. It started out as a sort of neighborhood crime watch or vigilante group, but by the 1970s it was carrying out violent actions against groups it considered to be oppressing Jews, attacking targets associated with the Soviet Union or Arab/Palestinian groups. The group is believed by some observers to be responsible for two attacks in 1985 on offices of the American-Arab Anti-Discrimination League.

Muslim Brotherhood (Ikwhan) The Muslim Brotherhood is an Islamic fundamentalist group that seeks to replace secular governments in the Muslim world with theocratic governments that would be ruled according to Muslim law (Sharia). There are actually several separate regional Muslim Brotherhood groups in Egypt, Syria, and other countries. The groups are active in domestic politics, where they are opposed by secularist governments or Moslems who disagree with their radical agenda. For example, when Syrian president Hafez al-Assad decided to enter the Lebanese civil war on the side of the Maronite Christians, Moslem Brotherhood radicals attacked al-Assad's younger brother Rifaat as well as police stations and offices of the ruling Bath party. Al-Assad cracked down on the group, which unsuccessfully attempted to assassinate him.

Palestine Liberation Organization (PLO) This umbrella organization for Palestinian nationalist groups has been recognized by the Arab nations as "the sole, legitimate representative of the Palestinian people" and has been increasingly seen around the world as a legitimate political institution that will serve as the foundation for an independent Palestinian state. The PLO was originally founded in 1964 as a nonmilitant organization. Following the disastrous defeat of the Arab participants in the Six-Day War in 1967, however, Yasir Arafat and his al-Fatah organization then forged the PLO into a weapon to be used directly against Israel. In the late 1960s, the PLO carried out guerrilla raids into Israel while functioning as a kind of quasi-state with local autonomy within Jordan. In 1970, Jordan's King Hussein expelled the Palestinian guerrilla groups, which established new bases in Lebanon and Syria. Following the 1973 Arab-Israeli war, the PLO split into moderate and militant factions, with the moderate faction announcing its willingness to accept a Palestinian state in the West Bank and Gaza Strip and the militant, or rejectionist faction still demanding the total destruction of the state of Israel.

Since the mid-1970s, the moderate, mainstream PLO gained increasing legitimacy both in the Arab world and farther afield through participation in the United Nations. The situation was complicated, however, by the civil war in Lebanon that started in 1975 and the Israeli invasion of Lebanon in 1982, when PLO forces split between those loyal to Arafat and those loyal to Syria. In 1988, however, the PLO took on a new role when King Hussein of Jordan transferred his claims to the territory occupied by Israel to the PLO, and the Palestine National Council (the PLO's policy-making body) accepted United Nations Resolutions 242 and 338, as Arafat officially accepted Israel's right to exist. The PLO was removed from the U.S. State Department's roster of terrorist groups soon after.

Popular Front for the Liberation of Palestine (PFLP) A Marxist-Leninist guerrilla organization founded by George Habash in 1967 as a leftist alternative to the Islamic nationalist al-Fatah. Between 1968 and 1970, the PFLP undertook a campaign of aircraft hijackings, mainly targeting Israel's El Al airline. The campaign culminated with the near-simultaneous hijackings of three airliners in September 1970, forcing them to land at Dawson's Field in Jordan, where they were subsequently destroyed. The PFLP also worked with the Red Army Faction in the Massacre at Israel's Lod Airport that resulted in 25 deaths. However, the PFLP hijacking in 1976 of an Air France plane to Entebbe, Uganda, failed after Israeli forces successfully raided on the airport. Similarly, a 1977 hijacking was thwarted by a rescue raid by West German commandos. The PFLP also recruited and worked with the infamous terrorist Carlos "The Jackal" (Ilyich Ramirez Sanchez). Later, the PFLP spearheaded the opposition to Yasir Arafat's moderate pronegotiation stance within the PLO.

Popular Front for the Liberation of Palestine-General Command (PFLP-GC) A splinter group of the PFLP founded in 1968 by Ahmed Jabril, this faction was resolutely committed to the destruction of Israel and specialized in cross-border raids against Israeli citizens. The PFLP-GC has worked and trained Armenian and European terrorist groups. The group accumulated a variety of sophisticated weapons including Soviet AS-7 antiaircraft missiles, antitank missiles, artillery, and even motorized hang gliders used to carry raiders. The PFLP-GC has hijacked airliners, bombed planes and buses, and set off bombs in Jerusalem and other parts of Israel. Its most spectacular success may have been its exchange of three captured Israelis for 1,150 Palestinian prisoners held in Israel. The group has also been linked to the bombing of Pan Am flight 103 in December 1988.

Popular Struggle Front (PSF; Palestine Popular Struggle Front) This Palestinian terrorist group broke from the Palestine Liberation Organization in 1974, joining "rejectionists" who opposed any moves toward settlement of the Arab-Israeli conflict. During the 1970s, the group engaged in hijackings and kidnappings, including the abduction of U.S. Army Colonel Ernest R. Morgan in Beirut. The group also launched bomb and rocket attacks against targets in Israel, leading to retaliatory attacks by the Israeli air force against PSF bases. In 1991, the group rejoined the PLO.

al-Qaida (in English, "The Base") A group established by Saudi Arabian millionaire Osama bin Laden around 1990, al-Qaida recruited mainly Arabs who had fought in Afghanistan against the Soviet invasion in the early 1980s. In February 1998, bin Laden issued a statement calling upon Muslims to kill U.S. citizens throughout the world. The group bombed the U.S. embassies in Nairobi, Kenya, and Dar es Salaam, Tanzania, on August 7, 1998, killing more than 300 persons and injuring more than 5,000 others. The United States retaliated with a cruise missile attack that damaged but did not destroy the group's training camp in

Afghanistan. Bin Laden's operatives are also suspected in the October 12, 2000 bombing of the U.S. destroyer *Cole*, which killed 17 sailors.

Stern Gang A Zionist terrorist group founded by Abraham Stern in the early 1940s. The group became known as Lehi after Stern's death in 1942. Two of the group's major leaders, Yitzhak Shamir and Menachem Begin, later became prime ministers of Israel. Two notorious actions by the Lehi group were the 1948 killing of the United Nations mediator for Palestine, Count Folke Bernadotte, who had been branded as "anti-Zionist," and the massacre that same year of more than 200 Palestinian civilians at the village of Deir Yassin, in which Irgun also participated.

AFRICA

Several dimensions of conflict in Africa have led to armed insurgency and outbreaks of terrorism. Geopolitically, the continent can be divided into two parts. Northern Africa, including Libya, Algeria, and Tunisia, is tied culturally to the Middle East through the common bond of Islam and has participated in the same dynamics that have motivated terrorism in the Middle East. The 1998 bombings of the U.S. embassies in Kenya and Tanzania by terrorists connected to Osama bin Laden also showed that Africa could be a theater for international as well as regional terrorism.

Algeria gained its independence from France through a bloody insurrection in the 1950s and early 1960s that saw much terrorism on both sides. Playing out a conflict common throughout the Islamic world, Islamic fundamentalists have unleashed terror against the moderate government since 1992. The government's failure to recognize the electoral victories of Islamist parties has only added fuel to the flames.

Libya, under Muammar al-Qaddafi, provided bases and support for many international terrorist groups (both Islamic and European) in the 1970s and early 1980s, but it may now be seeking closer ties with the West.

In sub-Saharan Africa, the principal dynamic in the 1950s and 1960s was the struggle of black majorities to gain independence from white-minority colonialist governments. This was complicated by the support given by the Soviets during the Cold War to left-leaning guerrilla groups and the support of western governments and corporations for authoritarian black leaders who could protect investments (such as oil production in Nigeria).

Weak, unbalanced economies, undemocratic leadership, and a general neglect by the developed world continues to create the conditions for insurgency and civil war through much of Africa. Indeed, the violence has typically been on the larger scale of guerrilla war (Mozambique), factional struggle (Sierra Leone), and near-genocidal ethnic conflict (Rwanda) rather than the actions of small terrorist groups.

Southern Africa continues to deal with the legacy of the vicious struggle between South Africa's white minority apartheid government and black insurgents represented by the African National Congress (ANC) and other groups—a struggle that was also carried out by proxy in Mozambique, where RENAMO (Resistência Nacional Moçambicana, or Mozambique National Resistence), backed by the South Africa and Rhodesian white regimes, fought through the 1980s against leftist FRELIMO guerrilla forces supported by the ANC. Yet despite the high crime rate, sporadic terrorism, and the unmet basic needs of millions of poor blacks, South Africa, under an ANC government since 1990, has avoided the chaos that many feared would ensue after the apartheid government ended.

GROUPS IN AFRICA

African National Congress (ANC) The major antiapartheid organization in South Africa, the ANC fought the apartheid regime by both political and guerrilla means. In 1961, following the Sharpesville massacre, the ANC formed a military offshoot, the Umkhonto we Sizwe ("Spear of the Nation"), headed by Nelson Mandela. During the 1960s and 1970s the guerrilla attacks generally avoided hurting innocent civilians. In 1986, however, the organization took a more militant turn when acting ANC president Oliver Tambo encouraged attacks on government facilities and officials and upon civilians viewed as supporters of the white regime. With the establishment of majority black rule in the 1994 elections in which Nelson Mandela became president of South Africa, the ANC has struggled to transform itself from an opposition group to the leading party in a government of national unity.

Eritrean Liberation Front (ELF) A Muslim separatist group founded in 1958, the ELF seeks independence for Muslim Eritrea from Ethiopia. In 1971 a more militant faction called the Eritrean People's Liberation Front emerged and became dominant. (There was also a guerrilla unit designated the Eritrean Liberation Army.) The ELF has hijacked several Ethiopian Airlines flights.

FLN (in French, Front de Liberation Nationale; in English, National Liberation Front) Founded in 1954, the FLN carried on a violent campaign consisting mainly of bombings against Algeria's French colonial rulers. The French settlers, through the OAS, retaliated with violent reprisals. The bloody fighting ended with the establishment of the independent Algerian state in 1962.

Islamic Salvation Front (FIS; in Arabic, Jabha al Islamiyah li-Inqadh) This group was the main fundamentalist Islamic party in Algeria. After the group won majorities in the 1991 elections, secular military leaders staged a coup on January 11, 1992, canceling follow-up elections and ruling by decree. Government forces cracked down on the FIS, arresting thousands of supporters. Throughout the 1990s, the FIS responded with armed attacks on Algerian officials and military, as well as terrorist attacks against civilians; eventually more than 100,000 people died in the conflict. In June 1999 the government and the FIS signed a cease-fire and amnesty agreement.

OAS ("Secret Army Organization") An organization of French and other European settlers in Algeria, the OAS fought against native Algerian nationalists who were seeking to overthrow French rule. In the early 1960s, the OAS took violent action to disrupt peace negotiations between the nationalists and the French government, killing the mayor of Evian, France, the site of the talks. Many members of the French military violently opposed the French decision to grant Algeria independence, and the OAS joined with four former French generals in an unsuccessful attempt to seize Algiers in April 1961. Their ensuing campaign of violence was met with equal violence by the Algerian National Liberation Front (FLN), and most Europeans fled the country.

RENAMO (in Portuguese, Resistência Nacional Moçambicana) or Mozambique National Resistance (MNR) The MNR was formed in the 1970s after Portugal granted independence to Mozambique and a leftist government sympathetic to the African Nationalist Congress took power. The anticommunist MNR was sponsored by the apartheid regime in South Africa and the white government of Rhodesia. Its goal was to destabilize the Mozambican government and to fight FRELIMO, the leftist Mozambican guerrilla movement that was aiding the African National Congress in South Africa. In 1982 the MNR changed its name to RENAMO and began to expand its activities into the nearby countries of Zimbabwe (formerly Rhodesia), Malawi, and Zambia. During the 1980s RENAMO guerrillas used brutal tactics including assassination and kidnapping of government officials and relief workers as well as outright massacres, such as the killing of more than 400 civilians in the town of Homoine. In the early 1990s RENAMO's fortunes declined when the African National Congress took over the South African government, drying up the group's major source of aid. RENAMO and the Mozambican government began to negotiate and signed an accord in 1992. Both RENAMO and FRELIMO participated in UN-supervised elections in 1994; despite disputes over the 1999 election, large-scale violence did not recur.

Zimbabwe African People's Union (ZAPU) The ZAPU was founded in 1961 and led by Joshua Nkomo. It fought for black liberation against the white-run government of what was then known as Rhodesia. During the 1970s the group carried out frequent attacks against Rhodesia's white settlers and blacks whom it viewed as enemy collaborators. The group eventually lost out militarily and politically to its larger black rival, ZANU (Zimbabwe African National Union).

ASIA

While it is difficult to generalize over such a wide area, most terrorism in Asia seems to stem from the conflict between ethnic or religious groups.

The breakup of the Soviet Union resulted in a number of independent Muslim republics in the volatile region bordered by Europe, Asia, and the Middle East. The Russians became concerned about the threat of terrorist or separatist activity resulting from the extension of Muslim influence. In the 1990s, Russia became embroiled in a war to suppress separatists in Chechnya, a mountainous Caucasian republic. The first Russian military campaign was unsuccessful and resulted in considerable Russian casualties. Following a series of Moscow bombings in 1999 that Russia attributed to Chechen terrorists, the Russians launched a new military campaign that seemed to achieve greater success.

In India, the sporadic conflict between Muslims and Hindus that has existed ever since the British partitioned the subcontinent into the mostly Hindu India and the mostly Muslim Pakistan has expressed itself in a number of actions, including the February 2000 hijacking of an Afghani jet on a domestic flight out of Kabul, and its diversion to an airport outside London. By that time the main focus of the conflict was the Indian province of Kashmir, which Muslims want to make either an independent state or part of Pakistan. Insurgencies by Muslim separatists also persist in Indonesia (and to a lesser extent) the Philippines.

Besides the Hindu-Muslim conflict, the Sikhs, a religious minority who live mainly in northern India, have also been in violent conflict with the Hindu majority. Demanding a separate state and reacting to Indian government actions such as the 1984 attack on one of Sikism's holiest temples (the Golden Temple of Amritsar), Sikh terrorists assassinated Indian prime minister Indira Gandhi in October 1984 and were accused of the bombing of an Air India jet in June 1985 that resulted in 329 deaths.

For many years Sri Lanka (formerly British Ceylon) has been the scene of a persistent terrorist campaign by a group known as the Tamil Tigers that seeks independence for the Tamil minority (the majority in the country are Sinhalese). Despite some victories by the Sri Lankan military, the insurgency continues.

Japan, perhaps the Asian nation most like the industrial West socioeconomically, has had its own indigenous left-wing terrorist groups, including the Japanese Red Army, but as with European groups such as the Red Army Faction, leftist terrorism has not been a major concern in recent years. Rather than a resurgence from the right, however, the mid-1990s witnessed the emergence of the idiosyncratic terror cult Aum Shinri Kyo, which made the first large-scale chemical weapons terrorist attack when it released Sarin nerve gas into the Tokyo subway. Japanese police arrested the cult's leader and have cracked down on the group's widespread facilities.

Another potential Asian terrorist trouble spot is North Korea. North Korea's communist government has long carried out sporadic state-sponsored terrorism against South Korea and has developed ballistic missiles and possibly nuclear weapons. North Korea's economy is very weak, and its leaders began in the late 1990s to seek better cooperation both with South Korea and the United States. In a possible breakthrough in June 2000, the presidents of the two Koreas had a cordial meeting and expressed hopes for closer cooperation and eventual unification.

There is also the potential for other ethnic-based conflict and terrorism in Southeast Asia. For example, the Molluccans, a distinct ethnic group in Indonesia, have sometimes engaged in separatist violence and terrorism (such as train hijackings).

GROUPS IN ASIA

Armenian Revolutionary Army This Armenian nationalist organization surfaced suddenly in 1983 to claim credit for the murder of two Turkish diplomats in Brussels. Later that year, the group seized the Turkish embassy in Lisbon. The terrorists blew up the building, killing themselves and two of their hostages. It remained unclear whether the group had any real existence or was a cover name.

Armenian Secret Army for the Liberation of Armenia (ASALA) An organization of Armenian nationalists founded in 1975, ASALA seeks an end to discrimination against and mistreatment of Turkey's Armenian minority. Its goal is the formation of an independent state in the traditional Armenian homeland in eastern Turkey, northern Iran, northern Iraq, and the former Soviet Armenian republic. The group was fueled by anger among many Armenians who feel that the West favors Turkey for geopolitical purposes and continues to ignore the 1915 Turkish genocide of Armenians that claimed an estimated 1.5 million victims. The group has engaged in several terrorist bombings including a 1983 attack on Orly Airport in Paris. By the end of the 1980s the organization was in decline, and many Armenian nationalists now oppose terrorism as being counterproductive.

Aum Shinri Kyo (Aum Supreme Truth) A Japanese religious cult established in 1987 by Soko Asahara, who formed a grandiose plan to take over the world. When the plan failed to materialize, Asahara gradually emphasized apocalyptic elements, including an Armageddon that he claimed would be triggered by the United States. Using the cult's considerable financial resources and technically trained members, the group began to research and develop chemical, biological, and even nuclear weapons. On March 20, 1995, cult members released Sarin, a nerve gas, into the Tokyo subway, killing 12 people and injuring more than 5,000. Despite the arrest of its leader, the cult continued to recruit members in the late 1990s and maintained a web site.

Chukaku-Ha (in English, the "Nucleus") A Japanese leftist extremist group, Chukaku-Ha seeks to overthrow Japan's constitutional monarchy and to sever ties with the United States. While the group is primarily political, it does have a terrorist wing that has focused on attacking infrastructure and property rather than killing. In 1988, the group attacked the Japanese National Railway to protest its privatization, as well as attacking the construction site for the Tokyo International Airport at Narita.

Harakat ul-Mujahadeen (HUM) This radical Muslim group is based in Pakistan but operates mainly in Kashmir, an area disputed between Muslim Pakistan and majority Hindu India. The group has attacked Indian troops and tourists in Kashmir and has been linked to some kidnappings. The HUM is believed to be part of Osama bin Laden's network. Its terrorist training bases in Afghanistan were damaged by U.S. cruise missile attacks in 1999.

Japanese Red Army (JRA; in Japanese, "Nippon Sekigun") This small but extremely violent Japanese left-wing terrorist group was founded in 1971 as an offshoot of radical student movements of the late 1960s. Its founder, Fusako Shigenobu, linked up with Palestinian terrorists and went with a group of followers to train in Lebanon. The JRA first became known to the world when it hijacked a Japanese airliner in 1970. It also carried out terrorist acts in the Middle East on behalf of the Popular Front for the Liberation of Palestine, such as the massacre at Lod Airport in Israel in 1972. In September 1974, the JRA seized the French embassy in the Hague and held 12 hostages until the French government freed an imprisoned comrade. Since the late 1970s, the JRA no longer seems to operate as a distinct group, but its members continued to carry out terrorist acts individually or under the umbrella name Anti-Imperialist International Brigade.

Kashmiri Liberation Front This is a separatist group representing Muslim Kashmiris who want independence from Hindu-dominated India. This and other separatist groups receive covert support from Muslim Pakistan, which also claims the Kashmir region and has fought repeated military skirmishes with India.

Komando Jihad This group, founded by Ali Moertopo in 1977, was a Muslim separatist group in Indonesia. Its terrorist activities included a 1980 hijacking of an Indonesian airliner, which was foiled by a raid by government forces. Many Komando Jihad terrorists were imprisoned in the 1980s and released in the 1990s.

Moro Liberation Front (MLF; also called the Moro National Liberation Front) This is a Muslim separatist group seeking a separate state for Muslims in the islands of Mindanao and the Sulu Archipelago in the southern Philippines. The group has received support from both Libya's Muammar al-Qaddafi and Iran. The group mainly conducted guerrilla operations, but in 1975 it hijacked two Philippine airliners. (The second hijacking resulted in the death or capture of the hijackers.) Government counterterrorism efforts and internal disputes weakened the group. In 1986 the new Philippine president, Corazon Aquino, signed a truce agreement with the MLF.

New People's Army (NPA) A Maoist guerrilla group in the Philippines, associated with the Communist Party of the Philippines. During the 1970s and early 1980s the group grew, spreading its influence from its rural roots into the cities. The repressive activities of the Marcos regime brought new supporters to the movement. The group engaged in relatively small-scale terrorist activities, primarily against government officials and police. In the late 1980s the group underwent internal splits and purges that weakened it, and the overthrow of the Marcos regime offered democratic alternatives, although continuing poverty still fueled unrest.

Tamil Tigers (Liberation Tigers of Tamil Eelam or LTTE) The Tamil Tigers are a Sri Lankan separatist guerrilla organization founded in 1972. The island nation of Sri Lanka (Ceylon) has seen bitter conflict between the Hindu Tamil minority and the Buddhist Sinhalese majority. The Tigers seek an independent Tamil state in the northern and eastern parts of the island. Despite receiving antiterrorist aid and troops from India in the late 1980s, the Sri Lankan government has been unable to defeat the Tigers, who have proven able to mount substantial attacks.

LATIN AMERICA

The story of terrorism in Latin America is woven from persistent strands. The countries in South America (as well as Mexico) were founded by Spanish and Portuguese colonizers starting in the 16th century. The conquest of extensive indigenous societies (the Aztecs, Mayas, and Incas) created a continually exploited underclass of Indian peoples. Colonialism ensured that an elite born in Europe and its descendents controlled vast lands worked by impoverished natives.

The invasion of Spain by Napoleon in the early 19th century triggered liberal, revolutionary sentiments in members of the Latin American elite who also looked for inspiration to the first American revolution, which had given birth to the United States in 1776. Despite brutal countermeasures by Spain, a series of successful revolutions swept Latin America, led by José de San Martín and Bernardo O'Higgins in the south, Simón Bolívar in the north. A successful revolution in Mexico overthrew European rule in 1821. But despite the idealism of leaders such as Bolívar, who sought to create something like a United States of the Americas, the new countries went their separate ways.

By the 20th century, the predominant influence on Latin America was its powerful northern neighbor, the United States. Ever since the United States had claimed the western Hemisphere as its "manifest destiny," and thus off limits to Europeans in the preceding century, American businesses and corporations had invested a lot of capital in South and Central America. They pressed the federal government to protect their interests with military force, including the U.S. Marines on occasion. Most Latin American countries remained poor and poorly governed. Typically, the military or a military-backed oligarchy brutally suppressed any political opposition.

Following World War II, the poor nations in Africa and Asia that had been ruled by Europeans struggled for independence and, with less success, economic self-sufficiency. During the Cold War, the Soviets generally supported insurgencies and guerrilla groups that at least claimed to represent the poor, while the United States, in the name of stability and the checking of worldwide communism, usually sided with the ruling oligarchs.

The Cuban revolution that brought Fidel Castro to power in Cuba in 1959 gave leftist insurgents a beachhead in the Western Hemisphere. Castro's victory inspired charismatic guerrilla leaders such as his compatriot Che Guevara, French revolutionary theorist and exponent of terrorism Frantz Fanon, and the Brazilian Carlos Marighella. To these thinkers, terrorism was not a blind striking out against injustice, but a weapon that, combined with guerrilla war in the countryside, could destabilize oligarchic governments. Much of their thinking, including the use of terrorism to trigger government repression that could in turn inspire a general uprising, would become the common currency of terrorist groups around the world.

Other than in Cuba, leftist insurgents achieved long-term results only in Nicaragua, where in 1979 the leftist Sandinistas overthrew U.S.–backed dictator Anastasio Somoza, a staunch anticommunist. The Sandinistas were then attacked by the Contras, U.S.–backed guerrillas, and they were defeated in a 1990 election by a U.S.–backed moderate candidate, Violetta Chamorro.

In Chile, the brief reign of the leftist government of Salvador Allende was overthrown in 1973 by the U.S.–backed Augusto Pinochet. In Chile, as in Argentina, right-wing "death squads" unleashed state terrorism on insurgents, political opponents, and random citizens. Similar tactics were also used in Guatemala and El Salvador. Some hope for democracy emerged, however, when Patricio Aylwin Azócar, leader of a democratic coalition, was elected president of Chile. While Pinochet still had a powerful position as head of the army, he stepped down in 1998. Later that year, he was arrested in London on charges of brutality against Spanish citizens in Chile during his regime. The British eventually declined to extradite him on grounds of his poor health, but he may still face charges in Chile.

In Colombia, the continuing three-sided struggle between the government, leftist rebels, and drug lords has brought calls for increased American aid, which opponents doubt would have any effect on the drug problem, and could involve the U.S. in a Vietnam-like quagmire.

Peru's Sendero Luminoso (Shining Path) became known for its unusual and ruthless tactics. The teachings of its founder, Abimael Guzman, are based on a Maoist model, focusing on gaining control of rural areas and ruthlessly eliminating opponents using both guerrilla and terrorist tactics. Guzman's arrest and successful campaigns by the Peruvian military had largely destroyed the Shining Path by the mid-1990s.

Latin America continues to struggle with poverty, insurgency, and outbreaks of terrorism, though economic growth in some areas such as Brazil, and the possibility of reform in others, such as Mexico, have brought some areas of hope.

Groups in Latin America

Bandero Roja (GBR; in English, "Red Flag") Was a small Venezuelan leftist guerrilla and terrorist group that operated mainly during the late 1970s and early 1980s. It primarily targeted wealthy business owners, kidnapping for them ransom and demanding protection money. In 1981 the group carried out its best-known action, the simultaneous hijacking of three domestic airliners, demanding the release of prisoners plus a ransom of $10 million. Following the failure of negotiations, some of the group then fled to Cuba, while others were arrested or killed by government forces.

Cinchoneros Popular Liberation Movement (MPL) This small Honduran leftist group was the armed wing of the People's Revolutionary Union, a communist splinter group. (Cinchoneros was the nickname of Serapio Romero, a Honduran peasant rebel apparently executed in the 19th century.) The group financed itself through robberies and kidnappings, as well as receiving support and cooperation from Cuba and Salvadoran FMLN guerrillas. In 1980, the MPL hijacked a Honduran

Airlines jet in an unsuccessful attempt to win freedom for 15 Salvadoran leftists imprisoned in Honduras. In 1982, the MPL raided an economic conference in San Pedro Sula, taking 105 hostages. Again failing to win their demands, they traded the hostages for safe passage to Cuba. The group conducted other attacks into the late 1980s.

Extraditables The terrorist arm of the Colombian drug cartels, the Extraditables emerged in the 1980s. By the end of the decade they had killed 261 people and wounded more than 1,200 in about 200 separate attacks, including the bombing of an Avianca airliner in November 1989 and the truck bombing of the Bogotá police headquarters the same month. The purpose of the terrorism was to pressure the Colombian government to back down from its antidrug efforts and to refuse to extradite drug lords to the United States.

Frente Farabundo Martí De Liberación Nacional (FMLN; in English, "Farabundo Marti National Liberation Front") FMLN is the umbrella organization for the five major Salvadoran left-wing guerrilla groups that fought to overturn the government of El Salvador during the 1980s. During that time the group received extensive support from Cuba and the Sandinista regime in Nicaragua. The group used terrorism as a core part of its strategy to destabilize the Salvadoran government and prevent the establishment of a western-style democracy. As with many other guerrilla groups, FMLN has used kidnapping and extortion (which it refers to as "taxes") to raise money in areas it controls.

Fuerzas Armadas de Liberación Nacional (FALN; in English, "Armed Forces of National Liberation") A militant Puerto Rican separatist organization, FALN has conducted terrorist bombings in both the United States and Puerto Rico. Its best known attacks were the bombing of five New York City banks on October 26, 1974, and the bombing of Fraunces Tavern in New York's Wall Street area, which killed 4 people and wounded more than 60. The group was disrupted in April 1980 by the arrest of 11 members in Evanston, Illinois, during an attempted armed robbery. The FALN set off additional bombs in New York on December 31, 1983, targeting the FBI, police, and court offices; the group largely became inactive in the 1980s. This group should not be confused with the Venezuelan FALN, a marxist guerrilla group active in the 1960s and early 1970s.

Fuerzas Armadas Revolutionarias de Colombia (FARC; in English, "Revolutionary Armed Forces of Colombia") The largest leftist guerrilla movement in Colombia, FARC was established in 1966 by the Colombian Communist Party as its military wing, and the organization had close relations with the Soviet and Cuban governments. During the 1980s, FARC conducted bombings of Colombian government targets as well as U.S.–owned businesses in Colombia and carried out killings and kidnappings. A May 1984 cease-fire ended large-scale military actions but did not stop the terror campaign. FARC has also cooperated with drug interests, offering protection in exchange for money to purchase weapons and supplies, and it has also kidnapped people for ransom, including the abduction of a U.S. Peace Corps worker, who was released after a $250,000 ransom was received. In 1998, FARC began sporadic peace negotiations with the Colombian government, but fighting continued.

Fuerzas Revolucionarios Populares Lorenzo Zelaya (FRP-LZ; in English "Lorenzo Zelaya Popular Revolutionary Forces") The FRP-LZ was a Honduran Marxist-Leninist group which sought to overthrow the Honduran government. Active mainly during the early 1980s, the FRP-LZ targeted Honduran government facilities (such as the National Assembly), U.S. diplomats, and diplomats from Argentina, Chile, and Peru (countries that the group accused of supporting U.S. interests). In 1982 the group hijacked a Honduran airliner. The hijackers failed to win their demands for $1 million and the release of 32 political prisoners, but they were allowed to flee to Cuba after releasing their hostages. The arrest and defection of the group's leader, Efraín Duarte Salgado, in 1983 led to the group's disintegration.

Movimiento 19 de Abril (M-19; in English, "Movement of April 19") A Colombian rebel group that combined leftist, nationalist, and populist appeals for the overthrow of the Colombian establishment and an end to U.S. imperialism. The group was active through the 1970s and 1980s, financing its plans with robberies and extortion of (and sometimes cooperation with) drug traffickers. The group also received considerable training and support from Cuba, Nicaragua, and Libya. In 1980, M-19 seized 15 diplomats and 16 other hostages at the embassy of the Dominican Republic, freeing them after 61 days in exchange for ransom and safe passage to Cuba. The group's largest attack was the 1985 seizure of the Justice Ministry building in Bogotá, involving about 500 hostages, including members of the Supreme Court and Council of State. Government forces counterattacked, killing the terrorists, but 11 Supreme Court justices and 50 other hostages died in the fighting. The M-19 also carried on a running skirmish with the drug cartels. In the 1990s M-19 signed several accords with the government and began to function as a regular political party.

Movimiento Revolucionario do Octobre 8 (MR-8; in English, "Revolutionary Movement of October 8") MR-8 was a Brazilian terrorist organization that was particularly active in the 1960s and 1970s. It was affiliated with the Brazilian Communist Party. It conducted numerous attacks, of which the most famous was the kidnapping of U.S. ambassador Charles Elbrick in 1969.

Movimiento Revolucionario Tupac Amaru (MRTA; in English, "Tupac Amaru Revolutionary Movement") A Marxist-Leninist guerrilla movement founded in Peru by radical university students and intellectuals in 1983, the MRTA is named after Tupac Amaru, an 18th-century anticolonialist leader. The group has emphasized a traditional marxist approach (as opposed to the Maoist approach of Peru's Shining Path). During the 1980s, the MRTA specialized in attacks on U.S. representatives and businesses and raised money through extortion of businesses and offering protection to drug traffickers. During the 1990s, many members were arrested and the group seemed to be in decline. However, in December 1996, MRTA terrorists seized the Japanese embassy in Lima, taking hundreds of hostages. Government forces retook the embassy and freed the captives, and MRTA mounted no further major attacks during the decade.

Puerto Rican Nationalists Throughout much of the 20th century the Puerto Rico Nationalist Party sought independence of the island from the United States. The party's most important leader, Pedro Albizo Campos, failed to win popular support in a 1932 election, and was subsequently imprisoned for plotting to overthrow the U.S. government. Freed and repatriated after World War II, Campos again attempted to gain political support, but the Nationalist Party did poorly in the 1948 election. Campos and the more radical nationalists abandoned politics in favor of terrorist action. In 1950 they attacked both the governor's house in Puerto Rico and Blair House in Washington, D.C., where President Harry Truman was staying during White House renovations. In 1954, armed Puerto Rican nationalist terrorists fired into the chambers of the U.S. House of Representatives, wounding five representatives.

Sendero Luminoso (in English, "The Shining Path") A Peruvian Maoist-inspired terrorist group founded by Abimael Guzman in 1969, Sendero Luminoso has been one of the most unpredictable and vicious terrorist groups. The group is rural-based and has sought to enlist the support of the native Quechua people through appeals to their heritage and traditions. With little support from Cuba or other outside forces, the group provides for its needs mainly through bank robberies and extortion ("war taxes.") Ironically, although the group has attacked Peruvian officials and foreign diplomats, the majority of its violence has been directed against the very peasants it claims to be fighting for, brutally punishing people suspected of collaborating with the authorities. In the 1990s, the group went into decline with the arrest of its leader Abimael Guzman in 1992, the arrest of other leaders in 1995, and a government amnesty for members who agreed to renounce terrorism.

Tonton Macoutes (in English, "Volunteers for National Security") Tonton Macoutes was an unofficial militia sponsored and used by Haitian dictator François "Papa Doc" Duvalier to eliminate enemies and silence dissent via state terror. After Duvalier was deposed in 1985, the Tonton Macoutes offered its services to another president, Henri Namphy. In 1988 the Tonton Macoutes attacked a church service in Port-au-Prince that included dissenters, killing 9 persons, wounding 77, and setting fire to the church. The church's pastor, Jean-Bertrand Aristide, survived the attack, however, and rallied supporters to fight the Tonton Macoutes. In 1990, Aristide briefly served as president, was deposed, and then restored to office in 1994 with the aid of international forces. The decade ended with a new spate of political violence.

Tupamaros (Movimiento de Liberación Nacional or MLN; in English, "National Liberation Movement") Tupamaros is a Uruguayan guerrilla and terrorist group founded in the early 1960s by Raul Sendic Antonaccio. Like the MRTA, the MLN derived its name from Tupac Amaru, an 18th-century Peruvian Indian chieftain who fought the Spanish. The group began its activities by robbing and attacking banks and other institutions, but by the mid-1960s it had broadened its base in the capital of Montevideo, gaining influence through propaganda exposing government corruption and by employing the Robin Hood–like tactic of giving the proceeds of robberies to the poor. In 1970, the Tupamaros kidnapped and killed USAID official Daniel A. Mitrione. The following year they kidnapped the British ambassador. The Uruguayan government successfully suppressed the group in 1972, but the battle also resulted in the reactionary imposition of military government until 1984. In 1985, the new civilian government declared an amnesty for Tupamaros prisoners, and Sendic, the founder, entered mainstream politics.

UNITED STATES AND CANADA

Despite such horrific acts as the Oklahoma City bombing in 1995, the United States in modern times has had a considerably lower rate of terrorist attacks than most parts of the world. But this is not to say that political and economic violence have not had a significant place in U.S. history.

During the first half of the 19th century, the bitter battle over slavery gave rise to terrorism on both sides, such as the violence over Kansas statehood that gave rise to the term *bleeding Kansas.* Following the Civil War, southern whites brutally repressed the freed blacks. Race remained a persistent source of terrorism in the United States.

In the later 19th and early 20th century, labor struggles were another major source of terrorism. In many industries the guns and clubs of private police forces were used to break up strikes and union organizations, and the municipal and state police often sided with the companies against the strikers. In turn, labor radicals such as the more militant members of the International Workers of the World (IWW) engaged in some sabotage and bombings.

In addition to the largely peaceful civil rights and antiwar movements, the social upheaval of the 1960s also spun off a variety of leftist terrorist groups. Their causes ranged from black power (Black Panthers, Black Liberation Army, some Black Muslims) to leftist anti-imperialism (the Weathermen, New World Liberation Front, and others) to the bizarre (Symbionese Liberation Army). However, the end of the Vietnam War and the prosperity of the 1980s led to a diminishment of left-wing terrorism in the United States.

In the late 1980s and 1990s, most terrorism came from the right wing. Its motivations included white supremacy (as with the Aryan Nations and the Ku Klux Klan, as well as Christian Identity groups that espoused a theology of whiteness) as well as a more generalized populist revolt against what many people, particularly in rural areas, perceived to be a too-powerful federal government that served alien economic interests. By the late 1980s, this sentiment had found its widespread expression in the founding of numerous militias. (Although most militias did not engage in overt violence, some fringe elements did. The Oklahoma City bombing, however, was the work of two men who had no real involvement with organized militia groups.)

Canada has had little terrorist activity, with the exception of some "spillover" activity from U.S. groups and the activities of some radical French Quebec separatists, which has diminished as Quebec has gained greater autonomy.

A few other issues have also caused persistent terrorism. Radical antiabortion groups have bombed women's health clinics and killed personnel. Buildings presumed to be associated with Jews or gays have also been attacked.

Even the Earth and its animals have found terrorist advocates. Ecoterrorists under the name Earth Liberation Front have destroyed lumber company facilities and even a Colorado ski resort. A related group, animal rights activists, such as the Animal Liberation Front, have freed laboratory animals and attacked facilities involved with animal or genetic research.

Although the actual damage caused by terrorists in the United States remains small, as the nation perhaps most committed to freedom of association and expression, the United States has struggled to reconcile constitutional rights with security. Recent developments in Congress, such as the passage of the 1996 Antiterrorism and Effective Death Penalty Act, suggest that in the aftermath of the Oklahoma City bombing the pendulum has swung somewhat in favor of counterterrorism.

GROUPS IN THE UNITED STATES AND CANADA

Animal Liberation Front (ALF) A radical animal rights organization founded in 1978, it has conducted several attacks on research and food facilities in Great Britain and the United States, notably the lacing of Mars candy bars with rat poison in 1984 and the destruction of a livestock disease research laboratory at the University of California, Davis, in 1987. In October 1999, the same group, under the name Earth Liberation Front, claimed responsibility for arson that caused $12 million in damage to a Vail, Colorado, ski resort.

Armed Resistance Unit A small U.S. left-wing organization that claimed credit for the November 6, 1983, bombing of the Senate wing of the U.S. capitol building. The group stated that the attack was in protest of the U.S. invasion of Grenada. The group faded away; it may have been a cover name for the United Freedom Front.

Aryan Nations A loose coalition of U.S. white supremacist, anti-Semitic radical right-wing groups. The organization was founded by Richard Girnt Butler in 1974 and attracted followers from the Ku Klux Klan and other racist groups. It seeks the formation of a "white homeland" in the northwest United States. Although it does not directly conduct terrorist operations, some observers suspect it is a haven or supporter of terrorist groups such as the Order as well as individual terrorists. By 2000 successful legal action by the Southern Poverty Law Center had resulted in the group's losing its compound and much of its resources.

Black Liberation Army An extremist U.S. Black Power group, the Black Liberation Army killed eight law enforcement officers between 1971 and 1973. A massive FBI effort led to the arrests of most of the group's leaders, and the group disintegrated.

Black Panther Party The most prominent U.S. Black Power group, the Black Panthers were founded in 1966 in Oakland, California, by Huey Newton and Bobby Seale. The Panthers attempted to be both a grassroots community organization, running schools and breakfast programs, and an urban guerrilla force that targeted law enforcement officers. In the late 1960s and early 1970s a series of violent confrontations with police and a massive FBI effort led to the death, arrest, or exile of most of the organization's leading members.

Covenant, The Sword, and The Arm of the Lord A U.S. white supremacist group, affiliated with Aryan Nations, this group was active in the 1980s. In 1985, police uncovered a large weapons cache and training camp used by the group.

Le Front de Libération du Québec (FLQ; in English, "Quebec Liberation Front") This violent separatist group bombed Canadian government and public facilities in the province of Quebec during the 1960s. On October 5, 1970, the group kidnapped British trade commissioner James R. Cross in Montreal and demanded $500,000 and the release of 23 FLQ prisoners for his return. When Canadian prime minister Pierre Trudeau refused to negotiate, the group kidnapped another official, Quebec's minister of labor and immigration, Pierre Laporte, and strangled him to death. Police found the kidnappers' hideout and negotiated for Cross's release in exchange for safe passage to Cuba.

Ku Klux Klan (KKK) A white supremacist, racist group, the KKK, was originally founded in the United States during the post–Civil War Reconstruction period as a way to intimidate and suppress the newly freed blacks and their white political allies. The group had a resurgence in the 1920s and it broadened its agenda to include anti-immigrant, anti-Catholic, and anti-Semitic activities. Klansmen sought to strike terror into their victims by wearing white sheets and hoods and burning crosses, and the group carried out hundreds of lynchings early in the 20th century. Starting in the 1980s, however, successful lawsuits brought by Morris Dees of the Southern Poverty Law Center and other plaintiffs bankrupted and dispersed the major Klan organizations, and the group is now more of a symbol of hatred than an active terrorist force.

New World Liberation Front (NWLF) A U.S. left-wing group, mainly active in California during the 1970s, the NWLF conducted numerous, mostly small bombings against public utilities, particularly targeting International Telephone and Telegraph (IT&T), which it accused of helping to overthrow the leftist Allende government in Chile.

The Order A violent, white supremacist, neo-Nazi organization, the Order had a brief but violent career in the mid-1980s. It was founded in 1983 by Robert Matthews, who died in a shootout with police in Puget Sound, Washington, in December 1984. The group raised money through robbery, notably an attack on a Brinks armored car outside Ukiah, California, in June 1983, which yielded $3.6 million, at that time the largest armored car robbery in U.S. history. The Order declared that its goal was to overthrow the U.S. government, which it claimed was "occupied" or controlled by secret Zionist forces, and to establish an independent "white nation" in the northwestern United States. The group assassinated Denver radio talk-show host Alan Berg (who was Jewish) in 1984 and bombed a Seattle theater and a synagogue in Boise, Idaho. Successful investigation by the FBI and subsequent prosecution essentially destroyed the group by 1987.

Posse Comitatus (in English, "Power of the County") A U.S. right-wing organization founded in 1969, it was one of the earliest expressions of a generalized movement on the radical right that rejected federal authority, taxation, and courts, insisting that only local, county-level authorities were legitimate. Although it has not carried out terrorist actions as a group, members have been implicated in shoot-outs with police and attacks on government facilities and officials.

Symbionese Liberation Army (SLA) A tiny, idiosyncratic, California-based left-wing terrorist group, the SLA surfaced with the killing of Oakland education superintendent Marcus Foster and the kidnapping and subsequent brainwashing of newspaper heiress Patricia Hearst in 1974. The SLA tried to build its image in the minority community by demanding ransom in the form of food distribution to the poor, but the group had no real popular support. On May 17, 1974, a gun battle and a fire killed six members of the small group, effectively destroying it.

United Freedom Front (UFF) The UFF was a small but active American radical left-wing organization that attacked U.S. military installations and major corporations during the early 1980s. A major effort by federal and local law enforcement agencies led to the arrest and imprisonment of virtually the entire group.

Weather Underground (popularly known as the Weathermen) The Weather Underground was a violent Marxist terrorist group formed in Chicago in 1969 by members of Students for a Democratic Society (SDS) who wanted a more militant, revolutionary program. (The name comes from a line in a Bob Dylan song: "You don't need a weatherman to know which way the wind blows.") The Weathermen conducted numerous bombings and arson attacks for about a year. In March 1970, however, seven of the group's top leaders were killed in an apparently accidental explosion in a New York City apartment they had been using for assembling bombs.

CHAPTER 3

LAWS AND COURT CASES RELATING TO TERRORISM

Because terrorism is a problem that crosses both state lines and national boundaries, it is generally a matter of federal law. However, state laws against anarchists and communists were passed in the 20th century, and states have laws against hate crimes, which can also apply to some terrorist acts.

FEDERAL LEGISLATION

Federal law is found in the United States Code. There are a number of provisions in the U.S. Code that relate to persons suspected of belonging to groups that use terrorism or advocate the overthrow of the U.S. government.

DEFINITION OF TERRORISM

18 U.S. Code Sec. 2331 defines "international terrorism" as follows:

(1) the term "international terrorism" means activities that
(A) involve violent acts or acts dangerous to human life that are a violation of the criminal laws of the United States or of any State, or that would be a criminal violation if committed within the jurisdiction of the United States or of any State;
(B) appear to be intended—
(i) to intimidate or coerce a civilian population;
(ii) to influence the policy of a government by intimidation or coercion; or
(iii) to affect the conduct of a government by assassination or kidnapping; and
(C) occur primarily outside the territorial jurisdiction of the United States, or transcend national boundaries in terms of the means by

which they are accomplished, the persons they appear intended to intimidate or coerce, or the locale in which their perpetrators operate or seek asylum

SEDITION

Sedition can be described as advocacy or action aimed at overthrowing the government. According to 18 U.S.C. Sec. 2384, "Seditious conspiracy" is defined as follows:

> If two or more persons in any State or Territory, or in any place subject to the jurisdiction of the United States, conspire to overthrow, put down, or to destroy by force the Government of the United States, or to levy war against them, or to oppose by force the authority thereof, or by force to prevent, hinder, or delay the execution of any law of the United States, or by force to seize, take, or possess any property of the United States contrary to the authority thereof, they shall each be fined under this title or imprisoned not more than twenty years, or both.

18 U.S.C. Sec. 2385 deals with advocating the overthrow of the government:

> Whoever knowingly or willfully advocates, abets, advises, or teaches the duty, necessity, desirability, or propriety of overthrowing or destroying the government of the United States or the government of any State, Territory, District or Possession thereof, or the government of any political subdivision therein, by force or violence, or by the assassination of any officer of any such government; or
>
> Whoever, with intent to cause the overthrow or destruction of any such government, prints, publishes, edits, issues, circulates, sells, distributes, or publicly displays any written or printed matter advocating, advising, or teaching the duty, necessity, desirability, or propriety of overthrowing or destroying any government in the United States by force or violence, or attempts to do so; or
>
> Whoever organizes or helps or attempts to organize any society, group, or assembly of persons who teach, advocate, or encourage the overthrow or destruction of any such government by force or violence; or becomes or is a member of, or affiliates with, any such society, group, or assembly of persons, knowing the purposes thereof—Shall be fined under this title or imprisoned not more than twenty years, or both, and shall be ineligible for employment by the United States or any department or agency thereof, for the five years next following his conviction.

If two or more persons conspire to commit any offense named in this section, each shall be fined under this title or imprisoned not more than twenty years, or both, and shall be ineligible for employment by the United States or any department or agency thereof, for the five years next following his conviction.

As used in this section, the terms "organizes" and "organize", with respect to any society, group, or assembly of persons, include the recruiting of new members, the forming of new units, and the regrouping or expansion of existing clubs, classes, and other units of such society, group, or assembly of persons.

In practice, the sedition laws (including those passed during the McCarthy era of the Cold War, such as the Smith Act of 1940 and the McCarran Act of 1950) are not generally enforced against persons who simply advocate the overthrow of the government. During the 1950s and 1960s, the Supreme Court gradually broadened the protections afforded by the First Amendment in such a way that mere belief, advocacy, or discussion was not illegal. Some knowledge of and participation in actual activity aimed at the overthrow of the government was required. However, recent cases stemming from later antiterrorist laws tend to suggest that immigrants or aliens in the United States have less protection, and can be kept out (or deported) for engaging in advocacy or other behavior that would be protected if done by U.S. citizens.

IMMIGRATION ACT

In general, aliens who engage in terrorist activities as defined in Sec. 1182 of the Immigration and Naturalization Act are excludable and deportable. Terrorist activity is defined as follows:

(I) The highjacking [sic] or sabotage of any conveyance (including an aircraft, vessel, or vehicle).

(II) The seizing or detaining, and threatening to kill, injure, or continue to detain, another individual in order to compel a third person (including a governmental organization) to do or abstain from doing any act as an explicit or implicit condition for the release of the individual seized or detained.

(III) A violent attack upon an internationally protected person (as defined in section 1116(b)(4) of title 18) or upon the liberty of such a person.

(IV) An assassination.

(V) The use of any—

(a) biological agent, chemical agent, or nuclear weapon or device, or

(b) explosive or firearm (other than for mere personal monetary gain), with intent to endanger, directly or indirectly, the safety of one or more individuals or to cause substantial damage to property.

(VI) A threat, attempt, or conspiracy to do any of the foregoing.

[As used in this chapter] [of the U.S. Code], the term "engage in terrorist activity" means to commit, in an individual capacity or as a member of an organization, an act of terrorist activity or an act which the actor knows, or reasonably should know, affords material support to any individual, organization, or government in conducting a terrorist activity at any time, including any of the following acts:

(I) The preparation or planning of a terrorist activity.
(II) The gathering of information on potential targets for terrorist activity.
(III) The providing of any type of material support, including a safe house, transportation, communications, funds, false identification, weapons, explosives, or training, to any individual the actor knows or has reason to believe has committed or plans to commit a terrorist activity.
(IV) The soliciting of funds or other things of value for terrorist activity or for any terrorist organization.
(V) The solicitation of any individual for membership in a terrorist organization, terrorist government, or to engage in a terrorist activity.

ANTITERRORISM ACT OF 1996

The Antiterrorism and Effective Death Penalty Act of 1996 has added or revised many provisions of the U.S. code that define terrorist activity and that deal with related matters such as deportation of immigrants and the regulation of chemical and biological weapons as well as explosives.

The following is a summary of the provisions that deal directly with terrorism (material in quotes is from the legislative summary; see Appendix D for the full text).

Jurisdiction for Lawsuits Against Terrorist States

Title II, Subtitle B gives victims of foreign terrorism greater ability to sue a foreign government that sponsored the terrorist attack, in cases where "money damages are sought against a foreign government for personal injury or death caused by an act of torture, extra judicial killing, aircraft sabotage, hostage taking, or the provision of material support or resources to terrorists," subject to a 10-year statute of limitations. (Such lawsuits have generally been barred on grounds of "sovereign immunity" in the past.)

However, the right to sue can be limited in cases in which "the Attorney General certifies will interfere with a criminal investigation or prosecution, or a national security operation, related to the incident that gave rise to the cause of action, subject to specified restrictions."

Assistance to Victims of Terrorism

Title II, Subtitle C, entitled the Justice for Victims of Terrorism Act of 1996, amends the Victims of Crimes Act of 1984 to provide money for states "(1) to provide compensation and assistance to State residents who, while outside U.S. territorial boundaries, are victims of a terrorist act or mass violence and are not eligible for compensation under the Omnibus Diplomatic Security and Antiterrorism Act of 1986; and (2) for eligible crime victim compensation and assistance programs to provide emergency relief, including crisis response efforts, assistance, training, and technical assistance, for the benefit of victims of terrorist acts or mass violence occurring within the United States and funding to U.S. Attorney's Offices for use in coordination with State victims compensation and assistance efforts in providing emergency relief."

Prohibitions on International Terrorist Funding

Title III, Subtitle A amends "the Immigration and Nationality Act (INA) to authorize the Secretary of State, in consultation with the Secretary of the Treasury (Secretary) and the Attorney General, to designate an organization as a terrorist organization upon finding that the organization is a foreign organization that engages in terrorist activity and such activity threatens the security of U.S. nationals or U.S. national security." The procedures for such designation are then given.

Section 303 sets "penalties for knowingly providing, or attempting or conspiring to provide, material support or resources to a foreign terrorist organization. Requires any financial institution that becomes aware that it has possession of, or control over, any funds in which a foreign terrorist organization or its agent has an interest, to retain possession of or maintain control over such funds and report to the Secretary the existence of such funds, with exceptions. Establishes civil penalties for knowingly failing to comply with such provision."

Prohibition on Assistance to Terrorist States

Title III, Subtitle B "[i]mposes penalties upon U.S. persons who engage in a financial transaction with a country knowing or having reasonable cause to know that such country has been designated under the Export Administration Act as a country supporting international terrorism." Existing language is amended in section 323 so that "humanitarian assistance to persons not directly involved in violations" is no longer an exception to the prohibition, but "medicine or religious materials" are allowed.

Sanctions Against Terrorist Nations

The ability of the President to impose sanctions on terrorist states is substantially enhanced.

Section 324 affirms the President's power to "use all necessary means, including covert action and military force, to destroy international infrastructure used by international terrorists."

Section 325 "[a]mends: (1) the Foreign Assistance Act of 1961 to authorize the President to withhold assistance to the governments of countries that aid (including providing military equipment to) terrorist states, with exceptions by presidential waiver when in the national interest; and (2) the International Financial Institutions Act to direct the Secretary to instruct the U.S. executive director of each international financial institution to oppose assistance by such institutions to terrorist states."

Subsequent sections define various types of assistance affected by the legislation and appropriate a small amount of funds for assistance to foreign countries in developing counterterrorism programs.

Terrorist and Criminal Alien Removal and Exclusion—Subtitle A: Removal of Alien Terrorists

This section provides additional powers to remove or exclude aliens who are associated with terrorism.

Title IV, Subtitle A "Directs the Chief Justice of the United States to publicly designate five district court judges from five of the U.S. judicial circuits to constitute a court with jurisdiction to conduct removal proceedings."

A controversial provision allows for the use of secret (classified) testimony in courts closed to the public ("in camera"). Further, it

> *"Allows a single judge of the removal court, in determining whether to grant an application, to consider, ex parte and in camera, in addition to the information contained in the application: (1) other (including classified) information presented under oath or affirmation; and (2) testimony received in any hearing on the application of which a verbatim record shall be kept."*

Exclusion of Members and Representatives of Terrorist Organizations

Title IV, Subtitle B "[m]akes being a member or representative of a foreign terrorist organization a basis for exclusion from the United States under the INA."

Modification to Asylum Procedures

Title IV, Subtitle C "[p]rohibits the Attorney General from granting asylum to an alien excludable as a terrorist unless the Attorney General determines that the individual seeking asylum will not be a danger to U.S. security." It has various provisions that limit the rights of such aliens to appeal.

Nuclear Weapons Restrictions

Title V, Subtitle A "[r]evises Federal criminal code provisions regarding prohibited transactions involving nuclear materials to cover specified actions involving nuclear byproduct material and actions knowingly causing substantial damage to the environment."

Expands jurisdiction by making such prohibitions applicable where an offender or victim is a U.S. national or a U.S. corporation or other legal entity. Repeals a requirement for jurisdiction that at the time of the offense the nuclear material must have been in use, storage, or transport for peaceful purposes.

Modifies the definition of "nuclear material" to mean material containing any plutonium (currently, with an isotopic concentration not in excess of 80 percent plutonium 238)."

Section 503 "[d]irects the Attorney General and the Secretary of Defense to jointly conduct a study and report to the Congress on the number and extent of thefts from military arsenals of firearms, explosives, and other materials that are potentially useful to terrorists."

Biological Weapons Restrictions

Title V, Subtitle B "[a]mends the Federal criminal code to include within the scope of prohibitions regarding biological weapons attempts, threats, and conspiracies to acquire a biological agent, toxin, or delivery system for use as a weapon. Authorizes the United States to obtain an injunction against the threat to engage in prohibited conduct with respect to such prohibitions.

Expanded definitions of biological agents and related items are given. Biological weapons are included in the category of "weapons of mass destruction" as used elsewhere in federal law.

The Secretary of Health and Human Services is directed to develop a list of biological agents that have potential to be dangerous weapons, to develop safety procedures and procedures for the use and access to such materials."

Chemical Weapons Restrictions

Title V, Subtitle C specifies criminal penalties for any person who "without lawful authority, uses or attempts or conspires to use a chemical weapon against: (1) a U.S. national while such national is outside the United States; (2) any person within the United States; or (3) any property that is owned, leased, or used by the United States, whether the property is within or outside of the United States." It also provides for studying the feasibility of developing a test facility for studying the effects of chemical weapons.

Implementation of Plastic Explosives Convention

Title VI: Implementing a treaty commitment, this provision generally requires that all plastic explosives be manufactured with a "detection agent" or taggant included. It also prohibits "any person (other than a U.S. agency or the National Guard of any State) possessing any plastic explosive on the effective date of this Act from failing to report to the Secretary the quantity of such explosives possessed, the manufacturer or importer, and any identification marks."

Criminal Law Modifications to Counter Terrorism

Title VII, Subtitle A provides increased penalties for "(1) conspiracies involving explosives; (2) specified terrorism crimes, including carrying weapons or explosives on an aircraft; and (3) the use of explosives or arson."

Subtitle B expands jurisdiction over persons involved with offenses committed while aboard an aircraft in flight, as well as over persons involved with bomb threats. It also specifies increased criminal penalties.

Section 725 adds chemical weapons to the legal category of "weapons of mass destruction."

Section 726 "[a]dds terrorism offenses to the money laundering statute."

Section 727 "Sets penalties for: (1) killing or attempting to kill any U.S. officer engaged in, or on account of, the performance of official duties or any person assisting such an officer or employee; and (2) threatening to assault, kidnap, or murder former Federal officers and employees."

Section 728 "Includes among the aggravating factors for homicide that the defendant intentionally killed or attempted to kill more than one person in a single criminal episode."

Section 732 specifies research into tagging explosives or making them inert, as well as the regulation of the use of fertilizer in making explosives.

USE OF MILITARY IN DOMESTIC TERRORIST ATTACK

A provision added to the 1997 Defense Appropriations Act (10 U.S.C. 382) allows the use of the U.S. military in response to an attack using a biological or chemical weapon of mass destruction.

Roving Wiretap Provisions (1999)

Provisions in the Intelligence Authorization Act for 1999 expanded the ability of federal agents to use court-ordered wiretaps. Rather than specifying a particular phone or other instrument, agents can follow the suspect and tap whatever instruments he or she is likely to use. These provisions are opposed by civil libertarians and privacy advocates who feel they weaken the Fourth Amendment, which requires that searches be conducted specifically.

Limitations on Counterterrorism

An executive order signed by President Reagan (executive order 12333, December 4, 1981) provides that "No person employed by or acting on behalf of the United States Government shall engage in, or conspire to engage in, assassination." This remains in force. However, "assassination" is generally interpreted as the intentional targeting of a specific person. As the attacks on Muammar al-Qaddafi in Libya in 1986 and Osama bin Laden in Afghanistan in 1999 seem to indicate, bombing or shooting missiles at an area where a foreign leader is likely to be residing is not interpreted as an attempt at assassination.

TERRORISM AND INTERNATIONAL TREATIES

The United States is party to a number of multilateral international treaties that involve subjects relevant to terrorism. A selection of such treaties is presented, organized by subject.

Citations

Citations following some treaty titles refer to the following:

Bevans Bevans, Charles. *Treaties and Other International Agreements of the United States of America, 1776–1949.* Washington, D.C.: U.S. Department of State, 1968–76.

LNTS *Treaty Series: Publications of Treaties and International Engagements Registered with the Secretariat of the League.* Geneva: League of Nations, 1920–46.

TIAS *Treaties and Other International Acts Series.* Washington, D.C.: Government Printing Office, 1946.

UNTS *United Nations Treaty Series.* New York: United Nations, 1946/47– . This can be accessed online at http://untreaty.un.org/ENGLISH/series/simpleunts.asp

UST *United States Treaties and Other International Agreements.* Washington, D.C.: U.S. Department of State, 1952– .

Aviation and Hijacking

Convention on International Civil Aviation. Done at Chicago December 7, 1944; entered into force April 4, 1947. 61 Stat. 1180; TIAS 1591; 3 Bevans 944; 15 UNTS 295.

This treaty resulted in the creation of the International Civil Aviation Organization (ICA). It established the general framework for international standards for the operation of civil aviation, to which later agreements would add provisions specifically relating to hijacking, sabotage, and other terrorist acts.

Convention on Offenses and Certain Other Acts Committed On Board Aircraft. Done at Tokyo September 14, 1963; entered into force December 4, 1969.

This treaty did not specify particular criminal acts, but gave an aircraft's pilot in command the authority to act if he or she had "reasonable grounds" to believe that an act has been or is about to be committed which is a threat to "safety" or "good order and discipline on board the aircraft". Such actions can include restraining the threatening passenger and calling upon the assistance of crew or passengers.

Convention for the Suppression of Unlawful Seizure of Aircraft (Hijacking). Done at The Hague December 16, 1970; entered into force October 14, 1971.

This treaty covers the procedures for the detention and investigation of persons accused of having unlawfully seized or attempted to seize an aircraft, including cooperation between the nation in which the person is apprehended, the state where the aircraft is registered, and the state where the accused person resides.

Convention for the Suppression of Unlawful Acts Against the Safety of Civil Aviation (Sabotage). Done at Montreal September 23, 1971; entered into force January 26, 1973. 24 UST 564; TIAS 7570.

This treaty is directed at a variety of forms of destruction or sabotage that would compromise the safety or operation of the civil aviation system, specified as: "Unlawfully and intentionally to perform an act of violence against a person either when that person is on board an aircraft in flight and the act is likely to endanger the safety of the aircraft or that person is at an airport serving international civil aviation and the act is likely to cause serious injury or death, to destroy an aircraft in service or to so damage it as to make flight unsafe or impossible; to place or cause to be placed on board an aircraft in service by whatever means a substance likely to destroy it or so to damage it that it cannot fly or that its safety in flight is likely to be endangered; to destroy, damage, or interfere with the operation of air navigation facilities if it is likely to endanger the safety of an aircraft in flight; to communicate knowingly false information thereby endangering the safety of such an aircraft; to destroy or damage the facilities or an airport serving international civil aviation or damage aircraft not in service located on such an airport or disrupt the services of such an airport."

Protocol for the Suppression of Unlawful Acts of Violence at Airports Serving International Civil Aviation, Supplementary to the Convention of September 23, 1971. Done at Montreal February 24, 1988; entered into force August 6, 1989; for the United States November 18, 1994.

This is a supplementary protocol to the Montreal Convention above.

Biological and Chemical Weapons

PROTOCOL FOR THE PROHIBITION OF THE USE IN WAR OF ASPHYXIATING, POISONOUS, OR OTHER GASES, AND OF BACTERIOLOGICAL METHODS OF WARFARE. DONE AT GENEVA JUNE 17, 1925; ENTERED INTO FORCE FEBRUARY 8, 1928; FOR THE UNITED STATES APRIL 10, 1975. 26 UST 571; TIAS 8061; 94 LNTS 65.

This is the original treaty against the use of poison gas (which had been extensively employed by both sides in World War I), and bacterial agents. In general, the treaty was adhered to during World War II.

CONVENTION ON THE PROHIBITION OF THE DEVELOPMENT, PRODUCTION AND, STOCKPILING OF BACTERIOLOGICAL (BIOLOGICAL) AND TOXIN WEAPONS AND ON THEIR DESTRUCTION. DONE AT WASHINGTON, LONDON, AND MOSCOW APRIL 10, 1972; ENTERED INTO FORCE MARCH 26, 1975. 26 UST 583; TIAS 8062; 1015 UNTS 163.

This treaty prohibits the development, production, and stockpiling of bacteriological and toxin weapons and requires the destruction of existing stockpiles.

CONVENTION ON THE PROHIBITION OF THE DEVELOPMENT, PRODUCTION, STOCKPILING, AND USE OF CHEMICAL WEAPONS AND ON THEIR DESTRUCTION, WITH ANNEXES. DONE AT PARIS JANUARY 13, 1993; ENTERED INTO FORCE APRIL 29, 1997.

This treaty provides a rigorous schedule for the destruction of chemical weapons stockpiled by signatory nations (more than 135 nations have ratified the treaty). It has been ratified by more than 140 nations.

Genocide and Human Rights

CONVENTION ON THE PREVENTION AND PUNISHMENT OF THE CRIME OF GENOCIDE. DONE AT PARIS DECEMBER 9, 1948; ENTERED INTO FORCE JANUARY 12, 1951; FOR THE UNITED STATES FEBRUARY 23, 1989.

This convention was enacted in the aftermath of the Holocaust and reflected the declaration of the crime of genocide in the Nuremberg Tribunal following World War II. It was applied in 1998 when the International Criminal Tribunal for Rwanda convicted a Rwandan army major for genocide for inciting Hutu mobs to rape and attack Tutsis. While it is unlikely this provision would be applied to ordinary terrorist groups, it could become relevant if the terrorist group is motivated by race hatred, or if a government attacked an ethnic group in the guise of counterterrorism.

HELSINKI FINAL ACT, CONFERENCE ON SECURITY AND COOPERATION IN EUROPE, 1975.

This treaty was signed by most European nations as well as the United States and the Soviet Union. Besides dealing with the peaceful resolution of international disputes, the agreement provides that:

> *"The participating States will respect human rights and fundamental freedoms, including the freedom of thought, conscience, religion or belief, for all without distinction as to race, sex, language or religion."*

It also provides that

> *"The participating States on whose territory national minorities exist will respect the right of persons belonging to such minorities to equality before the law, will afford them the full opportunity for the actual enjoyment of human rights and fundamental freedoms and will, in this manner, protect their legitimate interests in this sphere."*

While not directly dealing with terrorism, this agreement potentially could both restrict suppressive counterterrorism and improve the rights of ethnic minority groups and reduce the potential for terrorism. The agreement resulted in the creation of a network of national groups monitoring compliance with the agrement.

INTERNATIONAL COVENANT ON CIVIL AND POLITICAL RIGHTS. DONE AT NEW YORK DECEMBER 16, 1966; ENTERED INTO FORCE MARCH 23, 1976; FOR THE UNITED STATES SEPTEMBER 8, 1992.

This fundamental document, ratified by more than 140 nations, specifies civil and political rights including political and social self-determination, and equal and due process in legal proceedings. The agreement prohibits torture and scientific experimentation without a person's consent, as well as slavery. Theoretically, at least, it would prevent extrajudicial antiterrorism measures, though a clause in the agreement does allow for its abrogation "in time of public emergency."

Maritime

PROTOCOL FOR THE SUPPRESSION OF UNLAWFUL ACTS AGAINST THE SAFETY OF FIXED PLATFORMS LOCATED ON THE CONTINENTAL SHELF. DONE AT ROME MARCH 10, 1988; ENTERED INTO FORCE MARCH 1, 1992; FOR THE UNITED STATES MARCH 6, 1995.

This agreement declares it to be an offense to seize, destroy, or attempt to destroy fixed maritime platforms (such as oil rigs on the continental shelf) or to attack occupants of such facilities.

CONVENTION FOR THE SUPPRESSION OF UNLAWFUL ACTS AGAINST THE SAFETY OF MARITIME NAVIGATION. SIGNED AT ROME MARCH 10, 1988; ENTERED INTO FORCE MARCH 1, 1992; FOR THE UNITED STATES MARCH 6, 1995.

Similar to laws against sabotage of civil aviation, this agreement deals with offenses where an individual or individuals seize a ship, attack personnel on board, damage a ship, or otherwise interfere with its safe navigation and operation. It specifies the taking into custody of persons suspected of such offenses, and the cooperation of the nation where the arrest is made, the nation to whom the ship is registered, and the nation where the suspects reside, and encourages the promotion of extradition for such offenses.

Nuclear Materials

Convention on the Physical Protection of Nuclear Materials, with Annex. Done at Vienna October 26, 1979; entered into force February 8, 1987.

This treaty, signed by 45 nations, restricts the transport of nuclear materials to or through nonsignatory nations, and provides standards for protecting the integrity of shipments and recovering them in case of theft. Signatories are required to criminalize the theft or fraudulent obtaining of nuclear materials or the use of such materials in attacks or threatened attacks, and to make these extraditable offenses. The treaty was further affirmed in 1992.

Treaty on the Non-proliferation of Nuclear Weapons. Done at Washington, London and Moscow July 1, 1968; entered into force March 5, 1970.

This treaty, among other things, requires that "Each nuclear-weapon State Party to the Treaty undertakes not to transfer to any recipient whatsoever nuclear weapons or other nuclear explosive devices or control over such weapons or explosive devices directly, or indirectly; and not in any way to assist, encourage, or induce any non-nuclear-weapon State to manufacture or otherwise acquire nuclear weapons or other nuclear explosive devices, or control over such weapons or explosive devices." By attempting to restrict the possession of nuclear weapons to those nations already having them, the treaty attempts to make development of nuclear weapons by "rogue states" (some of whom support terrorism) less likely.

Terrorism (General)

Convention to Prevent and Punish the Acts of Terrorism Taking the Form of Crimes Against Persons and Related Extortion That Are of International Significance. Done at Washington February 2, 1971; entered into force October 16, 1973.

This treaty requires that signatories take "all the measures that they may consider effective, under their own laws, and especially those established in this convention, to prevent and punish acts of terrorism, especially kidnapping, murder, and other assaults against the life or physical integrity of those persons to whom the state has the duty according to international law to give special protection, as well as extortion in connection with those crimes." It provides for the extradition or prosecution of offenders.

Convention on the Prevention and Punishment of Crimes Against Internationally Protected Persons, Including Diplomatic Agents. Done at New York December 14, 1973; entered into force February 20, 1977. 28 UST 1975; TIAS 8532; 1035 UNTS 167.

This treaty deals with attacks or kidnapping against government officials or diplomats, who are "internationally protected persons."

International Convention Against the Taking of Hostages. Done at New York December 17, 1979; entered into force June 3, 1983; for the United States January 6, 1985. TIAS 11081.

This treaty deals with the taking of hostages "in order to compel a third party, namely, a State, an international intergovernmental organization, a natural or juridical person, or a group of persons, to do or abstain from doing any act as an explicit or implicit condition for the release of the hostage." Signatories are required to take measures against groups in their territory who may be planning such hostage-taking, to facilitate the freeing and repatriation of hostages, and to extradite or prosecute alleged hostage-takers.

International Convention for the Suppression of the Financing of Terrorism. Adopted by the General Assembly of the United Nations in resolution 54/109 of 9 December 1999.

This agreement defines and prohibits terrorist acts and prohibits individuals from participating in such acts or providing funds or other resources to groups known to be terrorist.

Torture

CONVENTION AGAINST TORTURE AND OTHER CRUEL, INHUMAN OR DEGRADING TREATMENT OR PUNISHMENT. DONE AT NEW YORK DECEMBER 10, 1984; ENTERED INTO FORCE JUNE 26, 1987; FOR THE UNITED STATES NOVEMBER 20, 1994.

Article 5 of the Universal Declaration of Human Rights and Article 7 of the International Covenant on Civil and Political Rights provide that no one shall be subjected to torture or to cruel, inhuman, or degrading treatment or punishment. This agreement requires signatories to take legal measures to prevent the use of torture within its territory. Torture may not be justified under any circumstances, even national emergency. The prosecution and extradition of persons accused of committing acts of torture is specified.

Warfare

CONVENTION RESPECTING THE LAWS AND CUSTOMS OF WAR ON LAND, WITH ANNEX OF REGULATIONS. SIGNED AT THE HAGUE OCTOBER 18, 1907; ENTERED INTO FORCE JANUARY 26, 1910. 36 STAT. 2277; TS 539; 1 BEVANS 631.

Among other things, this agreement dealt with the responsibilities of military forces, the treatment of prisoners of war, prohibition on the use of "poisoned weapons," and the responsibility of an attacker to avoid unnecessary damage to civilians or nonmilitary buildings.

CONVENTION RELATIVE TO THE TREATMENT OF PRISONERS OF WAR. DATED AT GENEVA AUGUST 12, 1949; ENTERED INTO FORCE OCTOBER 21, 1950; FOR THE UNITED STATES FEBRUARY 2, 1956. 6 UST 3316; TIAS 3364; 75 UNTS 135.

The famous "Geneva Convention" forms the basis for the rights of prisoners in modern war, specifying what may be demanded of prisoners and what treatment must be provided them. The treaty was reaffirmed and expanded in 1977.

CONVENTION RELATIVE TO THE PROTECTION OF CIVILIAN PERSONS IN TIME OF WAR. DATED AT GENEVA AUGUST 12, 1949; ENTERED INTO FORCE OCTOBER 21, 1950; FOR THE UNITED STATES FEBRUARY 2, 1956. 6 UST 3516; TIAS 3365; 75 UNTS 287.

This agreement requires the humane treatment of civilians and also combatants whose injuries or other circumstances have removed them from active combat. Hospitals and other facilities for the treatment of such persons are not to be attacked.

COURT CASES

The cases described below deal with key legal issues involving terrorism and counterterrorism. (It should be noted that as of this writing, a number of challenges to the 1996 Antiterrorism and Effective Death Penalty Act are still working their way through the courts.)

Some of these issues include:

- Can mere advocacy of the forceful overthrow of the U.S. government be outlawed, or does the advocacy have to be accompanied by some substantial action in furtherance of that goal?
- Can mere membership in a group associated with terrorism or revolution be outlawed, or is some active participation in a conspiracy required?
- Do immigrants (or potential immigrants) have the same rights as U.S. citizens with regard to the First Amendment (freedom of association or advocacy) and the Fifth Amendment (due process of law)?

Note that the trials of defendants such as Timothy McVeigh or Theodore Kaczynski are not included below because they are not of great legal interest, although they may be of great human interest.

DENNIS V. UNITED STATES, 341 U.S. 494 (1951)

Background

Eugene Dennis was a member of the American Communist Party between 1945 and 1948. He was arrested and convicted in New York for violation of the federal Smith Act, a product of the early Cold War, which forbade any person "knowingly or willfully to advocate the overthrow or destruction of the Government of the United States by force or violence, to organize or help to organize any group which does so, or to conspire to do so . . ." Dennis appealed his conviction, and the Supreme Court agreed to hear the case.

Legal Issues

The broad issue is whether advocacy of the overthrow of the government, or organizing a group with that aim, is protected under the First Amendment. Another issue concerned whether or not Dennis had received the due process of law to which he was entitled under the Fifth Amendment.

Decision

The Supreme Court ruled that Dennis's activities in the Communist Party were not protected by the First Amendment. The majority began on the basis that Congress had the power to protect the United States from armed rebellion or other attempts to overthrow the Constitution itself. The Court acknowledged that mere "discussion" or explanation of Marxist-Leninist doctrines was protected by the First Amendment, but that the Smith Act was directed not at mere discussion of the overthrow of the government, but actual "advocacy" of it. Further, the Court had already established that speech that interfered with vital matters of national security was not protected by the First Amendment. For example, the Court noted that in *Schenck v. United States* 249 U.S. 47 (1919) and *Debs v. United States* 249 U.S. 211 (1919) speech that interfered with armed forces recruitment or that advocated mutiny was not protected.

Impact

While *Schenk* and *Debs* arguably dealt with direct interference with the operation of the military in wartime, Dennis was accused of a much more generalized activity—advocating or working toward the overthrow of the government. Reflecting Cold War tensions, this decision represents a low ebb in the protection of advocacy under the First Amendment.

YATES V. UNITED STATES, 354 U.S. 298 (1957)

Background

In 1951, 14 persons including the appellant were charged with violating the Smith Act through their membership in the Communist Party in California.

Legal Issues

Although in *Dennis v. United States* the Court had already ruled that membership in a communist organization that advocated the overthrow of the government of the United States was not protected by the First Amendment, Yates argued that his activities did not involve the direct or immediate overthrow of the government. He may have expressed opinions about what would be desirable in the future but did not advocate that any specific action be taken against the government.

Decision

The Court overturned Yates's conviction. It ruled that to violate the Smith Act (and lose protection under the First Amendment), a person had to advocate some concrete action, not just express an abstract opinion.

Impact

By distinguishing between opinion and advocacy and between indefinite advocacy and immediate advocacy, this decision broadened First Amendment protections.

SCALES V. UNITED STATES, 367 U.S. 203 (1961)

Background

The defendant, a member of the Communist Party, was convicted under the Smith Act, "which makes a felony the acquisition or holding of membership in any organization which advocates the overthrow of the Government of the United States by force or violence, knowing the purposes thereof."

The jury had been instructed that it could convict Scales only if "(1) the Party advocated the violent overthrow of the Government, in the sense of present 'advocacy of action' to accomplish that end as soon as circumstances were propitious, and (2) petitioner was an 'active' member of the Party with knowledge of the Party's illegal advocacy and a specific intent to bring about violent overthrow 'as speedily as circumstances would permit' and not merely 'a nominal, passive, inactive or purely technical' member."

Legal Issues

One of Scales's arguments was that the Internal Security Act (McCarren Act) of 1950, which had a provision that "'the holding of office nor membership in any Communist organization by any person shall constitute *per se* a violation' of that or any other criminal statute" meant that the membership clause in the Smith Act had been superseded, and he could not be convicted simply for being a member of a communist organization.

Further, Scales argued that the Smith Act violated both the free speech guarantee of the First Amendment and the due process guarantee of the Fifth Amendment.

Decision

The Court upheld Scales's conviction. Because the Smith Act and jury instructions did require "not only knowing membership, but active and purposive membership, purposive that is as to the organization's criminal ends," the law was not punishing simply association (protected by the First Amendment) but the advocacy of the future overthrow of the U.S. government that acted to further the illegal objectives of the Communist Party.

Impact

This was a narrow interpretation of the First Amendment that basically protected "free association" only if the association was minimal and there was no actual participation in the organization.

Noto v. United States, 367 U.S. 290 (1961)

Background

As with *Scales v. U.S.*, the defendant Noto was convicted of illegal membership in the Communist Party, an organization that advocated the overthrow of the United States government.

Legal Issues

Unlike the case in *Scales*, the main issue in *Noto* was whether the government had shown that the Communist Party actually advocated the overthrow of the U.S. government in a concrete and direct way that would be furthered by action, rather than just as an abstract principle.

Decision

The majority of five justices overturned the conviction on the grounds that the government had not made a substantial showing that the Communist Party had the kind of active, direct advocacy that would be prohibited. They ruled that there must be substantial evidence of a call to violence, "now or in the future" that is both "sufficiently strong and sufficiently persuasive."

Impact

The combination of *Noto* and *Scales* suggested that the type of advocacy prohibited would be narrowly interpreted; however, if the organization were shown to have such advocacy, membership would be rather broadly interpreted as being illegal. However, recent First Amendment interpretation is considerably broader.

BRANDENBURG V. OHIO, 395 U.S. 44 (1969)

Background

The appellant, leader of a Ku Klux Klan (KKK) group, joined with other KKK members (some of them armed) around a burning cross, where they made racially inflammatory remarks about African Americans and Jews while a reporter filmed the proceedings. The appellant also said that "We're not a revengent [sic] organization, but if our President, our Congress, our Supreme Court, continues to suppress the white, Caucasian race, it's possible that there might have to be some revengeance taken." Based on the remarks made in the film, Brandenburg was charged under the Ohio Criminal Syndicalism Statute with "advocat[ing] . . . the duty, necessity, or propriety . . . of crime, sabotage, violence, or unlawful methods of terrorism as a means of accomplishing industrial or political reform" and for "voluntarily assembl[ing] with any society, group, or assemblage of persons formed to teach or advocate the doctrines of criminal syndicalism."

Brandenburg was convicted under the Ohio statute and his conviction was upheld on appeal. The case then went to the U.S. Supreme Court.

Legal Issues

Between 1917 and 1920, 20 states adopted similar "criminal syndicalism" laws in response to fears of communist or other agitation, particularly to guard against international communist activity resulting from the successful Russian Revolution of 1917. These laws criminalize the advocacy of violence or terrorism. The question is whether a prohibition so broad that it extends to mere advocacy is compatible with the First Amendment's guarantee of freedom of speech, as applied to the states via the Fourteenth Amendment.

Decision

In 1927, the Supreme Court had upheld a similar California statute (*Whitney v. California*, 274 U.S. 380). The Court ruled that advocating violence, sabotage, or other terrorist acts presented such great danger to the security of the state that the state may outlaw it. However, what had been the dissenting opinion at that time now won the support of the majority, which declared that speech can be criminalized only if it is intended to produce and is likely to produce "imminent lawless action." Thus threats made about some vague situation in the future, for example, were not criminal.

Impact

This decision expanded the protection afforded by the First Amendment, because in effect it shifted the burden: defendants did not have to show that their advocacy was acceptably vague; the government had to prove that the speech was likely to cause immediate lawlessness or violence. In other words, the standard became more similar to that which allowed anything short of "fighting words"—language that might provoke a reasonable person to violence.

RANKIN V. MCPHERSON, 483 U.S. 378 (1987)

Background

Ardith McPherson worked as a clerk in the Harris County, Texas, office of Constable Rankin. Although she, like all such employees, was technically a "deputy constable," she did not perform the duties of a peace officer. On March 31, 1981, McPherson and her fellow employees heard a report on the radio of an attempt to assassinate President Ronald Reagan. As a black person, she did not feel sympathetic toward Reagan, whose policies she felt were unfair to minorities. In response to a remark made by another employee (who happened to be her boyfriend), she replied, " . . . shoot, if they go for him again, I hope they get him." Another employee overheard this remark and reported it to Constable Rankin. After McPherson confirmed that she had made the remark, Rankin fired her. She sued in the Southern District Court of Texas for reinstatement, back pay, and other relief.

Legal Issues

The basic issue was whether McPherson's remark was "protected speech" under the First Amendment. Under standards established by the Supreme Court, speech about something "of public concern" is protected by the First Amendment, which was intended to guarantee people's right to speak freely on political matters. Generally, the Court has favored a broad interpretation of what constitutes such political speech. If a remark is protected, then the state must show a compelling interest that justifies firing the employee.

Decision

The District Court upheld McPherson's discharge, but the Federal Court of Appeals determined, and the Supreme Court affirmed, that McPherson's remarks were protected under the First Amendment. They were a matter of public concern in that the "statement was made in the course of a conversation addressing the policies of the President's administration, and came on the heels of a news bulletin regarding a matter of heightened public attention: an attempt on the President's life." The state, in turn, had failed to show a compelling interest that justified firing McPherson:

> *Petitioners have not met their burden of demonstrating a state interest justifying respondent's discharge that outweighs her First Amendment rights, given the functions of the Constable's office, respondent's position therein, and the nature of her statement. Although that statement was made at the workplace, there is no evidence that it interfered with the efficient functioning of the office. Nor was there any danger that respondent had discredited the office by making the statement in public. Her discharge was not based on any assessment that her remark demonstrated a character trait that made her unfit to perform her work, which involved no confidential or policymaking role. Furthermore, there was no danger that the statement would have a detrimental impact on her working relationship with the Constable, since their employment-related interaction was apparently negligible.*

Impact

This decision is relevant to terrorism because some terrorism legislation has sought to criminalize what could be called violent rhetoric rather than an actual threat. Here, the Court confirmed that merely wishing that a government official were killed does not put one beyond the bounds of the First Amendment.

U.S. v. Wang Kun Lue and Chen De Yian, U.S. 2d Circ., 96-1314 (1996)

Background

Defendant Chen De Yian originally pleaded guilty to "(1) violating 18 U.S.C. § 1203, the Act for the Prevention and Punishment of the Crime of Hostage-Taking ('Hostage Taking Act'), Pub. L. No. 98-473, Title II, § 2002(a), 98 Stat. 2186 (1984), and (2) carrying a firearm in relation to the hostage taking in violation of 18 U.S.C. § 924(c)." as part of a plea bargain. He later sought review of his conviction from the appeals court.

Legal Issues

These U.S. code provisions implement the International Treaty Against the Taking of Hostages, signed in 1979. According to the court record:

> *Defendant first argues that the district court erred in holding that Congress has the authority to pass the Hostage Taking Act under the Necessary and Proper Clause of Article I, as an adjunct to the Executive's acknowledged authority under Article II to enter into treaties, with the advice and consent of the Senate. Chen contends that (1) the Hostage Taking Act is unconstitutional because the Hostage Taking Convention upon which it is based exceeds the Executive's authority under the Treaty Clause and (2) even if entry into the Convention is in accord with the treaty-making authority, the Hostage Taking Act is not a "plainly adapted" means of effectuating the Convention's ends and thus exceeds Congress's authority under the Necessary and Proper clause.*

The defendant-appellant also argued that because the federal legislation involved hostage taking that occurred entirely within the United States, and involved only U.S. citizens, Congress had gone beyond the proper subject of an international treaty. Finally, he argued that the Hostage-Taking Act violated the equal protection requirements of the Fourteenth Amendment by denying immigrants recourse that is available to citizens.

Decision

The court quickly dismissed the challenge to the treaty-making power and Congress's implementation of it, as having been disposed of by well-settled law that gives broad scope to treaties. There are limits to the application of treaties to domestic affairs; the Court quoted constitutional expert Lawrence Tribe, who observed that "The President and the Senate could not. . . . create a fully operating national health care system in the United States by treaty with Canada. . . .") But the court concluded that "within such generous limits, it is not the province of the judiciary to impinge upon the Executive's prerogative in matters pertaining to foreign affairs."

In interpreting the international law, the court stated that according to the *Restatement (Third) of the Foreign Relations Law of the United States* § 302:

> *Contrary to what was once suggested, the Constitution does not require that an international agreement deal only with "matters of international concern." The references in the Constitution presumably incorporate the concept of treaty and of other agreements in international law. International law knows no limitations on the purpose or subject matter of international agreements, other than that they may not conflict with a peremptory norm of in-*

ternational law. States may enter into an agreement on any matter of concern to them, and international law does not look behind their motives or purposes in doing so. Thus, the United States may make an agreement on any subject suggested by its national interests in relations with other nations.

Dismissing the challenge to the treaty-making and implementation powers, the court concluded that the argument that the Hostage-Taking Act was not a "necessary and proper" implementation of the treaty was not valid. The law needs only to have a "rational relationship" to the objectives of the treaty, and a law against hostage-taking is rationally related to a treaty that is designed to deter hostage-taking. A challenge under the Tenth Amendment (which deals with powers reserved to the states) was ruled immaterial, because the treaty power is one specifically given to the executive.

Finally, the challenge on equal protection grounds argued that the Hostage-Taking Act, by treating citizens and aliens differently, impermissibly discriminated. The court ruled, however, that this equal treatment provision bound only state and local governments, not the federal government, which has sole authority to regulate immigration and aliens.

Impact

Based on this decision, any future attempt to overturn an antiterrorism law simply because it seems to be an overextension of an international treaty is likely to fail. The courts give great deference to the constitutional treaty-making power of the executive and to Congress's power to implement treaties.

RENO V. AMERICAN-ARAB ANTI-DISCRIMINATION COMMITTEE, 97-1252 (1999)

Background

In 1987, the Immigration and Naturalization Service (INS) began deportation proceedings against seven Palestinians and a Kenyan on the grounds that they were advocates of "doctrines of world communism" in violation of the Cold War–era McCarran Act. When the constitutionality of this law was questioned, prosecutors replaced the McCarran Act–related charges with other charges relating to involvement with groups that engage in destruction of property or terrorist attacks.

The INS sought to deport these aliens because they had been distributing literature and carrying out other work for the Popular Front for the Liberation of Palestine (PFLP), which has engaged in both terrorist and political activities.

Legal Issues

The defendants argued that the First Amendment protected their rights of association and political advocacy, and thus they could not be deported solely on grounds of their association with a particular group. They claimed they were engaged in lawful political activity and had no involvement with terrorism. They argued that the immigration laws were being enforced selectively against persons whose political views were considered objectionable by the authorities, and they objected to the use of secret testimony or evidence that was not disclosed to the defense.

Decision

The district court upheld the appellants, noting that the PFLP did engage in a range of peaceful activities. The circuit court of appeals affirmed the ruling and further, it asserted that "Because of the danger of injustice when decisions lack the procedural safeguards that form the core of constitutional due process, . . . the use of undisclosed information in adjudications should be presumptively unconstitutional. Only the most extraordinary circumstances could support one-sided process."

The Supreme Court, however, ruled on a matter of procedure that Congress had denied, in a 1996 immigration law, the right to appeal such immigration decisions in federal court. In response to the claim of selective prosecution, the Court ruled that an "alien unlawfully in this country has no constitutional right to assert such a claim as a defense against his deportation." The Court did not address the question of the use of secret evidence or proceedings.

Impact

Apparently, the First Amendment does not give immigrants protection for being targeted based on their views, as it would for U.S. citizens. On the other hand, the appeals court had expressed serious misgivings about the use of secret evidence, which were left unresolved by the Supreme Court.

KIARELDEEN V. RENO, 71 F. SUPP. 2D 402, 419 (D.N.J. 1999)

Background

Hany Kiareldeen, a Palestinian resident of the United States since 1990 and a student at Rutgers University, married a U.S. citizen in 1997 and applied for permanent residency status. In March 1998, however, Immigration and Naturalization Service (INS) and FBI agents arrested Kiareldeen, charging him with having stayed in the country too long after completing his studies. He was detained without bail. In removal proceedings Kiareldeen acknowledged that he had overstayed his visa, but that he had earlier asked for a "discretionary adjustment" of his status based on a claim for political asylum (he faced the threat of persecution or torture if he returned to his homeland). The INS, however, presented secret evidence to the judge that claimed that Kiareldeen was a member of a Palestinian terrorist group and thus a threat to U.S. national security.

At the conclusion of the first removal hearing, the judge ordered a reconsideration of whether Kiareldeen should continue to be detained pending conclusion of the legal process. At the second removal hearing, the judge determined that "[a]n evaluation of the evidence by a person of ordinary prudence and caution cannot sustain a finding that this respondent has engaged in terrorist activity." On April 2, 1999, the judge ordered that Kiareldeen's immigration status be adjusted and that he be freed on $1,500 bail pending completion of the proceedings.

The government appealed to the Board of Immigration Appeals (BIA), which stayed the order for Kiareldeen's release and then voted 2-1 to deny his release. The FBI announced that it had closed its criminal investigation, and although Kiareldeen had never been charged with any crime, he remained in INS detention. After another hearing, the BIA then reversed its ruling and ordered that Kiareldeen be freed, but the government appealed to the attorney general's office for review. Meanwhile, however, a habeas corpus petition that Kiareldeen had previously filed came before a federal district court in New Jersey.

Legal Issues

In the habeas petition, Kiareldeen argued that the use of secret evidence and hearings was not authorized by any of the immigration statutes. Further, he argued that even if the evidence were authorized, it would be unconstitutional under the Fifth Amendment, which guarantees due process of law in criminal proceedings.

The main legal issue is whether the use of secret evidence is permissible under the U.S. Constitution. Civil libertarians argue that the constitutional right to confront one's accusers and the state's evidence cannot be exercised if evidence (and even witnesses) are presented in secret. Defenders of the practice argue that in certain circumstances evidence must be kept secret in order to protect vital intelligence sources, while at the same time dangerous terrorists must be prevented from entering the country.

Decision

Judge William Walls granted the habeas petition, ruling that Kiareldeen was being held without justification, and freed him after 19 months of detention. He began by addressing the use of secret evidence:

> *[T]he court does not ignore the warnings of [the Rafeedie and Anti-Discrimination Committee cases]. . . . Minimally, these cases teach that the INS' reliance on secret evidence raises serious issues about the integrity of the adversarial process, the impossibility of self-defense against undisclosed charges, and the reliability of government processes initiated and prosecuted in darkness. . . . Review of the Service's [INS] procedures involving Kiareldeen leads the court to believe that the petitioner's case is an example of the dangers of secret evidence.*

The court noted that the unclassified summaries that the INS had provided to the defense were inadequate, because they were not specific enough for the defense to determine what evidence needed to be rebutted or countered. "Use of secret evidence creates a one-sided process by which the protections of our adversarial system are rendered impotent. [Kiareldeen] has been compelled by the government to attempt to prove the negative in the face of anonymous slurs of unseen and unsworn informers."

The court then responded to the government's assertion that it had an overriding interest in protecting national security. It replied that "even if the interest is deemed to be the unarguably weighty one of national security, as the government maintains, the court must inquire whether that interest is so all-encompassing that it requires that [Kiareldeen] be denied virtually every fundamental feature of due process." The court noted that the FBI had closed its investigation, leaving Kiareldeen in legal limbo. "Under these circumstances, the government's claimed interest in detaining [Kiareldeen] cannot be said to outweigh [his] interest in returning to freedom. . . . [T]he government's reliance on secret evidence violates the due process protections that the Constitution directs must be extended to all persons within the United States, citizens and resident aliens alike." The court made similar conclusions about the government's use of hearsay evidence and evidence from unsworn witnesses. The court granted the habeas petition, and a three-judge immigration panel granted Kiareldeen permanent residency status.

Impact

The lower courts seem to be increasingly concerned about and suspicious of the government's use of secret evidence and testimony, even when a person is accused of being a dangerous terrorist and a threat to national security. Another district court, in *Rafeedie v. INS*, had already come to a similar conclusion. On the other hand, in *Reno v. American-Arab Anti-Discrimination Committee*, the Supreme Court had refused to extend First Amendment rights to noncitizens. The question remains whether the Court, confronted with arguments based on fundamental due process and the Fifth Amendment, might agree with lower courts that the use of secret evidence is unacceptable. As of late 2000, the Supreme Court has not yet resolved this issue.

CHAPTER 4

CHRONOLOGY

This chapter presents a chronology of significant terrorist attacks and other developments in the history of terrorism since 1946. This starting date was chosen because it marks the beginning of the postcolonial cold war period that shaped the environment for modern terrorism.

1946

- ***January 7:*** The Jewish terrorist group Irgun blows up the King David Hotel in Jerusalem, which had contained the principal government offices for the British mandate of Palestine. The blast killed 91 people, including 17 Jews and 46 non-British citizens.

1947

- Unrest in Palestine continues, as Jewish terrorists attack British soldiers. Typically, they kill the soldiers and booby-trap their bodies. The terrorists' objective is to force the British to hand over Palestine to the Jewish settlers.

1948

- ***April 9:*** Members of the Jewish terrorist organizations Irgun and Lehi (also known as the Stern Gang at that time) kill more than 200 Arab men, women, and children, in the Palestinian village of Deir Yassin, near Jerusalem. This and other terrorist attacks drive many Palestinian Arabs out of what will become the state of Israel.
- ***September 17:*** Count Folke Bernadotte of Sweden, who had been serving as United Nations mediator for Palestine between Israel and the Arabs, is killed along with French colonel André Serot by three members of the Jewish terrorist Stern Gang.
- ***December 28:*** Egyptian Prime Minister Mahmoud Fahmy el-Nokrashy Pasha is assassinated by a member of the extremist Muslim Brotherhood who is frustrated at Egypt's inability to destroy the Israeli state.

Chronology

1950

- ***November 1:*** Puerto Rican nationalists get into a gun battle with White House Police and Secret Service personnel outside Blair House (the vice presidential mansion across the street from the White House, where President Harry Truman is in temporary residence). Their attempt to assassinate the president is unsuccessful.

1951

- ***July 20:*** King Abdullah I of Jordan is assassinated by a Palestinian gunman while visiting his father's tomb.

1954

- ***March 1:*** Four Puerto Rican nationalists in the visitors' gallery of the U.S. House of Representatives pull out guns and open fire on members of Congress. Five representatives are wounded, and all four terrorists are captured alive.

1955

- ***August 20:*** In Algeria, the insurgency against the French colonial government intensifies. The terrorist group FLN (Front de Libération Nationale, the National Liberation Front) murders and then mutilates 37 European men, women, and children in what becomes known as the Philippeville massacre.

1956

- ***March 15:*** Violence in Algeria continues, and the procolonial terrorist group OAS (Secret Army Organization) seizes and kills six men in a social center.
- ***October 21–22:*** Directed by Saadi Yacef, FLN assassins murder 49 people in Algeria.

1959

- ***August 31:*** Basque separatists found the "Basque Fatherland and Liberty Movement," whose initials in Basque are ETA.

1960

- ***March 20:*** Beginning a new era of state terrorism against the black population, in the township of Sharpesville, South Africa, police open fire on a civil rights demonstration and kill 69 blacks, including many women and children. In response, the African National Congress abandons non-violent action in favor of more militant means.

1963

- ***November 27:*** Venezuelan FALN insurgents kidnap a U.S. Army military attaché in Venezuela and demand the release of 70 political prisoners. The Venezuelan government releases the prisoners and the U.S. hostage is freed.

1966

- ***October:*** In the United States, the Black Power movement is on the rise. The Black Panthers are formed by Huey Newton and Bobby Seale. The group engages in community and political action but also becomes involved in violent clashes with police.

1968

- ***July 28:*** Three hijackers belonging to the Popular Front for the Liberation of Palestine-General Command (PFLP-GC) seize an Israeli El Al airliner flying from Rome to Tel Aviv and force it to land at Dar al-Bayda Airport in Algiers, taking 48 hostages. The terrorists release the 23 non-Israeli hostages. On September 1, the 25 Israeli hostages are released in exchange for 16 Arab prisoners in Israeli jails.
- ***November 22:*** A car bomb explodes in the Jewish sector in Jerusalem, killing 12 people.
- ***December 28:*** In apparent retaliation for attacks on its airliners, Israeli commandos attack the Beirut National Airport in Lebanon, destroying 13 airliners belonging to three Arab-owned airlines.

1969

- ***July 18:*** Palestinian terrorists bomb the Jewish-owned Marks and Spencer department store in London.
- ***July 29:*** Two members of the PFLP hijack an El Al jet on its way to Tel Aviv. They order the plane diverted to Damascus, where they release the passengers unharmed but destroy the plane. Syria, however, detains 6 Israeli passengers until December, when it exchanges them for 13 Syrians and 58 Egyptians held in Israeli prisons.
- ***August 29:*** The PFLP-GC diverts a TWA jet to Damascus, evacuating the passengers and crew and then destroying the plane.
- ***September 4:*** The U.S. ambassador to Brazil, Charles Elbrick, is abducted in Rio de Janeiro by MR-8 (Revolutionary Movement of October

8) and affiliated terrorists. He is freed after the Brazilian government agrees to release 15 political prisoners.

- ***October:*** Terrorist bomb attacks target several major U.S. corporation facilities in Argentina, including those of Pepsi-Cola, IBM, and General Electric. No specific group, though, has been affiliated with these attacks.

1970

- ***February 21:*** Swissair flight 330 explodes shortly after takeoff from Geneva. The PFLP-GC under Ahmed Jabril claims responsibility for the bombing.
- ***March 31:*** Nine members of the leftist terrorist group Japanese Red Army, led by Kozo Okamoto, hijack a Japan Air Lines flight from Tokyo to Kukuoka. They demand to be flown to P'yongyang, the North Korean capital.
- ***May 29:*** The former provisional president of Argentina, Pedro Eugenio Aramburo, is kidnapped by leftist guerrillas. On July 1, 1970, the guerrillas announce that he has been "executed."
- ***June 24:*** The Quebec separatist group Front De Libération du Québec (FLQ) sets off a bomb at the Defense Ministry in Ottawa.
- ***July 22:*** In Lebanon, five members of the Popular Struggle Front hijack an Olympic Airways flight from Beirut to Athens. After several weeks of negotiations mediated by the International Red Cross, the incident ends peacefully after the Greek government releases seven Palestinians held in Greek jails.
- ***July 31:*** In Uruguay, Tupamaros guerrillas kidnap a U.S. official, Daniel A. Mitrione, and Aloisio Gomide, a Brazilian diplomat. Mitrione is found dead but Gomide is released the following February after his family pays a ransom. In the following months the Tupamaros conduct several other kidnappings of diplomats and win the freedom of a number of prisoners.
- ***September 6:*** In a coordinated wave of hijackings, the PFLP seizes four planes in midair (a fifth attempt, on an El Al plane, is foiled by Israeli security personnel). Three of the planes are diverted to a field outside Amman, Jordan, while one is destroyed on the runway at Cairo. After three weeks of negotiations the hijackers release their collection of more than 400 hostages in exchange for the release of 8 Palestinians held in Western jails. The hijackings prove to be the last straw for King Hussein of Jordan, who has his army expel the PFLP guerrillas from the country.
- ***October:*** In Quebec, the FLQ (Front de Libération du Québec, Quebec Liberation Front) kidnaps a British trade official, demands ransom (which is refused), and finally releases him in exchange for passage to Cuba. A few days later the FLQ kidnaps and kills Pierre Laporte, Quebec's minister of labor.

Terrorism

1971

- ***January 30:*** Two members of the Kashmiri Liberation Front hijack an Indian Airlines flight to Lahore, Pakistan. When India refuses their demand for the release of 36 prisoners, they destroy the plane.
- ***March 1:*** The leftist terrorist group Weather Underground sets off a bomb that causes heavy damage to a wing of the U.S. Senate office building.
- ***December 4:*** In Northern Ireland, the loyalist terrorist group UVF (Ulster Volunteer Force) claims responsibility for a bomb attack that kills 15 people in a Belfast pub.

1972

- ***January 27:*** A new U.S. terrorist group, the Black Liberation Army, surfaces when it kills two New York City police officers.
- ***January 30:*** In what becomes known as Bloody Sunday, British troops in Londonderry fire on a Catholic demonstration, killing 13 marchers.
- ***February 22:*** Five Palestinian hijackers seize a German Lufthansa airliner flying from New Delhi to Greece. They divert the plane to Aden, South Yemen, and release their hostages in exchange for a $5 million ransom. South Yemeni authorities in turn release the hijackers after taking $1 million of the ransom money.
- ***May 8:*** Four members of Black September seize a Sabena airliner on the ground at Lod Airport in Tel Aviv, hoping to trade the plane for the freedom of 317 *fedayeen* (Arab fighters) being held in Israeli jails. However, Israeli commandos recapture the plane, killing two of the hijackers. One passenger also dies in the battle.
- ***May 11:*** The German Red Army Faction carries out six bombing attacks against U.S. Army personnel in Frankfurt. One serviceman is killed and 11 are injured.
- ***May 30:*** In an ominous example of cooperation between disparate terrorist groups, the Japanese Red Army, working on behalf of the PFLP, launches a machine gun attack in the passenger terminal at Lod Airport in Tel Aviv, killing 25 people and wounding 76. Two terrorists are killed and the third captured.
- ***July 8:*** In retaliation for the massacre at Lod Airport the preceding month, Israeli agents in Lebanon assassinate Ghassan Kanafani, a leader of the PFLP.
- ***July 21:*** The Troubles in Northern Ireland worsen when the Provisional Wing of the Irish Republican Army (PIRA) sets off a total of 22 bombs in the Belfast area, killing 11 people and wounding more than 100.
- ***September 5:*** In one of the most shocking terrorist incidents of modern times, 8 Black September terrorists kill 11 Israeli athletes and

coaches at the Olympic Games in Munich, Germany. Five of the terrorists are killed.

- ***October 29:*** Black September terrorists win the release of the three comrades captured in Munich by hijacking a Lufthansa flight from Beirut to Ankara, Turkey. The hijackers and the Munich terrorists meet in Libya, where they receive an enthusiastic reception. However, Israeli agents will hunt them relentlessly in years to come.
- ***November 8:*** Seven members of the Eritrean Liberation Army hijack an Ethiopian plane in an attempt to win the release of jailed comrades. Security personnel aboard the plane counterattack, however, and six of the seven hijackers are killed. The plane is damaged by a grenade blast during the battle, but it lands safely, with nine passengers injured.

1973

- ***March 1:*** Eight Black September terrorists seize the Saudi Arabian embassy in Khartoum, Sudan. They make a variety of demands, including the release of the surviving gunman from the Lod Airport massacre in 1972 and freedom for Red Army Faction leaders imprisoned in West Germany. When their demands are refused, they murder U.S. ambassador Claude Noel and two other diplomats.
- ***March 29:*** Irish authorities seize the freighter *Claudia* and find four members of the PIRA and a large quantity of arms and munitions that the terrorists had obtained from Libya.
- ***August 5:*** In Greece, two gunmen from the Arab Nationalist Youth Organization for the Liberation of Palestine attack passengers disembarking from a TWA flight from Tel Aviv. Five people are killed and 55 wounded.
- ***September:*** The PIRA carries out an extensive bombing campaign throughout the London area.
- ***December 17:*** Five members of ANYOLP (the Arab Nationalist Youth Organization for the Liberation of Palestine) kill 33 Pan Am passengers on the ground at Italy's Leonardo da Vinci Airport. They then hijack a Lufthansa jet, divert it to Kuwait, and surrender, whereupon they are turned over to the Palestine Liberation Organization (PLO).

1974

- ***February 3:*** The PIRA bombs a bus carrying British soldiers and their families, killing 12 people.
- ***February 4:*** Patricia Hearst, heiress of the Hearst publishing family, is kidnapped by members of the Symbionese Liberation Army (SLA) from her apartment in San Francisco. In the coming months she is brainwashed and transformed into "Tanya" and participates in robberies carried out by the terrorist group.

- ***March 26:*** In Ethiopia, members of the Eritrean Liberation Front seize crew and passengers from a private U.S. helicopter, holding the captives for several months.
- ***April:*** In Italy, public prosecutor Mario Sossi is kidnapped by Red Brigades members. He is later released in exchange for eight "political prisoners."
- ***April 11:*** Gunmen from the PFLP-GC attack the Israeli settlement of Qiryat Shemona, killing 18 settlers and wounding 16 others. The terrorists demand the release of 100 Palestinians being held in Israeli jails, but Israeli troops carry out an assault and kill them.
- ***April 13:*** In the Philippines, the New People's Army kills three U.S. Navy personnel near the Subic Bay naval base.
- ***May 15:*** Gunmen from the DFLP (Democratic Front for the Liberation of Palestine) seize a school in the village of Ma'alot, taking more than 100 students and teachers hostage. Israeli forces retake the school, but 27 children die during the gun battle.
- ***May 17:*** Los Angeles police attack an SLA safe house, killing six SLA members.
- ***June 17:*** The PIRA bombs the Tower of London, killing one tourist and injuring more than 40.
- ***August 4:*** The Italian fascist group Black Order claims credit for setting off a bomb on an Italian train traveling from Bologna to Munich. Twelve people are killed and about 50 wounded.
- ***September 7:*** A TWA airliner explodes just after taking off from the Athens airport. The attack is linked to ANYOLP.
- ***September 13:*** Three members of the Japanese Red Army seize the French embassy in The Hague, the Netherlands, and demand the release of a comrade being held by authorities. The four are given a plane and fly to Syria.
- ***September 13:*** The ETA bombs a Madrid cafe frequented by workers in the nearby national police headquarters. Twelve people are killed and more than 80 wounded.
- ***October 6:*** Starting a terror campaign, the Fuerzas Armadas de Liberación Nacional (FALN), a Puerto Rican separatist group, bombs five banks in New York City.
- ***November 9:*** The German Red Army Faction assassinates West German Supreme Court president Günther Drenkman in his home in Bonn.
- ***November 21:*** The PIRA bombs two pubs in Birmingham, killing 21 people and wounding almost 200.
- ***November 22:*** Four members of ANYOLP hijack a British Airways flight in the Dubai airport. They fly the plane to Libya and then to Tunis, demanding the release of Palestinian terrorists being held in Egypt and

the Netherlands. They kill a passenger and injure two crew members. Finally they are turned over to the PLO.

1975

- ***January 24:*** Puerto Rican FALN terrorists explode a bomb in New York's historic Fraunces Tavern, killing 4 patrons and wounding 60.
- ***January 29:*** The U.S. State Department headquarters in Washington, D.C., is badly damaged by a bomb planted by the Weather Underground.
- ***February 25:*** In Argentina, Monteneros terrorists kidnap John P. Egan, U.S. honorary consul to the city of Córdoba. He is found murdered two days later.
- ***March 1:*** Kurdish nationalists hijack an Iraqi Airways flight and divert it to Teheran, Iran, while engaging in a gun battle with Iraqi security forces aboard the plane. The hijackers surrender to Iranian authorities, who execute them on April 7.
- ***April 7:*** Three members of the Moro Liberation Front hijack a Philippine Airlines flight. They release the passengers in Manila but continue to hold the plane's crew and an airline executive hostage. They later free their hostages and are granted asylum in Libya. A similar hijack attempt the following month ends with 3 hijackers and 10 passengers dead after a gun battle with Philippine troops. The other three hijackers are captured and later executed.
- ***April 17:*** In Cambodia, one of modern history's worst reigns of state terror begins when the Khmer Rouge–controlled government forces city populations into the countryside, where many will die of starvation.
- ***August 4:*** A terrorist squad from the Japanese Red Army (JRA) takes over the U.S. consulate and the Swedish embassy in Kuala Lumpur, Malaysia. They threaten to destroy the buildings and kill their 52 hostages if their demand for freedom for seven imprisoned JRA members in Japan is not met. The Japanese government agrees to the demands, and five of the seven prisoners willingly join the hostage-takers in Tripoli, Libya.
- ***August 23:*** Three terrorists who say they belong to the Abu al-Nasir movement (not a known terrorist group) hijack an EgyptAir jet and demand the release of five Libyans in Egyptian jails. However during a refueling stop in Luxor, Egyptian troops storm the plane and capture the hijackers. No passengers are injured.
- ***September 15:*** Terrorists from the Black September group occupy the Egyptian embassy in Madrid, seize six diplomats, and demand that Egypt withdraw from its ongoing peace talks with Israel in Geneva, Switzerland, and repudiate agreements that had already been reached. The terrorists take their hostages to Algiers and release them without winning their demands.

- ***December 21:*** PFLP terrorists led by Ilyich Ramirez Sanchez (a.k.a. Carlos and "the Jackal") storm into an OPEC conference in Vienna, taking 81 hostages. They free the hostages in exchange for $50 million and a flight to safety in Algiers.
- ***December 23:*** In Athens, CIA station chief Richard Welch is assassinated by members of the Greek marxist group Revolutionary Organization 17 November.

1976

- ***January 4:*** In Northern Ireland, five Catholics are killed in two attacks by Protestant gunmen. The next day, gunmen from the IRA remove 10 Protestants from a bus in Armagh and execute them by the side of the road.
- ***May 23:*** Molluccan terrorists seize a Dutch school and a passenger train and use their hostages to demand that the Dutch government pressure Indonesia to give their region independence. The hostages at the school are freed four days later, but the train is stormed by Dutch marines who kill six terrorists. Two hostages also die.
- ***June 27:*** Seven terrorists from the PFLP and the Red Army Faction (RAF) hijack an Air France flight from Tel Aviv to Paris, diverting it to Entebbe, Uganda, where they are apparently aided by Ugandan dictator Idi Amin's soldiers. The hijackers demand the release of 53 terrorists who are being held in French, Swiss, Israeli, and Kenyan jails. But a planeful of Israeli commandos mount a daring raid and rescue most of the passengers, killing the terrorists and some Ugandan soldiers.
- ***July 21:*** Christopher Ewart-Biggs, British ambassador to Ireland, dies when his car passes over a land mine apparently planted along his route by the PIRA.
- ***August 11:*** PFLP gunmen attack an airport terminal in Istanbul, Turkey, killing four El Al passengers and wounding 20.
- ***September 10:*** Six Croatian nationalists hijack a TWA jet flying from New York to Chicago, diverting it first to Newfoundland, then to Iceland, and finally to Paris. After authorities yield to their demand to publish and distribute their propaganda statements, the terrorists direct police to a bomb in a locker in New York's Grand Central Station. When police attempt to disarm the bomb, it explodes, killing one policeman and injuring several others. French authorities turn the terrorists over to the U.S. for prosecution.

1977

- ***March 9:*** A Hanafi Muslim terrorist group seizes three buildings in Washington, D.C., holding 134 people hostage. The group surrenders peacefully two days later.

- ***August 3:*** The Puerto Rican separatist group FALN bombs two New York office buildings, killing one person.
- ***September 5:*** The RAF kidnaps German businessman Hans-Martin Schleyer after killing his driver and three bodyguards. They demand freedom for 11 imprisoned comrades, while their allies, the PFLP, hijack a Lufthansa jet and divert it to Mogadishu, Somalia. The situation unravels the following month, when German commandos recapture the plane and rescue the passengers. Many of the RAF prisoners commit suicide in their cells, and the RAF kills Schleyer in retaliation.
- ***September 28:*** The Japanese Red Army hijacks a Japan Air Lines plane and demands $6 million ransom and the freeing of nine prisoners. The Japanese government agrees to the demand and the hostages are released in batches as the plane makes several stops, ending up in Algeria, where the terrorists surrender.
- ***December 4:*** A hijacked Malaysian airliner crashes in Singapore during landing. Unidentified terrorists had apparently shot the pilot and copilot.

1978

- ***February 17:*** In Northern Ireland, the PIRA bombs the La Mon Restaurant, killing 12 and wounding more than 20.
- ***March 16:*** Red Brigades terrorists (possibly with the aid of the P2 group and the Mafia) kidnap Aldo Moro, former Italian prime minister and president of the Christian Democratic Party. The terrorists demand the release of 13 of their imprisoned comrades. The Italian government refuses to comply, and Moro's body is found in the trunk of a car parked on a Rome street.
- ***April 11:*** Eleven al-Fatah guerrillas make an amphibious landing outside the port of Haifa and hijack a passing bus in an attempt to reach Tel Aviv. Israeli security forces intercept the bus outside the capital. In the ensuing gun battle 25 passengers and 9 terrorists are killed.
- ***May:*** Two package bombs explode at Northwestern University, Evanston, Illinois. Each explosion injures one person. These are the first two known attacks by the person who will become known as the Unabomber.

1979

- ***February 12:*** In Rhodesia, guerrillas from the Zimbabwe African People's Union use a Soviet-made surface-to-air missile to shoot down an Air Rhodesia plane, killing all 59 people aboard.
- ***February 14:*** The U.S. ambassador to Afghanistan, Adolph Dubs, is kidnapped and murdered by Muslim terrorists.

- ***March 5:*** In Spain, the Maoist urban guerrilla group GRAPO kills General Agustin Munoz Vazquez in Madrid to protest Spain's entry into NATO.
- ***March 22:*** The PIRA reaches beyond the British Isles to assassinate Sir Richard Sykes, the British ambassador to the Netherlands, in front of his home in The Hague. Sykes had formerly been the British ambassador to the Republic of Ireland at Dublin.
- ***May 26:*** A group of Ku Klux Klan (KKK) members attacks civil rights marchers in Decatur, Alabama. Two civil rights workers and two Klansmen are killed.
- ***May 26:*** Egypt and Israel sign the Camp David Peace Accord. Israel hands the Sinai back to Egypt. Islamic extremists begin to target Egyptian president Anwar Sadat.
- ***June/July:*** A wing of the Basque ETA group begins a "tourist war," bombing Spanish coastal tourist resorts. Only two people are injured, but the bombings cause extensive property damage.
- ***August 27:*** The PIRA assassinates Louis, Earl Mountbatten; his grandson; and another person by setting off a remote-control bomb hidden aboard their fishing boat in Donegal Bay, Ireland. The same day, the PIRA sets off two bombs near Warrenpoint, Ireland, killing 19 people, mostly British soldiers.
- ***November 3:*** During an anti-Klan rally in Greensboro, North Carolina, five U.S. communists are killed in an attack by a KKK group.
- ***November 4:*** Ayatollah Khomeini's Revolutionary Guards seize the U.S. embassy in Teheran, holding 53 U.S. personnel hostage. What became known as the Iranian Hostage Crisis drags on for 444 days.

1980

- ***March 24:*** Members of the Cinchoneros Popular Liberation Movement hijack a Honduran jet and divert it to Managua, Nicaragua, demanding freedom for 15 Salvadoran leftists being held in Honduran jails. Negotiations fail, however, and the hijackers take the plane to Panama and surrender.
- ***March 24:*** The Roman Catholic archbishop of El Salvador, Oscar Romero, is assassinated by a right-wing death squad while he celebrates mass.
- ***March 28:*** Members of a new group called Komando Jihad hijack an Indonesian airliner and demand the release of 20 prisoners. Three days later government forces storm the aircraft. The pilot, one soldier, and four terrorists are killed.
- ***April 30:*** Members of an Iranian anti-Khomeini splinter group seize the Iranian embassy in London, holding more than 20 hostages and demanding international attention to the plight of Iran's Arab minority. The

British government refuses to negotiate, and six days later, the Special Air Service Regiment (SAS) elite counterterrorism force assaults the building. All five terrorists are killed, but two hostages also die.

- ***May:*** A new Portuguese leftist terrorist group called Popular Forces of 25 April (FP-25) launches a wave of murder, kidnapping, and bombing directed against the nation's government and elite, as well as U.S. embassies and NATO headquarters. The group sought to overthrow the Portuguese government and to sever all ties with NATO and the United States.
- ***August 2:*** A right-wing terrorist group bombs the railway station in Bologna, Italy, killing 84 people and causing a large number of injuries.
- ***September 26:*** The hijacking of a Yugoslav aircraft by Croatian separatists fails when the hostages fake a fire and escape to safety.
- ***October 13:*** A Turkish domestic flight is hijacked by Muslim extremists. Before the plane can fly to Iran, it is recaptured by Turkish troops; the hijackers are captured alive, though one passenger dies and 13 are wounded.
- ***December 4:*** Four U.S. citizens—including three Roman Catholic nuns—are found shot and strangled near San Salvador. They are believed to have been killed by a right-wing death squad associated with the Salvadoran military.
- ***December 7:*** The Venezuelan group Bandera Roja simultaneously hijacks three Venezuelan domestic airliners, demanding the release of seven prisoners and a ransom of $10 million. Their demands fail, and they fly to Havana and surrender to Cuban authorities.
- ***December 31:*** The PFLP takes credit for a bomb blast in the Norfolk Hotel in Nairobi, Kenya. Sixteen people are killed and 80 injured; and the historic building is devastated.

1981

- ***May 13:*** Turkish-born terrorist Mehet Ali Agca attempts to assassinate Pope John Paul II as the pontiff is entering St. Peter's Square in Rome. Although the pope is shot twice and seriously wounded, he makes a complete recovery. Ali Agca is convicted and sentenced to life in prison. In 2000 he is pardoned by Italy (at the pope's urging), but is imprisoned in Turkey for another past murder.
- ***August 31:*** A car bomb set off by the RAF injures 18 U.S. citizens and two West Germans at the U.S. Air Force base at Ramstein. Two weeks later, the RAF makes an unsuccessful attempt to assassinate General Frederick Kroesen, chief commander of U.S. forces in Europe.
- ***October 6:*** President Anwar al-Sadat of Egypt is assassinated by Muslim extremists while he is watching a military parade. Eight other people are also killed.

- ***October 10:*** A PIRA bombing attack on British troops kills two people and wounds 40 others.
- ***October 20:*** Following an unsuccessful armored car robbery near Nyack, New York, in which two policemen and a security guard are killed, Weather Underground fugitive Kathy Boudin is arrested and turned over to the FBI.
- ***November:*** The French leftist terrorist group Action Directe bombs a variety of business establishments.
- ***November 28:*** As part of its attempt to topple the government of Syrian President Hafez al-Assad, the Muslim Brotherhood sets off a bomb in Damascus, killing 64 people.
- ***December 17:*** U.S. Army general and NATO commander for southern Europe James Lee Dozier is kidnapped by Red Brigades terrorists from his home in Verona, Italy. He is held for 42 days but is then freed in a successful raid by Italian counterterrorism forces.

1982

- ***February 2:*** Syrian president Hafex al-Assad strikes back at the Moslem Brotherhood, attacking its bases in the city of Hamah. More than 20,000 people die in the fighting.
- ***February 26:*** Four members of the Revolutionary Youth Movement of Tanzania hijack an Air Tanzania flight, demanding the resignation of Tanzanian president Julius Nyerere. After making several stops, they land in Britain and surrender to authorities.
- ***April 28:*** Members of the Lorenzo Zelaya Popular Revolutionary Forces (FRP-LZ) hijack a Honduran airliner and demand $1 million and the release of 32 political prisoners. After 10 hostages escape through an emergency exit, the terrorists release the remaining 11 passengers in exchange for passage to Cuba. Meanwhile, the FRP-LZ attacks a number of embassies in Tegucigalpa.
- ***May 12:*** Members of the January 31 Popular Front, who oppose Guatemala's military junta, seize the Brazilian embassy in Guatemala City and take nine hostages. The group releases its hostages after being offered safe passage by the Mexican government.
- ***June 1:*** As President Ronald Reagan prepares to visit Germany, a group called Revolutionary Cells bombs a variety of U.S.–based businesses and U.S. military facilities.
- ***June 3:*** In London, the Black June group, instigated by Abu Nidal, seriously wounds Israel's ambassador to Britain, Shlomo Argov. A few days later Israel launches a full-scale invasion of Lebanon to root out terrorist bases.

- ***July 20:*** In London, the PIRA sets off a bomb in Hyde Park during the ceremonial changing of the guard. Two hours later, a second bomb goes off at a band concert in Regent's Park. Eleven people are killed in the two attacks.
- ***August 7:*** Armenian terrorists use a hand grenade and machine gun to kill seven people and wound more than 70 at the Esenboga Airport in Ankara, Turkey.
- ***August 9:*** Terrorists believed to be from the Abu Nidal group attack a Jewish restaurant and a synagogue in Paris, killing 6 people and wounding 27.
- ***September 6:*** A group of armed men seize the Polish embassy in Bern, Switzerland, demanding an end to martial law in Poland. Swiss police rescue the hostages and capture the gunmen.
- ***September 14:*** The newly elected president of Lebanon, Bashir Gemayel, is assassinated by a bomb at his Beirut headquarters. His killer is Habib Tanios Chartouny, a member of the Syrian Social Nationalist Party.
- ***September 16:*** Christian Phalangists allied with the Israeli occupation force in Lebanon massacre from 800 to 1,000 people in the Sabra and Shatila refugee camps outside Beirut.
- ***September 17:*** Members of the Cinchoneros Popular Liberation Movement, a Honduran leftist terrorist group, kill one person and take 105 hostages at an economic conference in San Pedro Sula. They demand the release of nine prisoners held in Honduran jails and the expulsion of foreign military advisers. Their demands are refused, but they gain asylum in Cuba.
- ***October:*** More than 20 bombs are set off at banks in the Basque regions of Spain. The bombings may have been the work of Terra Lliure ("Free Land"), a small leftist terrorist group.
- ***December 6:*** A tavern in Ballykelly favored by British security forces is bombed by the Irish National Liberation Army. Seventeen people are killed, 11 of them soldiers.

1983

- Throughout the year, the Revolutionary Cells group carries out 19 bombings against government facilities in West Germany.
- ***April 18:*** A suicide truck bombing kills 49 people and injures 120 at the U.S. embassy in Beirut. The group Islamic Jihad claims responsibility.
- ***July 27:*** A group called the Armenian Revolutionary Army seizes the Turkish embassy in Lisbon, Portugal. The terrorists blow up the building, killing themselves and two of their hostages.

- ***August 21:*** Benigno Aquino, Jr., leader of the opposition to President Ferdinand Marcos of the Philippines, is assassinated at Manila airport shortly after landing. His death is quickly linked to Marcos supporters.
- ***September 16:*** Puerto Rican FALN separatists rob a Wells Fargo armored car terminal in West Hartford, Connecticut, escaping with $7.2 million.
- ***October 9:*** A bombing during a South Korea delegation visit to Burma kills 19 people. South Korean president Chun Doo Hwan is slightly delayed and narrowly escapes the bombing. The bombers are suspected to be North Korean agents.
- ***October 23:*** In one of the worst terrorist attacks directed against U.S. forces, 241 U.S. servicemen are killed when a suicide truck bomb is driven into the U.S. Marine Corps barracks in Beirut. Another explosion moments later kills 58 at a French barracks. Islamic Jihad claims responsibility. Despite a very similar attack on the U.S. embassy the previous April, U.S. authorities had taken few security precautions.
- ***November:*** The Portuguese FP-25 terrorist group begins a bombing campaign around Lisbon, apparently to protest government labor policies.
- ***November 6:*** A left-wing group called the Armed Resistance Unit bombs the Senate wing of the U.S. Capitol Building to protest the U.S. invasion of Grenada.
- ***December 17:*** The PIRA sets off a bomb in a crowd of Christmas shoppers in front of Harrods department store in London, killing 5 people and wounding 90.
- ***December 31:*** The Puerto Rican separatist group FALN sets off bombs in New York City, attacking police, FBI, and federal court facilities.

1984

- ***January 18:*** Malcolm H. Kerr, president of the American University in Beirut, is killed by Islamic Jihad gunmen. The following month Frank Regier, a professor at the university, is kidnapped by Hezbollah.
- ***March 16:*** William Buckley, the CIA Beirut station chief, is kidnapped. Although his body is never found, he is believed to have been kidnapped, tortured, and killed by Islamic Jihad, which claimed responsibility for "executing" Buckley.
- ***April 17:*** A London police constable is killed outside the Libyan embassy by a gunman in the building (which Western observers believed harbored terrorists). Police surround the embassy, which eventually is surrendered, and diplomatic ties between Britain and Libya are broken.
- ***June 5–6:*** Indian troops assault the Golden Temple of Amritsar, a stronghold of Sikh extremists. Hundreds of people are killed, including Sikh leader Jarnail Singh Bhindranwale.

- ***June 18:*** Alan Berg, a controversial Denver talk show host who is Jewish, is murdered by members of the neo-Nazi white supremacist group the Order.
- ***July:*** The Spanish terrorist group GRAPO explodes 15 bombs in several Spanish cities during the summer, causing extensive property damage to the French consulate, General Motors, and a French bank. The group demands an end to Spain's involvement with NATO and the United States.
- ***August:*** In Chile, the Manuel Rodriguez Patriotic Front conducts a bombing campaign against American business interests.
- ***August–September:*** Trying to prevent people from voting against them in an upcoming referendum, members of the Rajneesh cult in Oregon contaminate salad bars with *Salmonella.* About 750 people get sick from this early attempt at bioterrorism.
- ***September 20:*** A truck bomb explodes at the U.S. embassy annex in East Beirut. A shadowy group called Islamic Jihad claims credit for the attack. Twenty-three people (including two U.S. citizens) are killed, and more than 60 are injured.
- ***October:*** A group called Communist Combatant Cells bombs a number of businesses in Brussels, as well as the Belgian Liberal Party Research Center.
- ***October 12:*** The PIRA bombs a Brighton hotel where important British officials are staying, narrowly missing Prime Minister Margaret Thatcher. Sir Anthony Barry, a member of Parliament, is killed, and several cabinet officials and Conservative Party leaders are injured.
- ***October 31:*** Indian prime minister Indira Gandhi is assassinated by two of her bodyguards, who are Sikhs. The killing is in retaliation for the earlier Indian attack on the Golden Temple of Amritsar.
- ***November:*** During the next three months, the communist New People's Army in the Philippines will murder two mayors, a deputy mayor, and a police chief.
- ***November 17:*** The radical animal rights group Animal Liberation Front causes a panic when they claim they have poisoned Mars brand chocolate bars. Millions of the bars are removed from store shelves and destroyed.
- ***December 3:*** Islamic Jihad hijacks a Kuwaiti airliner and kills two U.S. representatives of USAID. The Islamic Jihad members go to Iran and receive virtual asylum.
- ***December 11:*** The first of several bombings by European leftist terrorists (including Red Army Faction, Communist Combatant Cells, and Action Directe) damage NATO fuel pipeline facilities near Verviers, Belgium.
- ***December 25:*** Antiabortion terrorists simultaneously bomb three abortion clinics in Pensacola, Florida.

Terrorism

1985

- ***March 16:*** Terry A. Anderson, an Associated Press correspondent in Lebanon, is kidnapped by Islamic Jihad.
- ***June 9:*** Thomas M. Sutherland, acting Dean of Agriculture at the American University in Beirut, is also kidnapped by Islamic Jihad.
- ***June 14:*** Hezbollah terrorists hijack a TWA flight on its way to Rome and divert it to Beirut. They beat and kill U.S. Navy diver Robert Dean Stetham. The plane flies back and forth between Algiers and Beirut, with hostages being freed at each stop. The leader of the terrorists, Mohammed Ali Hamadei, is eventually convicted and sentenced to life in prison.
- ***June 23:*** An Air India flight mysteriously blows up on its way from Toronto to London, killing all 329 people on board. The wreckage is found off the coast of Ireland. Both the Kashmir Liberation Army and the Dashmesh Regiment, a Sikh group, claim responsibility. (The two groups are both obscure and their status is hard to determine.)
- ***July 10:*** French "counter terrorist" agents blow up the Greenpeace ship *Rainbow Warrior* in Auckland, New Zealand. The ship had been preparing to lead a flotilla to protest French nuclear tests.
- ***August 8:*** The RAF sets off a car bomb at the U.S. Air Force base at Rhein-Main, West Germany, killing two people and injuring 17. The previous day, the terrorists had killed an off-duty U.S. serviceman and used his identification to gain entry to the base.
- ***October 7:*** The Italian cruise ship *Achille Lauro* is hijacked by four terrorists from the PFLP, whose goal is unclear. Their brutal murder of Leon Klinghoffer, an elderly wheelchair-bound Jewish man, arouses public outrage. The terrorists receive long prison terms.
- ***October 25:*** Terrorists from the right-wing group RENAMO kidnap and murder two Jesuit priests in Mozambique as part of their campaign against missionaries and aid workers.
- ***November 6:*** The Colombian terrorist group M-19 seizes the Palace of Justice in Bogotá, taking 500 hostages including Supreme Court justices and members of the Council of State. Security forces retake the building next day in a bloody fight that takes the lives of all 20 or so terrorists, 11 Colombian soldiers, 11 Supreme Court justices, and 50 other hostages.
- ***November 23:*** Four members of an Abu Nidal splinter group hijack an EgyptAir jet flying from Athens to Cairo. They force the plane to land in Malta and free 13 female hostages. When the Maltese refuse to refuel the plane, the terrorists begin shooting their remaining hostages one by one. Egyptian commandos recapture the plane, but 57 people (including commandos, terrorists, and passengers) die in the gun battle and a fire that breaks out on the plane.

- ***December 11:*** A Sacramento, California, computer store owner is killed by a package bomb. This is the first fatality to be attributed to the Unabomber.
- ***December 23:*** Terrorists from the African National Congress set off a bomb in a shopping center in Durban, South Africa, killing five people and wounding 48.
- ***December 27:*** Abu Nidal terrorists kill 18 holiday travelers in the Rome and Vienna airports.

1986

- ***April:*** The U.S. Department of Justice under President Reagan sets up a secret task force to develop ways to use immigration procedures to deport "PLO activists who have violated their visa status." The group's use of secret evidence in deportation proceedings brings objections from civil liberties groups, who charge that such immigrants are unable to defend themselves effectively because they are denied access to the evidence being used against them. The targeting of individuals based on political beliefs is also seen as a violation of the First Amendment rights of free speech and association.
- ***April 5:*** A bomb explosion in the crowded La Belle Disco in West Berlin kills 3 people (including 2 U.S. soldiers) and injures more than 200. U.S. government investigators link the bombing to Libya, and on April 15 the U.S. Air Force conducts a retaliatory bombing raid on two Libyan cities.
- ***May 3:*** The Liberation Tigers of Tamil Eelam (also known as the Tamil Tigers) destroy an Air Sri Lanka plane, killing 17 people. Four days later, a bomb explodes in Colombo, the capital of Sri Lanka, killing 14 and wounding more than 100.
- ***June 18:*** About 200 prisoners belonging to Peru's Shining Path group riot in a prison outside Lima and are killed by authorities. About a week later Shining Path guerrillas bomb a tourist train near the Inca ruins of Machu Picchu, killing eight and injuring 40.
- ***July 14:*** In Spain, the Basque ETA kills 10 Civil Guard cadets with a truck bomb, wounding 56 bystanders.
- ***September 5:*** Abu Nidal terrorists attempt to hijack a Pan Am plane at Karachi Airport, Pakistan. When their efforts are thwarted, they open fire, killing 20 passengers.
- ***September 6:*** Two Abu Nidal terrorists kill 21 people in an Istanbul synagogue, then commit suicide.
- ***October 25:*** ETA terrorists kill General Rafael Garrido Gil, the military governor of the Basque province of Guipuzcoa, together with his wife and son, by blowing up their car.

- ***December 25:*** Iranian-sponsored terrorists attempt to hijack an Iraqi airliner, but the plane crashes in Saudia Arabia, killing 62 of the 107 people aboard, including two of the four hijackers.

1987

- ***January 20:*** Terry Waite, the personal emissary of the Archbishop of Canterbury, is abducted in Lebanon by Islamic Jihad while on a mission to seek the release of hostages.
- ***February 21:*** French police arrest the four top leaders of Action Directe in a farmhouse outside the city of Orléans, dealing a crushing blow to the terrorist group.
- ***March 23:*** The PIRA sets off a car bomb outside an officers' club at the British army base at Rheindahlen, injuring more than 30 people. Most of the people hurt are West Germans, however, not British military personnel.
- ***April:*** In a series of attacks, the Liberation Tigers of Tamil Eelam (Tamil Tigers) blow up four buses and the central bus station in Colombo, Sri Lanka, killing more than 200 people.
- ***September:*** Shining Path terrorists step up their efforts in Peru, setting off car bombs in Lima, killing 40 civilians in two villages in Tocache province, and assassinating leftist APRA (Alianza Popular Revolucionaria Americana) party leader Nelson Pozo.
- ***October 1:*** An Israeli air raid on the PLO's Tunis headquarters destroys the building and kills 65 people, many of whom are innocent bystanders.
- ***November 8:*** In Enniskillen, Northern Ireland, PIRA terrorists bomb a military ceremony, killing 11 people and wounding 60.
- ***November 25:*** In Zimbabwe, suspected members of the black guerrilla organization Zimbabwe African People's Union (ZAPU) murder 16 people (including 10 children) working on a farm run by Pentecostal missionaries. All victims but one are white.
- ***November 29:*** A bomb planted by two North Korean agents destroys South Korean airlines flight 858, killing 115 passengers and crew.
- ***December 8:*** The Intifada, a widespread campaign against the Israeli occupation of Palestine, begins.
- ***December 11:*** An ETA bomb attack on an apartment complex in Zaragosa that houses Spanish Civil Guard members kills 11 people and wounds 40.

1988

- ***March 11:*** Sinhalese terrorists kill 17 Tamils in apparent retaliation for an earlier attack by the Tamil Tigers that had killed 39 Sinhalese.

- ***April 5:*** Hezbollah terrorists supported by Iran hijack a Kuwaiti airliner and demand the release of 17 Shi'ite terrorists from prison. Negotiations fail, and the terrorists murder two hostages.
- ***April 12:*** Yu Kikumura, a member of the Japanese Red Army, is arrested in a rest area off the New Jersey Turnpike. His car contains three powerful bombs and other munitions. U.S. authorities believe he was preparing to bomb a U.S. facility in retaliation for the U.S. attack on Libya in April 1986. (The Japanese Red Army does make a successful retaliatory attack two days later against a USO club in Naples, Italy, killing a U.S. Navy enlisted woman and four other people.)
- ***April 16:*** Israeli agents kill Khalil al-Wazir, an al-Fatah commander also known as Abu Jihad.
- ***May 11:*** A suicide car bomb driven by an Abu Nidal terrorist kills two people and wounds 17 outside the Israeli embassy in Nicosia, Cyprus. The attack is said to be in retaliation for the killing of Khalil al-Wazir.
- ***May 15:*** Abu Nidal terrorists attack the Acropole Hotel and the British Sudan Club in Khartoum with grenades and automatic weapons, killing eight and wounding 21.
- ***July:*** The U.S. missile cruiser *Vincennes* accidentally shoots down an Iranian civil airliner while repelling an attack by missile boats. All 290 people aboard the plane are killed.
- ***July 11:*** In Greece, Abu Nidal terrorists set off a bomb aboard the cruise ship *City of Poros*, killing 9 people and injuring 100. A second bomb explodes prematurely, killing two terrorists in their car.
- ***September 7:*** Police in Rome arrest 21 suspected members of the Red Brigades, seriously disrupting the group.
- ***September 11:*** In Port-au-Prince, Haiti, members of the Tonton Macoute militia attack a church service. The attack, apparently aimed at dissident priest Jean-Bertrand Aristide, kills nine people and injures 77.
- ***October 26:*** Police raid an apartment in Neuss, Germany, used by the PFLP-GC, seizing plastic explosives and a pressure-sensitive detonator used for blowing up planes in flight. However, they later release most of the arrestees, citing lack of evidence, and fail to find the bomb that prosecutors would later charge was used later to destroy Pan Am flight 103.
- ***December 21:*** Pan Am flight 103 explodes as it is flying over Scotland, killing all 259 people on board and scattering wreckage over the village of Lockerbie, which kills 11 people on the ground. Investigators suspect the bomb was planted by the PFLP-GC, led by Ahmed Jabril.

1989

- ***February 14:*** Noted Indian-born British author Salman Rushdie goes into hiding after the Ayatollah Khomeini declares that Rushdie's novel

The Satanic Verses is blasphemous, and issues a *fatwa*, or religious order, authorizing Rushdie's execution.

- ***April:*** The Tamil Tigers and other militant groups kill more than 100 people in Sri Lanka with bomb attacks.
- ***April 3:*** Members of the Animal Liberation Front break into a research facility at the University of Arizona and free more than 1,200 rabbits, mice, frogs, and other animals. They then set fire to the laboratory and a nearby administration building.
- ***September 19:*** A plane of the French airline UTA explodes shortly after takeoff in Chad, killing all 171 people aboard. Islamic Jihad terrorists take credit for the bombing, saying that it is in retaliation for Israel's kidnapping of Hezbollah leader Sheikh Abdel Karim Obeid.
- ***November 11:*** More than 1,000 FMLN guerrillas launch an offensive against El Salvador's capital city, San Salvador. The Salvadoran army eventually drives the guerrillas out of the city.
- ***November 16:*** Six Roman Catholic priests and two employees are dragged from their rooms in the José Simeón Cañas University of Central America and executed by a right-wing death squad. The Salvadoran government will later charge nine military personnel with the killings.
- ***November 22:*** Rene Moawad, a Christian and one of three copresidents of Lebanon, and 23 other people are killed by a bomb as their motorcade passes through a Beirut street. No one claims responsibility for the attack, but some observers suggest it is the work of General Michel Aoun, a Maronite Christian who claims to be the rightful leader of the country.
- ***November 27:*** The Extraditables, the terrorist arm of the Medellín drug cartel, blow up an Avianca plane in midair, killing all 107 people on board. The group claims it destroyed the plane to kill five police informants said to be among the passengers.
- ***November 30:*** A remote-controlled bomb kills Alfred Herrhausen, head of Germany's powerful Deutsche Bank, as his limousine passes through a Frankfurt suburb. The RAF claims responsibility for the attack.
- ***December 6:*** A truck bomb set off by the Extraditables (Colombian narcoterrorists) kills more than 50 people and injures 250 in front of the headquarters of the Colombian police.
- ***December 13:*** An Italian court dismisses charges against 168 members of the Red Brigades, saying that the group was not a serious security threat.
- ***December 16:*** Colombian troops and police strike back at the Medellín cartel, killing drug lord Jose Gonzalo Rodriguez Gacha, his son, and 15 henchmen.
- ***December 16:*** Terrorists apparently motivated by race hatred send mail bombs to people associated with civil rights enforcement, killing Judge Robert S. Vance of the 11th Circuit Court and civil rights attorney Robert

Robinson of Savannah, Georgia. Two more bombs, sent to the Circuit Court and to an office of the National Association for the Advancement of Colored People (NAACP) in Jacksonville, Florida, are disarmed.

1990

- ***January 7:*** Terrorists working for the Medellín cartel kidnap more than 20 wealthy Colombians over a one-week period. They hope to turn the nation's elite against the war on drugs.
- ***March 9:*** More than a thousand members of the Colombian M-19 terrorist group turn over the weapons to authorities. Their leader, Carlos Pizarro Leon-Gomez, renounces violence and becomes a candidate for president, but he is assassinated on April 26.
- ***March 28:*** British police discover five people at Heathrow Airport who are attempting to smuggle nuclear weapons components to Iraq.
- ***April 6:*** In Peru, Shining Path guerrillas kill 24 people in the village of Alto Pauralli. Fifty villagers are killed in Sonomoro six days later.
- ***April 19:*** Sikh terrorists are believed to be responsible for the bombing of a bus near the northern Indian city of Pathanakot. Thirteen people are killed and 42 wounded.
- ***May 5:*** FBI agents in Florida arrest members of Pablo Escobar's Medellín cartel who were attempting to purchase 24 Stinger anti-aircraft missiles capable of shooting down airliners.
- ***May 21:*** An apparently deranged Jewish gunman kills seven Palestinians in the Gaza Strip. The attack causes renewed unrest in the occupied territories.
- ***May 24:*** A car bomb set off by Medellín cartel terrorists in front of Medellín's Inter-Continental Hotel kills 11 people and wounds 25.
- ***May 24:*** Two members of the radical environmental group Earth First! are injured by a bomb placed under the front seat of their car. Police claim that the activists were planning to use the bomb to disrupt logging operations, but the activists believe that it was planted by lumber interests. No charges are filed.
- ***June 30:*** As the East German communist government that had sheltered them falls, the identities of 10 RAF terrorists are revealed, and they are arrested by the new united German government. The fall of other Eastern European communist governments produces similar problems for the RAF and the infamous terrorist known as Carlos the Jackal.
- ***July 14:*** Tamil Tigers terrorists kill 35 Muslims after dragging them from passenger buses near the city of Kalmunai, Sri Lanka.
- ***September 6:*** Reports from Amnesty International and the Brazilian Institute for Social and Economic Analysis charge that death squads

operated by the Brazilian government have killed hundreds of homeless children whom they regarded as nuisances.

- *October 9:* In India, People's War Group terrorists lock a railroad coach and set fire to it, killing 47 passengers.
- *October 11:* In the northern Spanish province of Galicia, an organization called the Guerrilla Army of the Free Galician People bombs a disco, killing three people and wounding 46.
- *October 19:* Three members of the white supremacist Aryan Nations group are convicted of conspiring to bomb a Seattle disco frequented by gays.
- *October 24:* The IRA attempts a new terrorist tactic: forcing a person they consider to be a British collaborator to make a suicide bomb attack, by holding the bomber's family hostage. Of three such attacks, one in Londonderry succeeds, killing five soldiers and the bomber and wounding 26 others.
- *November 5:* Meir Kahane, leader of the extremist Jewish Defense League (JDL), is assassinated in New York. A year later, Arab terrorist El Sayyid Nosair is tried for the killing. He is convicted only of the charge of assault with a deadly weapon.

1991

- *February 7:* IRA gunmen fire shots into British Prime Minister John Major's residence while he is meeting with his cabinet. There are no injuries.
- *February 18:* IRA terrorists bomb Victoria and Paddington railway stations in London, killing one person and injuring 40.
- *August–December:* The remaining six U.S. hostages (including Terry Waite) held in Lebanon by Islamic Jihad are released. The remains of William Buckley and Colonel William R. Higgins are returned to the United States.

1992

- *January 11:* Secular military leaders stage a coup in Algeria, preventing the newly elected Islamic fundamentalist legislators from taking power. The secularists conduct a massive crackdown on the fundamentalist Islamic Salvation Front, which responds to the state terror with ongoing terrorist attacks.
- *March 17:* Islamic Jihad claims credit for the car bombing of the Israeli embassy in Buenos Aires, killing 20 and wounding more than 200. The attack is a reprisal for Israeli air raids on Hezbollah bases.
- *June 29:* Algerian president Muhammad Boudiaf is assassinated by members of the Armed Islamic Group.

- ***July 16:*** The Shining Path begins a new offensive against the Peruvian government with two car bomb attacks in Lima, killing 18 people and wounding more than 140.
- ***August 31:*** Randall Weaver, a white separatist who had fled to a remote cabin in Ruby Ridge, Idaho, after being charged with selling an illegal gun to federal agents, surrenders after a long siege. During the siege by federal forces, Weaver's wife, Vicki, is killed by a federal sniper while carrying their infant son. Weaver's older son, Sam, and Deputy Marshal William Degan had died in an earlier gun battle. Weaver is eventually acquitted of most charges, but his case becomes a rallying cry for right-wing antigovernment extremists. Evidence suggests Weaver had been approached originally by agents in an attempt to get him to inform on Aryan Nations meetings.
- ***September 13:*** Abimael Guzman, the founder of Shining Path, and his top lieutenants are captured by Peruvian security forces while holding a meeting in Lima.
- ***October 3:*** Neo-Nazis conduct anti-immigration demonstrations in the cities of Dresden and Arnstadt, Germany.
- ***October 9:*** A Russian nuclear engineer is arrested just before selling a large quantity of highly enriched uranium to terrorists. The material could have been used to make a nuclear bomb.
- ***October 14:*** Two former U.S. hostages in Lebanon, Joseph Cicippio and David Jacobsen, file a civil suit against the government of Iran, claiming that their kidnapping had been financed by Iran in order to force the United States to unfreeze Iranian assets.

1993

- ***January 25:*** A gunman, later identified as Pakistani terrorist Mir Aimal Kansi, opens fire with an automatic weapon on employees waiting to enter the CIA headquarters at Langley, Virginia. He kills two people and wounds three. He is captured more than three years later after an intensive investigation and a raid by FBI and CIA agents in Pakistan. A Virginia jury convicts him of capital murder.
- ***February 26:*** The World Trade Center in New York is bombed by followers of Egyptian fundamentalist spiritual leader Sheikh Omar Abdel Rahman, who drove a van containing a 1,200-pound bomb into one of the building's underground parking garages. Four persons are convicted by a federal jury on March 4, 1994, while two others remain at large.
- ***April 1:*** The United States indicts four Palestinian terrorists associated with the Abu Nidal organization for plotting to blow up the Israeli embassy in Washington, D.C.

- *April 19:* The federal siege of the compound of the Branch Davidian sect ends when the building explodes in flames after a tank assaults it and injects tear gas. Seventy-three people die, including cult leader David Koresh and many children. Authorities claim that the Branch Davidians had set fire to their own building, but critics accuse the FBI of having caused the disaster. As with Ruby Ridge, Waco becomes a battle cry for the extreme right-wing in America, who consider it another example of state-sponsored terrorism.
- *September 13:* A major Israeli-Palestinian peace agreement is signed in Washington, D.C., by Israeli prime minister Yitzhak Rabin and PLO chairman Yasir Arafat. Radical groups such as Hamas on the Palestinian side and Israeli ultranationalists launch terrorist attacks in an attempt to disrupt the peace process.
- *December 2:* Pablo Escobar, fugitive head of the Medellín drug cartel and organizer of a narcoterrorist bombing and kidnapping campaign against Colombian officials, is tracked down and killed in a gun battle with Colombian security forces in Medellín.

1994

- *February 25:* Baruch Goldstein, a militant follower of Rabbi Meir Kahane, opens fire on a group of Palestinian Muslims praying at the Tomb of the Patriarchs in Hebron, Israel. He kills about 30 people and wounds approximately 150. In response, riots break out in the occupied territories and negotiations on Palestinian autonomy are temporarily suspended.
- *March 14:* Nidal Ayyad, Ahmad Ajaj, Mohammad Salameh, and Mahmud Abouhalima are convicted on all four counts for their roles in the bombing of the World Trade Center in February 1993.
- *May–August:* In three separate incidents, German police seize nuclear materials being smuggled to European terrorists, possibly for eventual construction of a nuclear bomb.
- *August 15:* The notorious terrorist Carlos the Jackal (Ilyich Ramirez Sanchez) is captured in the Sudan by French counterterrorist agents. He is swiftly extradited to France for trial.
- *August 31:* The IRA agrees to a cease-fire, though some extremists continue terrorist attacks.

1995

- *January 22:* Islamic Jihad terrorists claim credit for a bombing outside a military camp in Israel. Nineteen people (including 18 Israeli soldiers) are killed, and another 65 injured.
- *January 30:* A car bomb explodes in Algiers, killing 42 people and injuring about 300 others.

- ***February 6:*** The trial of Sheikh Abdel Rahman and eleven other Islamic terrorists for the World Trade Center bombing and related conspiracies begins in U.S. Federal Court in New York City.
- ***February 7:*** Ramzi Ahmed Youssef, accused mastermind of the World Trade Center bombing, is arrested in Islamabad, Pakistan, and flown to the United States to stand trial.
- ***March 20:*** Members of the apocalyptic religious terrorist cult Aum Shinri Kyo release deadly Sarin nerve gas into the Tokyo subway system. Twelve people are killed and about 5,000 injured to varying degrees. Japanese authorities begin a massive hunt for the terrorists and their leaders.
- ***April 2:*** Terrorists from the Hamas group accidentally set off a bomb in Gaza while assembling it. Eight people are killed and 30 wounded.
- ***April 19:*** A massive truck bomb explosion demolishes the Alfred P. Murrah Federal Building in Oklahoma City in the worst domestic terrorist attack in U.S. history. The blast kills 168 people, including children in a day care center. Two days later, Timothy McVeigh and Terry Nichols are charged with the bombing. They are not connected to any known terrorist group.
- ***June 26:*** An attempt by radical Islamic gunmen to kill Egyptian president Hosni Mubarak during his visit to Addis Ababa, Ethiopia, fails, but two Ethiopian policemen and two terrorists are killed, and many bystanders are injured.
- ***August 15:*** The U.S. Department of Justice agrees to pay $3.1 million to settle a civil suit brought by Randall Weaver for the wrongful death of his wife and son.
- ***September 19:*** The *Washington Post* publishes a rambling, anonymous 35,000-word anti-industrial manifesto by a person claiming to be responsible for the Unabomb attacks. The writer had offered to cease the attacks if it was published. Authorities hope that someone will be able to identify the person by his writing style.
- ***October 1:*** In one of the most important terrorist trials in U.S. history, 10 Islamic fundamentalist terrorists are convicted in a New York federal court of conspiracy to destroy U.S. public buildings and structures. Their spiritual leader, Sheikh Omar Abdel Rahman, is convicted of directing the conspiracy and also of conspiring to assassinate Egyptian president Hosni Mubarak. El Sayyid Nosair is convicted of the 1990 murder of Rabbi Meir Kahane (earlier, in state court, he had been convicted only of assault with a deadly weapon.)

1996

- ***February 14:*** Believing that the "Unabomber Manifesto" had been written by his brother Theodore, David Kaczynski contacts the FBI. Theodore Kaczynski is arrested at his Montana cabin on April 3.

- ***June:*** A truck bomb kills 19 U.S. personnel and wounds 500 at a military camp in Dhahran, Saudi Arabia. Hani al-Sayegh is arrested in Canada and held for the attack. A controversy over the adequacy of U.S. military security develops, but the investigation bogs down due to lack of cooperation by Saudi Arabia.
- ***July 17:*** TWA flight 800 blows up just off the coast of Long Island, New York, just minutes after taking off. Many speculate that the plane had been destroyed by terrorists, and some witnesses claim that they saw missile trails intersecting the plane. Investigators eventually conclude, however, that the plane had been destroyed by a design flaw in the center fuel tank.
- ***July 27:*** In the midst of the 1996 Summer Olympics, a pipe bomb goes off in Atlanta's Centennial Olympic Park, killing one person and injuring 112. Guard Richard Jewell, who had reported a suspicious knapsack and helped other guards clear the area before the explosion, is first hailed as a hero but then becomes the FBI's chief suspect. Although he is later cleared, his life and reputation are disrupted and he sues various media organizations for reckless reporting. The bombing is eventually linked to antiabortion terrorist Eric Robert Rudolph, still at large in mid-2000.
- ***December 18:*** MRTA (Tupac Amaru) terrorists seize the Japanese embassy in Lima, Peru, taking 490 hostages, including many prominent international diplomats. They release 225 of the hostages as a Christmas gesture and enter into prolonged negotiations with authorities, demanding the release of imprisoned comrades.

1997

- ***January 16:*** Two bombs explode at an abortion clinic in Atlanta, Georgia. The first bomb causes only property damage, but when investigators and reporters reach the scene, a second bomb injures six people. Eric Robert Rudolph is sought for both this attack and the Olympic Park bombing.
- ***January 20:*** Islamic terrorists in Algeria attack a village, killing 36 residents, some of whom are decapitated. The same terrorists then go to Algiers, where they set off a bomb that kills more than 30 people and wounds many more.
- ***February 28:*** A gay/lesbian bar in Atlanta, Georgia, is bombed, injuring five people. This attack is also linked to Eric Robert Rudolph.
- ***March 21:*** A suicide bomb attack on a Tel Aviv cafe kills five people including the terrorist and wounds many more. It also interrupts ongoing Israeli-Palestinian peace negotiations.
- ***April:*** White supremacist and microbiologist Larry Wayne Harris is sentenced to probation and community service for illegally obtaining bubonic plague cultures. He had claimed to be doing research to protect the

United States from biological attack, but authorities suspected him of plotting an attack of his own.

- ***April 22:*** After months of fruitless negotiation with the MRTA, Peruvian troops burst into the Japanese embassy in Lima, freeing the diplomatic hostages. All 14 terrorists, one soldier, and one hostage are killed.
- ***June 13:*** A federal jury in Denver sentences Timothy McVeigh to death for the 1995 Oklahoma City bombing. His coconspirator, Terry Nichols, receives a life sentence.
- ***June 29:*** FBI agents in Pakistan arrest Mir Aimal Kansi, accused of a shooting on January 25, 1993, which killed two people and injured three outside the CIA headquarters in Langley, Virginia.
- ***July 30:*** Two bomb-carrying terrorists kill themselves and 13 bystanders in a crowded Jerusalem market. Another 150 people are injured. It is unclear whether the bombing was a suicide attack or an accident, but Hamas takes credit for the attack.
- ***September 4:*** Another Hamas suicide bomb attack on a Jerusalem market kills the three bombers and one bystander while injuring another 200 people.
- ***September 23:*** In Algeria, terrorists from the Islamic Salvation Front carry out a number of attacks, killing 85 and injuring 67 persons.
- ***September 30:*** Israel, hoping to aid the peace process, releases 20 terrorists from prison, including Sheikh Ahmed Yassin, founder of Hamas.
- ***October 8:*** The United States issues an expanded list of 30 terrorist groups, making entry of their members into the U.S. illegal and banning U.S. citizens from contributing to the groups.
- ***November:*** A terrorist campaign against the Egyptian government by the Islamic Group (Al-Gama'at al-Islamiyya) culminates in the killing of 58 tourists in Luxor.
- ***December 24:*** Carlos the Jackal (Ilyich Ramirez Sanchez) is convicted in Paris of murder and kidnapping and sentenced to life in prison.

1998

- ***January 29:*** An unknown terrorist bombs an abortion clinic in Birmingham, Alabama, killing off-duty police officer Robert Sanderson and injuring a nurse.
- ***March*** The family of Alisa Flatow, killed in an attack by Islamic Jihad gunmen on a bus in the Gaza Strip in 1995, wins a judgment for $247.5 million against Iran in a U.S. federal district court. However, Iran refuses to pay the judgment, and the administration of President Bill Clinton seeks to block efforts to collect the judgment from Iranian assets frozen by the U.S. government.

- ***April 10:*** A historic peace agreement is ratified by voters in both Northern Ireland and the Republic of Ireland. It calls for a Northern Ireland legislative council made up of both Protestants and Catholics, and the sharing of decision-making power between Northern Ireland and the Republic in areas such as transportation and the environment.
- ***May 4:*** Accepting a plea bargain, Theodore Kaczynski, the Unabomber, is sentenced to four consecutive life terms for his mail bombings. Kaczynski had sought to represent himself and had resisted any attempt by his attorneys to mount an insanity defense.
- ***August 7:*** In nearly simultaneous attacks, the U.S. embassies in Nairobi, Kenya, and Dar es Salaam, Tanzania, are bombed. The explosion in Kenya is larger, and destroys a building next door to the embassy after the truck carrying the bomb is turned away by an alert guard. Twelve U.S. citizens and 250 Kenyans are killed, and thousands of people are wounded. The explosion in Tanzania is considerably smaller but kills 10 people and wounds several times that number. The attacks are soon linked to terrorist multimillionaire Osama bin Laden, who is indicted in absentia.
- ***August 15:*** Slow but steady peace progress in Northern Ireland is threatened by a car bomb explosion in Omagh that kills 28 people and wounds 220. The perpetrators, a splinter group called the Real IRA, had given authorities a bomb warning with misleading information which caused bystanders to be evacuated in the direction of the bomb. The terrorists are vigorously condemned by the mainstream IRA, Sinn Féin, and Protestant groups.
- ***August 20:*** In retaliation for the earlier attacks on U.S. embassies in Africa, President Clinton orders cruise missile attacks on a pharmaceutical plant reportedly linked to terrorist nerve gas production in Khartoum, Sudan and Osama bin Laden's terrorist training camp in Afghanistan. Although bin Laden's camp is damaged, he escapes without injury. Later reports suggest that the pharmaceutical plant was actually just a pharmaceutical plant.
- ***October 19:*** A fire set by ecoterrorists causes $12 million in property damage to prime ski resort areas on Vail Mountain, Colorado. A group calling itself the Earth Liberation Front (believed to be the same as the Animal Liberation Front) claims responsibility for the blaze, demanding an end to expansion of the facilities.
- ***November 4:*** A New York federal court returns indictments against Osama bin Laden and other members of the al-Qaida group in connection with the bombings of the two U.S. embassies in Africa.

1999

- ***August:*** Jordan expels Hamas, arresting four members and closing the militant Islamic group's offices.

- ***September–October:*** A series of bomb blasts in Moscow are linked by authorities to Chechen terrorists who were demanding independence for the former Soviet Caucasian republic. Russian authorities respond with random police sweeps, curtailment of civil liberties, confused announcements, and a renewed military offensive in Chechnya.
- ***September 6:*** Israel's Supreme Court rules that government interrogators cannot be authorized to use torture or physical pressure beyond that "inherent in the interrogation process itself," even to get information about a pending terrorist attack.
- ***December:*** Government planners prepare heightened security measures, fearing that terrorists will strike during the holiday season, either from millennial beliefs or to take advantage of large gatherings of New Year's revelers.
- ***December 14:*** Ahmed Rassam, an alleged Algerian terrorist, is arrested for plotting to smuggle explosives into Port Townsend, Washington. Another Algerian, Abdelmajid Dahoumane, remains at large. The two are indicted on January 20, 2000, by a Seattle grand jury. The U.S. government announces a $5 million bounty for Dahoumane's capture. The authorities link the two suspects to the Armed Islamic Group.
- ***December 31:*** Ecoterrorists set fire to a genetic research facility partly funded by Monsanto Corporation at Michigan State University. The fire causes $400,000 in damages, and the Earth Liberation Front claims responsibility.

2000

- ***February:*** The House Judiciary Committee's Subcommittee on Immigration holds hearings to examine provisions of the 1996 Antiterrorism and Effective Death Penalty Act that would allows the INS to arrest, detain, or deport immigrants based on secret evidence of terrorist links. Arab-American and civil libertarian groups charge that such proceedings violate the fundamental right in American law to confront one's accusers.
- ***February:*** A federal jury in Washington state convicts a group of Freemen and Washington State Militia members of weapons charges but deadlocks on charges that they had conspired to blow up radio towers, a bridge, and a train tunnel to stop UN troops from "invading" from Canada.
- ***February:*** Hezbollah guerrillas and Israeli forces continue to battle with rockets and bombs as the Israelis prepare to leave Lebanon. Israel had hoped Syria would restrain the guerrillas during and after the withdrawal. Israelis are divided on whether to pull out sooner or exert more pressure to stop the attacks.

- ***February 14:*** During this week hackers launch "denial of service attacks" that tie up major Internet commerce sites such as Yahoo! and eBay. While not tied to particular terrorist groups, the attacks illustrate the vulnerability of the growing U.S. e-commerce sector to cyberterrorism.
- ***March:*** U.S. officials consider whether to lift a ban on U.S. citizens traveling to Libya. Libya's decision to hand over two men suspected of involvement in the 1988 bombing of Pan Am flight 103 over Lockerbie, Scotland, has led to improved relations between the two nations, and the United States has suspended sanctions against Libya.
- ***April 8:*** U.S. Secretary of Defense William Cohen says that if Iran wants better relations with the United States, it must stop backing terrorism. He notes that relations have been thawing between the two countries: The previous February, liberal reformers had won victories in Iranian parliamentary elections, and the United States in turn removed a ban on imports of some Iranian goods (but not oil).
- ***April 20:*** Jordan puts 28 alleged terrorists on trial for plotting to attack U.S. and Israeli tourists in Jordan over the New Year's holiday.
- ***May 1:*** The U.S. State Department's 1999 annual report on terrorism points to South Asia (including Pakistan and Afghanistan) as the emerging source of support for international terrorism. The report also notes that loosely organized terrorist groups based on religion or ideology are supplanting the political and state-sponsored terrorism of the past.
- ***June 5:*** The U.S. National Commission on Terrorism, created after the 1998 U.S. embassy bombings, issues recommendations for fighting terrorism. These include increased spending, tighter controls on financial transactions, and allowing the CIA to recruit informants who may have "unsavory" backgrounds. Civil libertarians respond with concern about potential abuses.
- ***August 12:*** A bomb explodes in an underpass at Moscow's Pushkin Square, killing at least eight persons and injuring more than 90. Some Russian officials attribute the bombing to Chechen terrorists, while others are more reticent.
- ***August 18:*** Libya, seeking to participate in an Eastern Mediterranean summit, agrees to pay $25 million to Muslim rebels in the Philippines in exchange for the ransom of 16 hostages.
- ***October:*** Weeks of widespread violence follow right-wing Israeli politician Ariel Sharon's visit to the Temple Mount (called Haram ash Sharif by Muslims). Israeli helicopter gunships attack Palestinian headquarters and Hamas claims responsibility for a Jerusalem car bombing. More than 170 people are killed, mostly Palestinians.
- ***October 12:*** A suicide boat attack blows a gaping hole in the side of the U.S. Navy destroyer *Cole* while the ship is taking on fuel in Aden harbor, Yemen. The attack kills 17 sailors.

- ***October 30:*** Basque ETA terrorists set off a large bomb that kills a Spanish judge, his driver, and a bodyguard. Sixty passengers aboard a nearby bus are also injured. A growing wave of ETA attacks has shattered the cease-fire signed earlier in the year.
- ***November 6:*** The arrest of four suspects in the Cole bombing is said to reveal links between the attackers and Islamic Jihad, and suspicion grows that the attack was masterminded by terrorist organizer Osama bin Laden.
- ***November 12:*** The hijacking of a Russian airliner ends peacefully when the plane arrives in Moscow after being diverted by a hijacker to Israel. Akhmed Amirkhanov, a citizen of Dagestan, is charged with the crime but is reported to be mentally deranged.
- ***November 13:*** A summit of moderate Islamic leaders in Doha, Qatar, condemns Israel for the killing of Palestinians, but it also denounces terrorism "from all sources" and refuses to declare a *jihad* against Israel.

2001

- ***January 16:*** Federal officials set May 16, 2001, as the date of execution of Timothy J. McVeigh, convicted of murder and conspiracy for the April 1995 bombing of the Alfred P. Murrah Federal Building in Oklahoma City.
- ***January 31:*** Abdelbaset Ali Mohmed al-Megrahi is found guilty of the bombing of Pan Am flight 103 by a Scottish court. However, the other defendant, Al Amin Khalifa Fhimah, is not convicted.

CHAPTER 5

BIOGRAPHICAL LISTING

This chapter provides brief biographical sketches of some of the more significant figures in the history of terrorism. More information about many of these individuals can be found on the Internet resource sites discussed in Chapter 7 and in the bibliographies in Chapter 8.

Abu Abbas (also know as Abdul Abbas and Mohammad Abbas), flamboyant leader of the Palestine Liberation Front and member of the Executive Committee of the Palestine Liberation Organization (PLO). Born shortly after the founding of Israel, Abbas grew up in Palestine refugee camps and became involved in Palestinian extremist activities in the 1960s, becoming a member of the Popular Front for the Liberation of Palestine (PFLP) and its more militant spinoff, the General Command. Abbas is best known for masterminding the *Achille Lauro* hijacking in October 1985. In an interview with the *New York Times*, he later expressed his relish at the death of elderly passenger Leon Klinghoffer. Abbas became known for brutality but also for innovative (if not totally successful) methods, such as attempting to raid Israel with hot air balloons and hang gliders. He thus acquired a reputation among PLO leaders as being something of a loose cannon.

Osama bin Laden, a Saudi multimillionaire. Bin Laden emerged at the end of the 1990s as the financial power behind terrorist actions that included the attacks on U.S. embassies in Africa. Bin Laden first became involved in conflict when the Soviets invaded Afghanistan in 1979. He moved his company and workers into the country and built the training infrastructure for the guerrilla resistance to the invasion. He and other Afghan leaders received substantial covert support from the CIA, which saw the conflict as an opportunity to mire the Soviets in an unwinnable war in Afghanistan. After the Soviets were defeated, bin Laden and his trained veterans went back to Saudi Arabia where they turned their radical Islamic focus to fighting the country's secular government. In 1994, the Saudis expelled bin Laden and his group, and he moved to Sudan, where he set up extensive bases staffed by his fellow Afghani veterans. In 1996, however, with Sudan seeking better relations with the United States, bin Laden moved again—back to Afghanistan. In February 1998, bin Laden announced a new group called the Islamic World Front for the Struggle Against the Jews and the Crusaders and declared that U.S. citizens throughout the world would be fair game for terrorist attack. In August 1998, bin Laden's terrorists bombed U.S. embassies in Nairobi, Kenya, and Dar es Salaam, Tanzania. Retaliatory U.S. attacks on a factory in Sudan that bin Laden had allegedly used for chemical weapons and on bin Laden's base in Afghanistan aroused controversy (evidence of chemical weapons in Sudan proved elusive). U.S. officials believe that extensive surveillance of bin Laden's agents, leading to arrests in Britain, Germany, Canada, the United States, Jordan, and Pakistan, have weakened bin Laden's network. However, he is suspected of masterminding that October 12, 2000 attack on the U.S. destroyer *Cole*.

Abu Daoud (nom de guerre for Mohammed Daoud Oudeh), a founder of the extremist Palestinian group Black September. He has been linked to the assassination of Jordanian prime minister Wasfi al-Tal in Cairo on November 28, 1971; the massacre of Israeli athletes at the Munich Olympics in 1972; and the assassination of U.S. ambassador Claude Noel and a Belgian diplomat at the Saudi Arabian embassy in Khartoum on March 1, 1973. In 1977, Daoud was arrested in connection with the Munich massacre, but a French court refused to extradite him to Israel and ordered him released. In 1981, he was wounded by gunmen, and speculation linked his attackers to either the Abu Nidal organization or the Israeli Mossad secret service. As of 1999, Abu Daoud remained free, touring to promote his forthcoming book, *Memoirs of a Palestinian Terrorist.*

Abu Nidal (nom de guerre for Sabri al-Banna), one of the most notorious modern terrorists. Born in Jaffa, Palestine, al-Banna saw his family lose its holdings following the establishment of the state of Israel in 1948. Nidal joined the al-Fatah group after the Six Day War with Israel in 1967 and served with the PLO in Baghdad in the early 1970s. However, he considered the PLO to be ineffective and started a new organization, the Fatah Revolutionary Council (FRC), which was backed by Iraq as a way to counteract the Syrian-backed PLO. Eventually the council evolved into a loose association of terrorist groups known in the West as the Abu Nidal Organization. The PLO passed a death sentence against Nidal, and Nidal's FRC in turn has made several unsuccessful assassination attempts against PLO leader Yasir Arafat. Terrorists organized by Abu Nidal have conducted more than 100 attacks in nations around the world, including attacks on airport passengers in Rome and Vienna in December 1985, the massacre of worshippers in an Istanbul synagogue in 1986, and the attack on the Greek cruise ship *City of Poros* in 1988. Intense Western pressure on Nidal's backers led to Syria expelling his agents in 1987, but he continues activities from bases in Lebanon.

Yasir Arafat, chairman of the PLO, leader of al-Fatah, its largest constituent group, and since 1996, president of the Palestine Authority. In the 1960s, as leader of al-Fatah, Arafat conducted guerrilla raids into Israel. In 1964, al-Fatah joined with other groups to form the PLO. During the 1970s Arafat consolidated his position as chief spokesperson for the Palestinian cause, despite opposition from more radical factions that accused him of being too moderate and too accommodating toward Israel. In 1988, Arafat announced his willingness to renounce terrorism in keeping with United Nations resolutions and to negotiate a settlement of the Palestinian question with Israel. In 1993, Arafat signed a peace agreement with the Israeli government, and in 1994, he and Israeli leaders Yitzhak Rabin and Shimon Peres were jointly awarded the Nobel Prize for Peace. As leader of the Palestine Authority, which rules Arab-controlled portions of the West Bank and the Gaza Strip, Arafat seems poised to become the first president of a true Palestinian state.

Andreas Baader, West German terrorist and cofounder of the Red Army Faction (RAF), also called the Baader-Meinhof Gang. Active in radical student politics in the 1960s, Baader committed his first terrorist act by bombing a Frankfurt department store with fellow terrorist Gudrun Ensslin in 1968. Arrested, he escaped with the aid of Ensslin and Ulrike Meinhof. They went to the Middle East and trained with other European terrorists in camps set up by the Popular Front for the Liberation of Palestine (PFLP). Returning to Germany in the early 1970s, Baader and his comrades carried out a string of bombings, kidnappings, and assassinations. In 1972, Baader and his associates were arrested by German authorities. In 1977, RAF terrorists tried to win their freedom by hijacking a Lufthansa airliner, but West German commandos freed the hostages. In despair, Baader, Ensslin, and a comrade committed suicide in their prison cells.

Menachim Begin, a leader of the Jewish Irgun terrorists in the 1940s and prime minister of Israel 1977–83. Begin's life demonstrates the complexity of the Middle East conflict. While Begin was in the Irgun's leadership, the group committed two notorious terrorist acts, the bombing of the King David Hotel and the massacre at Deir Yassin. Entering politics in the new state of Israel, he founded the right-wing Herut party and served in the Knesset (parliament) as leader of the opposition from 1948 to 1967. He helped form a national unity government in 1967–70 and became prime minister in 1977 as part of a right-wing coalition that included the Likud party. Despite his hard line against the Arabs, Begin opened the negotiations with Egypt in 1977 that under the mediation of U.S. president Jimmy Carter led to the Camp David Accords in 1978 and the 1979 Egypt-Israeli peace treaty, for which Begin shared the 1978 Nobel Peace Prize with Egyptian president Anwar Sadat. However, Begin's 1982 invasion of Lebanon to suppress continuing guerrilla activity led to political opposition at home and Begin's decision to retire in 1983.

Carlos (also known as "The Jackal," aliases for Ilyich Ramirez Sanchez) an infamous Venezuelan-born international terrorist. Carlos worked most extensively with the Popular Front for the Liberation of Palestine (PFLP) but is believed to have also coordinated efforts with the Red Army Faction, Japanese Red Army, Basque ETA, and other groups during the 1970s. He may have also had connections with the KGB and Cuban intelligence. His most successful action was probably his leadership of the PFLP kidnapping of the oil ministers of 11 nations at an OPEC meeting in Vienna, Austria, in 1975. In August 1995, Carlos was tracked down in the Sudan and extradited to France. On December 24, 1997, he was convicted of murder and kidnapping and sentenced to life in prison.

Eldridge Cleaver, U.S. Black Panther, leader of the party's most violent faction. After being released on bail following a 1968 arrest, he fled to Cuba and then to Algeria, where he sought to develop ties between the Black Panthers and Middle Eastern and African radical groups. In 1975, he returned to the United States, renounced his radical beliefs, and returned to private life.

Pablo Gaviria Escobar, probably the most infamous of the Colombian drug lords of the 1980s. When Colombian president Virgilio Barco Vargas launched an all-out war against the drug cartel in late 1989, Escobar went into hiding. The cartel tried to force the government to abandon its antidrug efforts by engaging in a campaign of "narcoterrorism" that included not only bombings but also assassinations and kidnappings of government officials and wealthy persons. The terrorism did prevent the Colombian government from extraditing Escobar to the United States to face charges. In June 1991, Escobar surrendered to Colombian authorities and was housed in a luxurious prison, from which he escaped in 1992 and went underground. On December 2, 1993, a commando force trapped Escobar on a rooftop and killed him in the ensuing firefight.

Abimael Guzman Reynoso, former professor of philosophy; founder of and major intellectual influence on Sendero Luminoso ("The Shining Path") guerrillas of Peru. He based his organization on radical Maoist principles; it became known for extreme brutality. In September 1992, Guzman and his top lieutenants were captured by Peruvian security forces, and Guzman was sentenced to life in prison. Sendero Luminoso subsequently lost much of its influence.

George Habash, leader and founder in 1968 of the Popular Front for the Liberation of Palestine (PFLP), a radical faction of the PLO. He was born in Lydda (now Lod, Israel) to a Greek Orthodox family. He studied medicine and earned his M.D. degree at the American University in Beirut. Under his leadership, the PFLP carried out major terrorist attacks including the hijacking of four planes over a three-day period starting September 6, 1970, which eventually backfired and resulted in Jordan expelling Palestinian guerrillas from the country. Habash and Yasir Arafat became longtime rivals, as Habash accused Arafat of being too moderate and not sufficiently grounded in leftist ideology. In 1980, Habash suffered a massive stroke; he recovered, but his health remained frail. He turned toward policy-making and away from direct involvement in terrorist activity. In 1999, Habash met with Arafat to discuss issues relating to the emerging Palestinian state. In 2000, Habash announced his retirement.

Meir Kahane, American rabbi who founded the Jewish Defense League (JDL) in 1968. The JDL staged violent attacks on Palestinian, Arab, and other groups it perceived to be "anti-Jewish." In 1971, Kahane emigrated to Israel, where he became a right-wing member of the Knesset (parliament). His party's platform called for the expulsion of all Arabs from Israel and the occupied territories. Kahane's supporters tried to intimidate Palestinian residents into leaving Israel. On November 5, 1990, Kahane was assassinated by an Egyptian Arab in New York while giving a speech to U.S. Jewish supporters.

Theodore Kaczynski, reclusive U.S. former mathematics professor known as the Unabomber. Kaczynski retreated to a Montana cabin where he built and, from 1975 to 1995, dispatched letter bombs targeting people he associated with computer and other high-tech industries. The bombs killed three persons and injured 23. Kaczynski believed that modern industrial civilization was destroying nature and alienating humanity. In 1995, he demanded that newspapers publish his antitechnology manifesto, and both the *Washington Post* and *New York Times* agreed to do so after consulting with law enforcement authorities. When Kaczynski's brother read the manifesto, he recognized the writing style as his estranged brother's. This led to Kaczynski's arrest, trial, and conviction for the Unabomber killings. After a tumultuous trial, Kaczynski pled guilty in January 1998, receiving four life sentences plus 30 years in prison. He later unsuccessfully appealed his sentence, claiming that his attorneys had not given him good counsel.

Leila Khaled, member of the Popular Front for the Liberation of Palestine (PFLP) and one of the few women to reach the front ranks of modern terrorism. Khaled played an important role in the multiple aircraft hijackings in September 1970 that became known as the Dawson's Field affair.

In this incident, she was captured during an attempted hijacking in London but was released in exchange for hostages aboard a BOAC airliner at Dawson's Field. Since then, she has become a heroine to many Palestinian activists, and she has brought a strongly feminist viewpoint to the internal debates of the PFLP and related groups.

Timothy McVeigh, served with some distinction as a U.S. soldier in the Persian Gulf War, but became disillusioned and then enraged at the federal government because of its actions toward the family of Randy Weaver at Ruby Ridge, Idaho, and against the Branch Davidians at Waco, Texas. He eventually decided to strike back by setting off a fuel-oil-and-fertilizer bomb in front of the federal building in Oklahoma City. The 1995 attack, which killed 168 people, was the worst incident of domestic terrorism in American history. McVeigh was sentenced to death for the crime and is residing on federal death row for the appeals process. His convicted coconspirator, Terry Nichols, is serving a life sentence.

Muammar al-Qaddafi (sometimes spelled Gadafy or Khadafy) ruler of Libya since 1969. When he took power, he seemed at first to be a staunch anticommunist allied with U.S. cold war interests. But when Egypt expelled Soviet advisers in 1972, the Soviets turned to Libya and built a sustained, if volatile, relationship with Qaddafi, in which they provided weapons and aid to Libya and Qaddafi opposed Western interests. Qaddafi's chief role in terrorism has been to provide weapons (including massive amounts of explosives), training bases, and other support to the more radical Palestinian terrorist operations such as Black September, the PFLP (under George Habash), and the Abu Nidal Organization. Since 1985, the United States has imposed sanctions on Libya and lists Libya as a "terrorist state." In 1986, the United States, accusing Qaddafi of masterminding attacks on the Vienna and Rome airports, retaliated by bombing the Libyan cities of Tripoli and Benghazi. Qaddafi reportedly narrowly escaped the bombs, which killed his adopted daughter. Since then Qaddafi has kept a relatively low profile. In 1999 he appeared to be cooperating somewhat with U.S. authorities when he surrendered two Libyans accused of bombing Pan Am flight 103 over Lockerbie, Scotland, in 1988.

Sheikh Omar Abdel Rahman, Islamic fundamentalist cleric. Abdel Rahman, though blind and not a direct participant, was implicated in the assassination of Egyptian president Anwar Sadat in 1981 because he had issued an Islamic judicial decree authorizing the killing. After his acquittal, he founded a group, Jamaa al Islami, with the purpose of overthrowing the Mubarak regime and replacing it with an Islamic state. He entered the United States and became leader of a small mosque in Jersey City, New Jersey. Following the World Trade Center bombing in February

1993, Abdel Rahman was implicated in both the bombing and a wider conspiracy to bomb key installations in New York including the Holland and Lincoln Tunnels and the United Nations building, as well as a plot to assassinate U.S. senator Alfonse D'Amato and U.N. secretary-general Boutros Boutros-Ghali. On October 1, 1995, Rahman was convicted of directing these conspiracies.

Ramzi Ahmed Yousef, Islamic terrorist and associate of Sheikh Omar Abdel Rahman. While Rahman, a blind cleric, provided theological inspiration for the New York World Trade Center bombing in 1993 and related terrorist plots, Yousef, an electrical engineer who learned to make bombs in an Afghanistan terrorist training camp, constructed and planted the bomb. Besides bombing the World Trade Center, Yousef bombed an airliner in the Philippines in December 1994 (while plotting to assassinate Pope John Paul II during his visit there). Philippine police uncovered Yousef's bomb-making operation there, but he fled to Islamabad, Pakistan. When Yousef tried to recruit South African Muslim theology student Istiaq Parker in 1995, the latter refused to smuggle a bomb into the United States and, fearing reprisal, went to U.S. authorities in Islamabad. U.S. and Pakistani agents arrested Yousef in his room in February 1995 and quickly flew him back to the United States, where he was convicted with two coconspirators and sentenced to life without parole.

CHAPTER 6

GLOSSARY

The following are some terms and events that frequently arise in the discussion of international terrorism.

active measures A Soviet euphemism for direct attempts to manipulate public opinion in western countries (such as through propaganda, disinformation, and campaigns by "front" groups), as well as support and encouragement of terrorists.

amnesty An official act of forgiveness by which a government agrees to ignore criminal offenses that have been committed by a group of people (such as a rebel force) as part of a process of peace and reconciliation.

anarchism The political philosophy asserting that government is inherently corrupt and abusive and should be replaced by arrangements arrived at through the voluntary cooperation of individuals. Starting in the 19th century, some anarchists, such as Mikhail Bakunin in Russia, advocated the use of violence and terrorism against political leaders.

ANFO (ammonium nitrate-fuel oil) A powerful explosive made by mixing ordinary fertilizer with fuel oil; used in the Oklahoma City bombing.

antiterrorism assistance (ATA) A U.S. State Department program that provides assistance to more than 40 foreign governments in the fight against terrorism, including training for border guards and customs officials and the strengthening of airport security.

assassination Deliberate murder of a politically or socially prominent person, especially when done for political purposes. It is illegal for the United States government to target individuals for assassination, but (as in the attack on the home of Libya's Muammar al-Qaddafi in 1986), military raids have been launched that might be expected to kill terrorist leaders.

attentat clause A provision of an extradition treaty in some nations that says that a nation holding the accused murderer of a head of state (or a head of state's family member) will not treat the accused as a "political" criminal and will extradite without considering any appeals on grounds of political protest or persecution.

bioterrorism The use of biological weapons (such as disease pathogens or toxins) in terrorist attacks.

Bloody Sunday The killing of 13 Catholic demonstrators by a British army unit in Londonderry, Northern Ireland, on July 21, 1972. The incident became a rallying cry for the IRA, which enacted bloody reprisals.

Bonn Declaration The Joint Statement on International Terrorism, issued July 17, 1978, by Italy, France, West Germany, the United Kingdom, Canada, the United States, and Japan. The nations agreed that other nations that did not cooperate in the extradition and prosecution of aircraft hijackers would have their airlines boycotted by the signatory nations.

Camp David Accords A peace agreement forged in 1978 and signed in 1979 between Egypt and Israel, mediated by U.S. president Jimmy Carter. As part of the agreement, Israel returned the Sinai to Egypt.

cell The smallest unit of organization of a guerrilla or terrorist group, usually consisting of five or fewer people. Typically, members of a given cell have no knowledge of or contact with other cells, thus minimizing vulnerability to exposure or infiltration.

chemical weapons Weapons that primarily work through the effects of toxic agents, such as nerve gas.

COINTELPRO (Counterintelligence Program) An FBI effort to turn public opinion against political opposition groups during the 1960s and early 1970s. In 1974, a committee investigation under the leadership of Senator Frank Church found that COINTELPRO had conducted illegal surveillance and disinformation campaigns against Martin Luther King Jr. and other dissident leaders.

commando tactics Use of small, highly trained and motivated armed forces inserted into enemy territory. Many nations have elite antiterrorism forces trained in commando tactics, while terrorists themselves could be said to be irregular commandos.

counterinsurgency General term for military, political, legal, economic, or other measures taken by a government to suppress or defeat revolutionaries. Counterinsurgency forces seek to gain intelligence about guerrilla activity and also to win the support of the public so it will turn against or expose the guerrillas.

counterterrorism The attempt to prevent terrorist attacks and root out and punish terrorist leaders and groups. As with counterinsurgency, intelligence is of key importance. Use of military or paramilitary forces and extrajudicial actions is commonplace in many nations, but problematic in democratic societies that support basic civil liberties.

Glossary

cyberterrorism The damaging or compromising of computer systems by hackers working as or for terrorists. Such activities can include introducing computer viruses, stealing sensitive information, and flooding web sites with bogus information requests.

death squad A vigilante, paramilitary group, often operating with the covert support of government officials or military leaders. Many right-wing Latin American governments (such as Chile under Agusto Pinochet) have used death squads to kill political opponents, usually leftist guerrillas. The killings are often indiscriminate, however.

Delta Force The elite counterterrorist task force of the U.S. Army, established in 1977 and based in Fort Bragg, North Carolina. The Delta Force has had only limited success against terrorists. In 1980, its attempt to mount an airborne rescue of U.S. hostages in Iran failed when a U.S. helicopter and plane collided.

Dirty War Colloquial term for the brutal program of repression undertaken by Argentina's military junta when it took power in 1976, which lasted until 1983. All types of opponents on the left and labor groups were targeted; many victims were killed and their bodies disposed of clandestinely.

disappeared A term often used in Latin America to refer to victims of death squads and other government campaigns to eliminate opposition. Victims are kidnapped and often secretly killed, leaving their fate unknown to their families, who have not even a body to bury.

euroterrorism Term applied to left-wing European terrorists who targeted NATO and American facilities, such as Action Directe, the Red Army Faction, and the Red Brigades.

extradition The legal process of transferring a prisoner from the country in which he or she is arrested to the country that has placed criminal charges. Countries often resist requests for extradition of accused terrorists, either because they fear reprisals from terrorist groups or out of concern for the civil liberties of the accused.

fedayeen Arabic term meaning commandos or guerrilla fighters.

Gaza Strip a narrow area between Egypt and Israel, consisting of about 140 square miles. Israel occupied the area following its victory over its Arab neighbors in the 1967 Six-Day War. In 1988, the Palestine National Council declared the Gaza Strip to be part of the future independent Palestinian state, and the Intifada (uprising) of the late 1980s took place in the Gaza Strip and West Bank. Any final settlement of the Palestine issue would have to involve the Gaza Strip.

Good Friday Agreement Irish political settlement agreed to by voters in both the Irish Republic and Northern Ireland on April 10, 1998.

Greensboro Five Five members of the U.S. Communist Workers Party who were killed by Ku Klux Klan members and other white supremacists at a "Death to the Klan" march held in Greensboro, North Carolina, on November 3, 1979. Most of the accused killers were acquitted by an all-white jury.

guerrilla warfare Military operations carried out by irregular forces against a government or occupying power. Guerrillas try to avoid direct, large-scale confrontations with forces that outmatch them and instead try to control the countryside and gain popular support while raiding government installations and supply convoys. While operating on a larger scale than terrorists and usually enjoying greater popular support, guerrillas frequently resort to terrorist acts such as killing people who collaborate with the government, using bombings and shootings to demonstrate that the government cannot protect the people, or extorting "taxes" from businesses or farms in areas that they control.

infrastructure The facilities a society uses to provide governance, distribute resources, maintain communications, and otherwise keep a country running. Terrorists and guerrillas often attack infrastructure targets such as railroads, power plants, police stations, and perhaps in the future, computer facilities. Infrastructure can also refer to the training camps, weapons and supply caches, and other facilities used by a terrorist group.

insurgency An armed uprising against a government, usually carried on by means of guerrilla warfare tactics.

Intifada Arabic for "Uprising," this term refers to the spontaneous outbreak of unrest that was triggered in December 1987 by the killing of several Arabs in the Gaza Strip when their vehicle collided with an Israeli vehicle. Rumors that the killing was deliberate inflamed riots and demonstrations, and attempts by the Israeli occupation forces to suppress the demonstrations further inflamed and expanded the Intifada.

Iran-Contra Affair The complicated interaction between members of the Reagan administration, Iran, and Nicaraguan rebels (contras). Some Reagan administration officials had sold weapons to Iran in the hope that Iran would use its influence to gain the release of American hostages in Lebanon. The profits from the weapons sales were then used to support contra rebels in Nicaragua in an attempt to circumvent restrictions on such aid passed by the U.S. Congress.

Iranian Hostage Crisis The taking of 53 hostages when the U.S. embassy in Teheran was overrun by Islamic revolutionaries on November 4, 1979. The hostages were held for 444 days. Political observers suggest that the Carter administration's inability to gain the freedom of the hostages paralyzed and weakened it, contributing to Ronald Reagan's decisive victory in the 1980 presidential election.

jihad An Arabic term usually translated as "holy war." While Islamic terrorists frequently invoke this concept to justify their violent campaigns against the enemies of Islam, some Islamic scholars believe that such use is illegitimate.

kneecapping Breaking or shooting a person's kneecaps, crippling the victim. Used by some terrorist groups in Northern Ireland and elsewhere to punish persons believed to be turncoats or collaborators.

narcoterrorrism A theory that international drug traffickers and terrorists are natural allies who increasingly cooperate to achieve their ends. Proponents point to the similarities of the two groups in their clandestine nature, use of weapons, and killing and intimidation of opponents. The term is also applied to acts of terrorism carried out by drug lords, such as the Extraditables, the terrorist arm of the Colombian Medellín cartel.

nationalism The development of a national identity in culture, politics, and society. The development of such an identity by an ethnic group living in a country controlled by another group frequently results in guerrilla warfare or terrorism when the national aspirations of such a small group are not accepted by the dominant group.

necklace A burning, gasoline-soaked tire placed around the neck, which severely burns or kills the victim. Some black terrorist groups in South Africa used the necklace as a way to punish people who cooperated with the apartheid regime.

neo-Nazis Post–World War II groups that have adopted the ideology of National Socialism (Nazism) espoused by Adolf Hitler. Neo-Nazi activity is strictly banned in Germany. In the United States, under constitutional protections of freedom of speech and assembly, the small neo-Nazi groups (including some skinheads) can operate freely unless they actually engage in crimes such as vandalism or assault. Nazi symbols and doctrine are a common feature of the loosely organized racist and white supremacist network in the United States.

nom de guerre (French, literally "name of war") In terrorism, a pseudonym used by a terrorist leader, often for symbolic purposes more than for concealment. For example, Yasir Arafat used the name Abu Amar, derived from an Arabic word for "builder."

nuclear terrorism The potential use of nuclear weapons by terrorists. Unsettled conditions in the former Soviet Union during the early 1990s fueled speculation that impoverished or disgruntled Soviet military or nuclear experts would be willing to sell their expertise or even nuclear materials or warheads to terrorist groups. By mid-2000, there seems to be little concrete sign of this happening, but the potentially devastating consequences of terrorists obtaining nuclear weapons have kept nuclear terrorism high on the agenda of counterterrorist planners.

Occupied Territories Generally refers to the areas that came under Israeli control following the Six-Day War in 1967: the West Bank of the Jordan, the Gaza Strip between Israel and Egypt, and the Golan Heights between Israel and Syria.

Orange, Orangemen Irish Protestants.

paramilitary General term for forces that share many characteristics of an army (training, weapons, tactics, etc.) but are not officially constituted. Examples include death squads and some militias. Paramilitary forces have often been used as way to repress political dissidents or the general population while denying government involvement.

plastic explosive A putty-like explosive substance manufactured under designations such as C-4 and Semtex. Easily shaped and embedded in innocuous objects, it is hard to detect, even with X rays, vapor sniffers, or other technologies. Under Muammar al-Qaddafi, Libya obtained a large amount of plastic explosive and distributed it to a variety of terrorist groups.

political risk The likelihood of losing a foreign investment due to factors such as government confiscation of facilities, currency manipulation, or terrorist action.

postcolonial period The period of roughly 30 years following World War II, when many developing nations that were once European colonies or protectorates gained independence.

safe house A house or building where a terrorist group can reside or store weapons while remaining concealed from authorities.

separatist General term for a person or group who seeks political independence or autonomy.

Shi'ites Followers of a sect that split off from the mainstream Sunni sect of Islam in the seventh century in a dispute over who would inherit spiritual leadership. Their theology and minority status (about one-tenth of the world's Muslims are Shi'ites) have encouraged militancy. In Iran, the only Muslim state where Shi'ites are the majority, this militancy has been embodied in a fundamentalist government that at least until recently aggressively promoted both fundamentalist movements in neighboring countries and terrorist action against the United States and its allies.

skinheads A subculture of mainly young white males with shaved heads, found in the United States, Great Britain, and, to some extent, other countries in Europe. Many skinheads espouse neo-Nazi or other white supremacist ideas and attack minorities and immigrants. Established white supremacist groups such as Aryan Nations and the Ku Klux Klan have made extensive efforts to recruit skinheads as "shock troops." However there are also some left-wing, antiracist skinheads.

skyjacking Hijacking of aircraft, a common terrorist practice in the 1960s and early 1970s. Tighter airport security has greatly reduced the incidence of skyjacking.

spillover terrorism The spread of terrorist activity from one area (such as the Middle East) to another (such as western Europe). Many Palestinian terrorist groups forged links with western European counterparts, and each group carried out operations in the other's territory.

state terrorism The use of terror and intimidation by a state against its own citizens. Throughout the 20th century, the number of victims of state terrorism in Germany, the former Soviet Union, China, and other countries was vastly greater than the toll taken by what are commonly considered to be terrorist groups.

state-sponsored terrorism The support (through training, weapons, money, or provision of safe havens) of terrorism as a means to carry out a nation's foreign policy. Libya, for example, has provided extensive support to a variety of Palestinian and European terrorist groups.

Stockholm syndrome A psychological process, first noted in four Swedish bank robbery hostages, by which hostages sometimes become sympathetic to, and identify with, their captors.

Sunni The orthodox sect of Islam. Sunni Muslims are in the majority in all Islamic countries except Iran. Tension often exists between the Sunni majority and the Shi'ite minority.

supergrass A term, probably derived from "snake in the grass," referring to the network of Irish informers that British authorities have been able to use to gather evidence against IRA terrorists.

truth commission A body charged with determining responsibility for atrocities committed by all sides in a conflict, usually as a part of a reconciliation or unification following a civil war or rebellion. South Africa's Truth and Justice Commission is probably the best-known example.

undetectable firearms Guns such as the Glock-17 that are mainly plastic with few metal parts. Such guns are a problem for counterterrorism because they are hard to detect in airport X-ray screenings.

urban guerrillas Guerrillas who operate within cities rather than in the countryside as do traditional guerrillas. Urban guerrilla theory is based on the works of Abraham Guillen and Carlos Marighella. Urban guerrillas emphasize terrorism as a strategy for provoking the government into repressive countermeasures and thus undermining popular support for it. As with the Tupamaros in Uruguay, this strategy has often backfired, resulting in the destruction of the guerrillas.

vigilantism Unofficial actions taken by private groups to violently suppress criminals. Vigilantism is a common response to the failure of a country's authorities to prevent attacks by terrorist groups. For example, the Ulster Volunteer Force in Northern Ireland arose as a vigilante response to Irish Republican Army terrorism. However, vigilantes often carry out terrorism themselves and can also be used by repressive governments as death squads, targeting not only terrorists but dissidents and innocent civilians.

weapons of mass destruction Weapons capable of killing large numbers of people at one time, such as large conventional or nuclear bombs, chemical weapons such as nerve gases, or biological weapons such as infectious diseases or toxins. The threat of terrorists gaining access to such weapons is a major focus of modern counterterrorism.

white supremacists Persons or groups, such as the Aryan Nations or Ku Klux Klan, who believe that the white race is superior and should dominate all other races. A related belief, white separatism, advocates a separate white state from which people of other races would be excluded.

PART II

GUIDE TO FURTHER RESEARCH

CHAPTER 7

HOW TO RESEARCH TERRORISM

This chapter presents some suggestions for further research into news, analysis, and scholarship on terrorism and related topics. Because the World Wide Web is now truly ubiquitous as a research tool and the text of most government documents, many scholarly works, and much of the popular press is available online, this guide will emphasize online sources.

A few cautions are still in order concerning the web. First, one cannot assume that any web search is exhaustive. No search engine currently indexes more than a fraction of the pages available on the web, so trying multiple search engines is always a good idea. Also, while some older papers or articles have been scanned or transcribed onto web pages, most material found on the web dates from the mid-1980s or later—about the time that computer-readable academic publications and full-text databases of popular periodicals became available.

Most online documents are short works: the full text of books is usually not available online, except for some historical and older works that are no longer under copyright. Therefore, the library remains a very important tool for the researcher. Fortunately, the nearly universal use of online (and often, remotely accessible) library catalogs has also made libraries easier to use.

Web pages, like all intellectual products, reflect the agenda and possible biases of their creators. Terrorism is a particularly sensitive topic, one that is intimately involved with political viewpoint. Government sources generally define terrorism very narrowly to refer to violence carried out by individuals or nongovernmental groups for political motives. Many extremist and even terrorist groups now have their own web sites. Scholars, of course, have many points of view on traditional terrorism and state terrorism. It is best to include a variety of sources and viewpoints in one's research.

TERRORISM ON THE WORLD WIDE WEB

There are a variety of government and private web sites that offer background material, news, analysis, and other material on terrorist groups, their leaders, and terrorist attacks as well as counterterrorism. The following are some of the more useful major sites, broken down by category.

GOVERNMENT SITES

The U.S. State Department offers several important sources of information on terrorism. The Office of the Coordinator for Counterterrorism (http://www.state.gov/www/global/terrorism/index.html) provides information about conferences and meetings, news updates, official statements, and advisories for travelers. The Reports page provides three annual reports:

- *Foreign Terrorist Organizations Designations* explains the process for designating organizations as terrorist and gives the current list.
- *Patterns of Global Terrorism* provides regional and country overviews of terrorist activities and related conflicts. It also provides a chronology of terrorist incidents during the year, background information on the major terrorist groups, and a variety of statistics about terrorist attacks.
- *Significant Incidents of Political Violence Against Americans* focuses specifically on attacks against U.S. citizens.

The Federal Bureau of Investigation (FBI) at http://www.fbi.gov has information on domestic terrorism that complements the State Department's reports on international terrorism. See the annual report *Terrorism in the United States* at http://www.fbi.gov/publish/terror/terroris.htm.

ACADEMIC SITES

The following sites are primarily involved with research or the maintenance of archives. The Terrorism Research Center, a consultancy group (http://www.terrorism.com/welcome.htm) has one of the most comprehensive sites, which includes links to many other organizations and agencies.

The Air University Library at Maxwell Air Force Base in Alabama has a page at http://www.au.af.mil/au/aul/bibs/tergps/tg98tc.htm that nicely supplements the background information on terrorist groups found in *Patterns of Global Terrorism.* It includes a book and periodical bibliography for each group.

The International Policy Center for Counter-Terrorism in Israel (http://www.counterror.org.il/) offers background materials, including databases of terrorist incidents, terrorist group profiles, and special sections on the Arab-Israeli conflict and counterterrorism.

Civil Liberties Groups

Because antiterrorism legislation frequently raises civil liberties issues, civil liberties groups are a good source for news and advocacy materials.

The American Civil Liberties Union site at http://www.aclu.org/ has a number of issues pages that are relevant to terrorism. See, for example, the following:

Criminal Justice: http://www.aclu.org/issues/criminal/hmcj.html
Free Speech: http://www.aclu.org/issues/freespeech/hmfs.html
Immigrants' Rights: http://www.aclu.org/issues/immigrant/hmir.html
National Security: http://www.aclu.org/issues/security/hmns.html

Because proposed antiterrorism legislation often includes provisions for allowing eavesdropping, monitoring, or restrictions on private use of encryption, civil liberties groups that focus on computer-related issues are also relevant here. The Electronic Privacy Information Center (http://www.epic.org/), the Electronic Frontier Foundation (http://www.eff.org/), and the Center for Democracy and Technology (http://www.cdt.org/) are all useful for keeping up with these issues.

Human Rights Organizations

The international human rights organization Amnesty International (http://www.amnestyusa.org/) is also a good source about human rights issues, including allegations of state terrorism. Another source is Human Rights Watch at http://www.hrw.org/.

Antihate Groups

Two groups focus on terrorism and related hate crimes based on ethnicity, gender, and other biases. The Anti-Defamation League site at http://www.adl.org/ includes statistics and reports on anti-Semitic attacks. The Southern Poverty Law Center (http://www.splcenter.org) monitors the activities of the Ku Klux Klan and other racist groups. Its Intelligence Project page at http://www.splcenter.org/intelligenceproject/ip-index.html includes a list of hate groups, a list of militia groups, and a chronology of hate incidents.

TERRORIST GROUPS

As noted, many terrorist groups, guerrilla movements, political extremists, and similar organizations have their own web sites. There's an extensive listing at Terrorists, Freedom Fighters, Crusaders, Propagandists, and Mercenaries on the Net at http://rvl4.ecn.purdue.edu/~cromwell/lt/terror.html. Discretion is advised when deciding whether to visit or use sites that may be involved in the promotion of terrorist groups.

BIBLIOGRAPHIC RESOURCES

As useful as the Web is for quickly finding information and the latest news, in-depth research still requires trips to the library or bookstore. Getting the most out of the library requires the use of bibliographic tools and resources. *Bibliographic resources* is a general term for catalogs, indexes, bibliographies, and other guides that identify the books, periodical articles, and other printed resources that deal with a particular subject. They are essential tools for the researcher.

LIBRARY CATALOGS

Access to the largest library catalog, that of the Library of Congress (LC), is available at http://lcweb.loc.gov/catalog/. This page explains the different kinds of catalogs and searching techniques available.

Yahoo offers a categorized listing of libraries at http://dir.yahoo.com/Reference/Libraries/. Of course, for materials available at one's local public or university library, that institution will be the most convenient source.

Online catalogs can be searched not only by the traditional author, title, and subject headings, but also by matching keywords in the title. Thus a title search for *terrorism* will retrieve all books that have that word somewhere in their title. (Of course a book about terrorism may not have that phrase in the title, so it is still necessary to use subject headings to get the most comprehensive results.)

Relevant LC subject headings for terrorism include the following:

- crimes against peace
- genocide
- mass murder

- security, international
- state sponsored terrorism
- terrorism
- terrorism—[subdivided by country]
- terrorism—prevention
- terrorism—prevention—international cooperation

Once the record for a book or other item is found, it is a good idea to see what additional subject headings and name headings have been assigned to it. These in turn can be used for further searching.

BIBLIOGRAPHIES, INDEXES, AND DATABASES

Bibliographies in various forms provide a convenient way to find books, periodical articles, and other materials. How far to go in one's reading depends, of course on one's research topic and goals. Some subjects, such as cyberterrorism or information warfare will not have useful materials more than a few years old. When consulting encyclopedias and handbooks, too, a researcher would generally want materials published after 1990. (For one thing, the fall of the Soviet Union is a watershed between the terrorism of the Cold War era and the more chaotic and diverse recent terrorism. Older books will also lack the considerable amount of information on Soviet clandestine activity that has now emerged from the archives.) On the other hand, many older works, both scholarly and primary sources, may be vital for doing research on earlier periods of terrorist activity such as lynchings in the post–Civil War south or labor terrorists and anarchists of the 19th century.

Popular and scholarly articles can be accessed through periodical indexes that provide citations and abstracts. Abstracts are brief summaries of articles or papers. They are usually compiled and indexed—originally in bound volumes, but increasingly available online. Some examples of printed indexes that might include literature related to terrorism include:

- Criminal Justice Abstracts
- Criminal Justice Periodical Index
- Index to Legal Periodicals and Books
- Social Sciences Citation Index
- Social Sciences Index
- Sociological Abstracts

Some of these indexes, especially for recent years, are available online. Generally, they can be accessed only through a library by a cardholder, and cannot be accessed over the Internet (except by users on a college campus). Consult with a university reference librarian for more help.

Two good indexes have unrestricted search access, however. UnCover Web (http://uncweb.carl.org/) contains brief descriptions of about 8.8 million documents from about 18,000 journals in just about every subject area. Copies of complete documents can be ordered with a credit card, or they may be obtainable for free at a local library.

Perhaps the most valuable index for topics related to criminal justice, including terrorism and hate crimes, is the National Criminal Justice Reference Service Justice Information Center, at http://www.ncjrs.org/. It offers a searchable abstract database containing 150,000 criminal justice publications, and it can be a real gold mine for the more advanced researcher.

FREE PERIODICAL INDEXES

Most public libraries subscribe to database services such as InfoTrac that index articles from hundreds of general-interest periodicals and some moderately specialized ones. The database can be searched by author or by words in the title, subject headings, and sometimes words found anywhere in the article text. Depending on the database used, "hits" in the database can result in just a bibliographical description (author, title, pages, periodical name, issue date, etc.), a description plus an abstract (a paragraph summarizing the contents of the article), or the full text of the article itself. Before using such an index, it is a good idea to view the list of newspapers and magazines covered and determine the years of coverage.

Many libraries provide dial-in, Internet, or Telnet access to their periodical databases as an option in their catalog menu. However, licensing restrictions usually mean that only researchers who have a library card for that particular library can access the database (by typing in their name and card number). Check with local public or school libraries to see what databases are available.

For periodicals not indexed by Infotrac or another index, or for which only abstracts rather than complete text is available, check to see whether the publication has its own web site (most now do). Some scholarly publications are putting all or most of their articles online. Popular publications tend to offer only a limited selection. Some publications of both types offer archives of several years' back issues that can be searched by author or keyword.

BOOKSTORE CATALOGS

Many people have discovered that online bookstores such as Amazon.com at (http://www.amazon.com) and Barnes & Noble.com (http://www.bn.com) are convenient ways to shop for books. A less-known benefit of online bookstore catalogs is that they often include publisher's information, book reviews, and readers' comments about a given title. They can thus serve as a form of annotated bibliography.

KEEPING UP WITH THE NEWS

It is important for the researcher to be aware of currently breaking news. In addition to watching TV news and subscribing to local or national newspapers and magazines, there are a number of ways to use the Internet to find additional news sources.

NEWSPAPERS AND NET NEWS

Like periodicals, most large newspapers now have web sites that offer headlines and a searchable database of recent articles. The URL is usually given somewhere in the local newspaper. Yahoo! is also a good place to find newspaper links: See http://dir.yahoo.com/News_and_Media/Newspapers/Web_Directories/.

Net news is a decentralized system of thousands of newsgroups, or forums organized by topic. Most web browsers have an option for subscribing to, reading, and posting messages in newsgroups. The Dejanews site (http://www.dejanews.com) also provides free access and an easy-to-use interface to newsgroups.

Some newsgroups related to terrorism include the following:

alt.security.terrorism
alt.security.terrorism.atlanta
alt.security.terrorism.flight800
clari.news.terrorism
clari.news.usa.terrorism
clari.usa.terrorism
clari.world.terrorism

Mail lists offer another way to keep up with and discuss recent developments. Some organizations offer a mail list that can keep you posted about current developments. Check the organization's web site for information on how to subscribe to the list.

Net news and mail lists are generally most valuable when they have a moderator who keeps discussions focused and discourages "flaming" (exchanges of heated or personally insulting statements).

SEARCHING THE WEB

A researcher can explore an ever-expanding web of information by starting with a few web sites and following the links they offer to other sites, which in turn have links to still other sites. But because this can be a hit-and-miss way to research, some important sites may be missed if the researcher only "web surfs" in this fashion. Two other, more focused techniques can fill in the information gaps.

WEB GUIDES AND INDEXES

A web guide or index is a site that offers a structured, hierarchical outline of subject areas. This enables the researcher to zero in on a particular aspect of a subject and find links to web sites for further exploration.

The best-known (and largest) web index is Yahoo! at http://www.yahoo.com. The home page gives the top-level list of topics, and the researcher simply clicks to follow them down to more specific areas.

In addition to following Yahoo's outline-like structure, there is also a search box into which the researcher can type one or more keywords and receive a list of matching categories and sites.

Web indexes such as Yahoo! have two major advantages over undirected surfing. First, the structured hierarchy of topics makes it easy to find a particular topic or subtopic and then explore its links. Second, Yahoo! does not make an attempt to compile every possible link on the Internet (a virtually impossible task, given its size). Rather, sites are evaluated for usefulness and quality by Yahoo's indexers. This means that the researcher has a better chance of finding more substantial and accurate information. The disadvantage of Web indexes is the flip side of their selectivity: the researcher is dependent on the indexer's judgment for determining what sites are worth exploring.

To explore terrorism via Yahoo!, the researcher should click on the Society and Culture link, then Crime, then Types of Crime, then Terrorism. A variety of sites selected by the editors are available for browsing.

Yahoo's "Full Coverage" news service page on the subject of terrorism is at http://fullcoverage.yahoo.com/Full_Coverage/US/Terrorism/. In addition to news stories and related web links, it also features audio and video versions of stories that can be viewed online.

About.com (http://www.about.com) is rather similar to Yahoo!, but gives a greater emphasis to overviews or guides prepared by experts in various topics. To find information on terrorism on About.com, browse to News/Issues, Conspiracies and Extremism, then Terrorism, or enter a direct keyword search on terrorism or a relevant phrase. (Remember, with guide sites it is often a good idea to supplement browsing with a direct search to ensure the most comprehensive results.)

New guide and index sites are constantly being developed, and capabilities are improving as the web matures. One example is AskJeeves, at http://www.askjeeves.com. This site attempts to answer a researcher's plain-English question, such as "Who bombed the World Trade Center?" Sometimes it directly answers the question, and other times it returns a number of possibly useful links that it obtains by querying a series of search engines.

There are also an increasing number of specialized online research guides that are something like traditional bibliographical essays with the added bonus of having many of the materials discussed already linked so they are just a click away. The Louisiana State University Law Library, for example, has "Terrorism: a Pathfinder & Select Bibliography" at http://www.law.lsu.edu/library/biblio/terrsm1.htm

SEARCH ENGINES

Search engines take a very different approach to finding materials on the web. Instead of organizing topically in a "top down" fashion, search engines work their way from the bottom up scanning through web documents and indexing them. There are hundreds of search engines, but some of the most widely used include:

- AltaVista (http://www.altavista.com)
- Excite (http://www.excite.com)
- Go (http://www.go.com)
- Google (http://www.google.com)
- Hotbot (http://hotbot.lycos.com)
- Lycos (http://www.lycos.com)
- Magellan (http://www.magellan.excite.com)
- Northern Light (http://www.northernlight.com)
- WebCrawler (http://www.webcrawler.com)

Search engines are generally easy to use by employing the same sorts of keywords that work in library catalogs. There are a variety of web search tutorials available online (try "web search tutorial" in a search engine to find some). One good one is published by the Web Tools Company at http://www.thewebtools.com/tutorial/tutorial.htm.

Here are a few basic rules for using search engines:

- When looking for something specific, use the most specific term or phrase. For example, when looking for information about extradition, use the specific term "extradition", since this is the standard term. (Note that phrases should be put in quotes if you want them to be matched as phrases rather than as individual words. In this book all search terms are shown in quotes to separate them from the rest of the sentence, but that doesn't mean quotes should be used in actual searches other than for phrases.)
- When looking for a general topic that might be expressed using several different words or phrases, use several descriptive words (nouns are more reliable than verbs); for example, "international terrorism statistics". (Most engines will automatically put pages that match all three terms first on the results list.)
- Use "wildcards" when a desired word may have more than one ending. For example, terroris* matches both "terrorism" and "terrorist."
- Most search engines support Boolean (*and, or, not*) operators that can be used to broaden or narrow a search. (These operators are shown in all caps for clarity, but can usually be typed in lowercase.)
- Use AND to narrow a search. For example "chemical AND weapon" will match only pages that have both terms.
- Use OR to broaden a search: "information warfare" OR "cyberterrorism" will match any page that has *either* term, and since these terms are often used interchangeably, this type of search is necessary to retrieve the widest range of results.
- Use NOT to exclude unwanted results: "bombings NOT Israel" finds articles about bombings except those in or relating to Israel.

Because each search engine indexes somewhat differently and offers somewhat different ways of searching, it is a good idea to use several different search engines, especially for a general query. Several "metasearch" programs automate the process of submitting a query to multiple search engines. These include the following:

- Metacrawler (http://www.metacrawler.com)
- Inference FIND (http://www.infind.com)
- Search.com (http://www.search.com)

There are also search utilities that can be run from the researcher's own PC rather than through a web site. A good example is Mata Hari, a shareware ("try before you buy") program available for download at http://thewebtools.com/.

FINDING ORGANIZATIONS AND PEOPLE

Chapter 9 of this book provides a list of organizations that are involved with the issue of terrorism, but new organizations emerge now and then. A good place to look for information and links to organizations is the U.S. State Department, the Terrorism Research Center, and other resource sites mentioned at the beginning of this chapter. If such sites do not yield the name of a specific organization, the name can be entered into a search engine. Generally, the best approach is to put the name of the organization in quote marks such as "National Committee Against Repressive Legislation".

Another approach is to take a guess at the organization's likely web address. For example, the American Civil Liberties Union is commonly known by the acronym ACLU, so it is not a surprise that the organization's web site is at www.aclu.org. (Note that noncommercial organization sites normally use the .org suffix, government agencies use .gov, educational institutions use .edu, and businesses use .com.) This technique can save time, but doesn't always work.

There are several ways to find a person on the Internet:

- Put the person's name (in quotes) in a search engine and you may find that person's home page on the Internet.
- Contact the person's employer (such as a university for an academic, or a corporation for a technical professional). Most such organizations have web pages that include a searchable faculty or employee directory.
- Try one of the people-finder services such as Yahoo People Search at http://people.yahoo.com or BigFoot at www.bigfoot.com. This may yield contact information such as E-mail address, regular address, and/or phone number.

LEGAL RESEARCH

It is important for researchers to be able to obtain the text and summary of laws and court decisions relating to terrorism. Because of the specialized terminology of the law, legal research can be more difficult to master than bibliographical or general research tools. Fortunately, the Internet has also come to the rescue in this area, offering a variety of ways to look up laws and court cases without having to pore through huge bound volumes in law libraries (which may not be easily accessible to the general public, anyway).

FINDING LAWS

Most legislation relating to terrorism is federal, since terrorism is usually national or international in scope. When federal legislation passes, it eventually becomes part of the United States Code, a massive legal compendium. Title 18 of the U.S. Code deals with crimes and criminal procedure. Part I of this title defines crimes and penalties, and can be used together with the summary in Chapter 3 of this book, "Laws and Court Cases Relating to Terrorism," to look up specific sections relating to terrorism. (Since so many new provisions and amendments have been passed, it may be better to work "backward" from the summaries of the Antiterrorism and Effective Death Penalty Act of 1996 in Chapter 3 and the complete summary in Appendix D to the existing sections of the U.S. Code.)

The U.S. Code can be searched online in several locations, but the easiest site to use is probably the web site of the Cornell University Law School at http://www4.law.cornell.edu/uscode/. The fastest way to retrieve a law is by its title and section citation, but phrases and keywords can also be used.

KEEPING UP WITH LEGISLATIVE DEVELOPMENTS

Pending legislation is often tracked by advocacy groups, both national and based in particular states. See Chapter 9, "Organizations and Agencies," for contact information.

Proposed federal legislation on terrorism normally turns up as part of a large bill often called an "omnibus crime bill," although provisions can also be added to appropriations bills for defense, intelligence, or other activities.

The Library of Congress "Thomas" web site (http://thomas.loc.gov/) includes files summarizing legislation by the number of the Congress (each two-year session of Congress has a consecutive number: for example, the 105th Congress was in session in 1997 and 1998 and the 106th will be in session in 1999 and 2000). Legislation can be searched for by the name of its sponsor(s), the bill number, or by topical keywords. (Laws that have been passed can be looked up under their Public Law number.)

For example, selecting the 106th Congress and typing the phrase "airport security" into the search box retrieved a list that began with the following bill:

> *1. H.R.700 : To amend title 49, United States Code, to provide enhanced protections for airline passengers.*

Sponsor: *Rep Shuster, Bud*—***Latest Major Action:*** *3/18/1999 House committee/subcommittee actions*
Committees: *House Transportation and Infrastructure*

Clicking on the bill number brings up a screen of information that starts with the following:

H.R.700
Sponsor: Rep Shuster, Bud (introduced 2/10/1999)
Latest Major Action: 3/18/1999 House committee/subcommittee actions
Title: To amend title 49, United States Code, to provide enhanced protections for airline passengers.

Underneath this heading, a series of hyperlinks follows. Clicking on any of these links brings up the appropriate details, including the bill's current status, a summary of provisions, or the complete text of the bill.

FINDING COURT DECISIONS

If legislation is the front end of the criminal justice process, the courts are the back. The U.S. Supreme Court and state courts make important decisions every year that determine how the laws are interpreted. Like laws, legal decisions are organized using a system of citations. The general form is: *Party1 v. Party2* volume reporter [optional start page] (court, year).

Here are some examples:

Brandenburg v. Ohio, 395 U.S. 44 (1969)

Here the parties are Brandenburg (the defendant who is appealing his case from a state court) and the state of Ohio. The case is in volume 395 of the *U.S. Supreme Court Reports*, beginning at page 44, and the case was decided in 1969. (For the Supreme Court, the name of the court is omitted.)

Fierro v. Gomez 77 F.3d 301 (9th Cir. 1996)

Here the case is in the 9th U.S. Circuit Court of Appeals, decided in 1996.

A state court decision can generally be identified because it includes the state's name. For example, in *State v. Torrance*, 473 S.E.2d. 703 (S.C. 1996) the S.E.2d refers to the appeals district, and the S.C. to South Carolina.

Once the jurisdiction for the case has been determined, the researcher can then go to a number of places on the Internet to find cases by citation and sometimes by the names of the parties or by subject keywords. Some of the most useful sites are:

- **The Legal Information Institute** (LII; http://supct.law.cornell.edu/supct/) has all Supreme Court decisions since 1990 plus 610 of what the LII considers the most important historic decisions.

- **Washlaw Web** (http://www.washlaw.edu/) has a variety of courts (including states) and legal topics listed, making it a good jumping-off place for many sorts of legal research. However the actual accessibility of state court opinions (and the formats they are provided in) varies widely.

LEXIS AND WESTLAW

Lexis and Westlaw are commercial legal databases that have extensive information including an elaborate system of notes, legal subject headings, and ways to show relationships between cases. Unfortunately, these services are too expensive for use by most individual researchers unless they are available through a university or corporate library.

MORE HELP ON LEGAL RESEARCH

For more information on conducting legal research, see the "Legal Research FAQ" at http://www.cis.ohio-state.edu/hypertext/faq/usenet/law/research/top.html. After a certain point, however, the researcher who lacks formal legal training may need to consult with or rely on the efforts of professional researchers or academics in the field.

GENERAL RESEARCH STRATEGY

It can be hard to know where to begin when there are so many kinds of information sources available. Unless one is researching a very specific topic, it is probably best to gain an overview and working knowledge of the topic by using some of the resource sites, web indexes, and guides and then pursue specific interests by using bibliographical tools (library and bookstore catalogs and periodical indexes) to obtain appropriate books, news articles, and scholarly papers. When legal research is required, having the general topic, context, and citations in hand will save time and frustration.

CHAPTER 8

ANNOTATED BIBLIOGRAPHY

This chapter presents a representative selection of books, journal and magazine articles, web (Internet) documents, and videos relating to terrorism. The bibliography is divided into four broad categories of materials outlined as follows:

General Background Materials
Encyclopedias, dictionaries, and handbooks
Bibliographies
Introductions, overviews, and anthologies
Theoretical or analytical works

Regional Developments
Northern Ireland
Europe
Middle East
Africa
Asia
Latin America
United States and Canada

Key Issues
Counterterrorism (theory and practice)
Legal issues (including civil liberties issues)

Specific Types of Terrorism
Weapons of mass destruction (general)
Chemical and biological terrorism
Nuclear terrorism
Ecoterrorism and animal rights
Cyberterrorism

The following general principles were used for selecting materials for this bibliography:

- **Utility:** While most materials are for the general reader, high school through adult, a representative sampling of more specialized or professional literature (legal, medical, etc.) is also included.
- **Currency:** Most publications are 1990 or later, except for historical or theoretical works.
- **Variety:** Materials represent a wide variety of viewpoints.

Note that many of the newspaper and magazine articles listed here are available from full-text databases accessible on the Internet or at one's local library, or on web sites maintained by publications. Such material can sometimes be accessed free of charge through one's public or academic library. Many publications charge a few dollars for access to articles that are more than a month or so old. Of course, many libraries also keep paper copies of back issues of publications.

Finally, it should be noted that web addresses change frequently and sites can disappear altogether. In the entries for web material, a "downloaded" date refers to when the site was last verified as existing online. "Posted" refers to either the date the material was posted on the web or (if the material was originally in some other form) the date the material was originally published. In general, listings are current as of mid-2000.

GENERAL BACKGROUND MATERIALS

Encyclopedias, Dictionaries, and Handbooks

BOOKS

Anderson, Sean, and Stephen Sloan. *Historical Dictionary of Terrorism.* Metuchen, N.J.: Scarecrow Press, 1995. This dictionary and reference handbook provides an A–Z listing of terrorist groups and incidents, as well as a brief chronology and an unannotated bibliography.

Courtois, Stephane, (and others). *The Black Book of Communism: Crimes, Terror, Repression.* Cambridge, Mass.: Harvard University Press, 1999. This widely acclaimed volume tabulates the killings, terror, and repression unleashed by communist regimes throughout the 20th century. Ranging from Lenin's use of terror following the Bolshevik revolution to the bizarre policies of Pol Pot, this book is relevant to students of terrorism for both the connection between Soviet and Communist Chinese policies and the activities of terrorist groups, and the use of state terrorism against internal dissent.

Crenshaw, Martha, ed. *Encyclopedia of World Terrorism.* Armonk, N.Y.: Sharpe Reference, 1997. 3 vols. A comprehensive encyclopedia covering all aspects of terrorism including both modern terrorist activities and its precursors, terrorist strategies and tactics, counterterrorism, and theoretical approaches to understanding terrorism. Includes a chronology of world terrorist activities since 1945, an A–Z listing of terrorist leaders and groups, and a select bibliography.

Nash, Jay Robert. *Terrorism in the 20th Century: A Narrative Encyclopedia from the Anarchists through the Weathermen to the Unabomber.* New York: M. Evans, 1998. A narrative history of terrorism in America during the 20th century, written in a popular journalistic style and providing useful overviews. Each of the 10 chapters describes events during one decade, including both domestic terrorism and attacks on U.S. interests abroad. Includes a chronology, glossary, and bibliography.

Political Risk Services. *Political Risk Yearbook, 2000.* East Syracuse, N.Y.: PRS, 2000. An eight-volume set (also available on CD-ROM) giving background on key political and other groups in each country and detailed assessment and rating of the risks of conflict and terrorism in each country. Designed and priced primarily for corporate and academic use, but may be available in large libraries.

Schmid, Alex P., and Albert J. Jongman. *Political Terrorism: A New Guide to Actors, Authors, Concepts, Data Bases, Theories and Literature.* Revised, expanded, and updated ed. New York: North-Holland Publishing Co., 1988. This handbook and research guide for students and professionals in the field of international terrorism includes a survey of 50 leading experts who offer a variety of definitions and theories about terrorism. It also includes a list of databases and an extensive, though unannotated, bibliography and a world directory of terrorist organizations.

Shafritz, Jay M., E. F. Gibbons, Jr., and Gregory E. J. Scott. *Almanac of Modern Terrorism.* New York: Facts On File, 1991. This reference handbook provides a chronology of terrorism from 1946 through 1990, an A–Z guide to organizations and concepts, a selection of quotes about and definitions of terrorism, and an unannotated bibliography of suggested readings.

INTERNET DOCUMENTS

"ERRI Counter-Terrorism Archive." Available online. URL: http://www.emergency.com/cntrterr.htm. Updated February 2000. Web site provided by the Emergency Response and Research Institute. Describes itself as "A Summary of World-Wide Terrorism Events, Groups, and Terrorist Strategies and Tactics." Highlights news articles and research reports on terrorism categorized by region and listed in chronological order, as well as special sections on terrorist leaders and tactics.

Franklin, Raymond A. "The Hate Directory." Available online. URL: http://www.bcpl.lib.md.us/~rfrankli/hatedir.pdf Release 3.0. March 15, 2000. A compilation of web links to dozens of extremist or hate groups including racist, anti-Semitic, antigay, and others. Includes some mailing lists, newsgroups, and IRC (Internet Relay Chat) channels. The last page is devoted to groups that are combating hate on the Net.

International Policy Institute for Counter-Terrorism. "Terrorist Group Profiles." Available online. URL: http://www.ict.org.il/. (linked under International Terrorism). Posted on April 27, 2000. A useful compilation that lists about 50 terrorist groups, including background, chronology of terrorist activity, and news updates, including links to articles.

Jane's Online. Available online. URL: http://fore.thomson.com/janes. A database service that provides access to information and articles from a variety of Jane's publications. Jane's is one of the foremost providers of military and intelligence materials to the general public. Access to bibliographic information requires free registration. Publications related to counterterrorism include *Jane's Islamic Affairs Analyst* and *Jane's Terrorism and Security Monitor.*

"Political Science: International and Comparative Politics Reference Sources." Available online. URL: http://www.lib.depaul.edu/subject/polisci/pscintnl.htm. Downloaded on April 27, 2000. A bibliography and resource list useful for researching the background of regional conflicts and terrorism. Prepared by the DePaul University Library. Topics include arms, war and political violence; biography; diplomacy; human rights; organizations; regional; and statistics.

Southern Poverty Law Center Intelligence Project. "Active Hate Groups in the U.S. in 1999." Available online. URL: http://www.splcenter.org/centerinfo/ci-index.html (follow link "List of Hate Groups"). Downloaded on April 27, 2000. Provides a list of 457 hate groups categorized under Klan, Neo-Nazi, Skinhead, Christian Identity, Black Separatist, and Other. For each group, lists cities where it is active. Also includes a map showing the distribution of hate groups in the United States.

Southern Poverty Law Center Intelligence Project. "Active Patriot Groups in 1998." Available online. URL: http://www.splcenter.org/intelligenceproject/ip-index.html. (Follow link "List of Patriot Groups.") Downloaded on April 27, 2000. Provides a list of 435 "Patriot" groups (these are separate from the "hate groups" also listed by the Intelligence Project). The list includes 171 militias and 31 "common law courts." Groups are listed by state.

Southern Poverty Law Center Intelligence Project. "Hate Incidents, 1999." Available online. URL: http://www.splcenter.org/intelligenceproject/ip-index.html. (follow link "Hate Incidents 1999"). Downloaded on April 27, 2000. A list of hate crimes and hate group activities, retrievable by state. Gives location, date, and brief description of each incident.

"Terrorist and Insurgent Organizations." Air University Library. Available online. URL: http://www.au.af.mil/au/aul/bibs/tergps/tg98tc.htm. Posted on August 1998. A comprehensive listing of books, research papers, articles, and periodicals on all aspects of terrorism and insurgency, prepared by a U.S. Air Force academic library. Organized by subtopic.

"Terrorist Group Profiles." Dudley Knox Library, Naval Postgraduate School. Available online. URL: http://web.nps.navy.mil/~library/tgp/tgp2.htm. Updated on August 31, 1999. Site includes links to the U.S. Department of State report "Patterns of Global Terrorism" starting with 1993, as well as links to terrorist group profiles.

United States Central Intelligence Agency. "World Factbook." Available online. URL: http://www.odci.gov/cia/publications/factbook/. Posted on January 1, 1999. This useful reference source provides basic information on the geography, demographics, economics, and infrastructure of each of the world's countries. It is a good first step in researching regional issues.

United States Department of Justice. Bureau of Justice Statistics. "The World Factbook of Criminal Justice Systems." Available online. URL: http://www.ojp.usdoj.gov/bjs/abstract/wfcj.htm. Downloaded on April 27, 2000. Provides a summary of the criminal justice system of each nation, including courts and criminal procedures, criminal code, law enforcement, and crime statistics.

United States Department of Justice. Federal Bureau of Investigation. "Terrorism in the United States 1997." http://www.fbi.gov/library/terror/terr97.pdf. Issues an annual report describing major terrorist incidents, arrests, and convictions, and highlighting particular issues of concern, such as terrorist use of delayed, secondary explosions, the right-wing "common law courts" movement, and hoaxes involving weapons of mass destruction.

United States Department of State. Office of the Coordinator for Antiterrorism. "Foreign Terrorist Organizations." Available online. URL: http://www.state.gov/www/global/terrorism/fto_1999.html. Posted on October 8, 1999. Lists those organizations officially designated as "terrorist" by the Department of State, gives background information about the organizations, and explains the legal criteria used for this designation.

United States Information Agency. "Fact Sheet: U.S. Government Views on Terrorism." Available online. URL: http://usinfo.state.gov/topical/pol/terror/99120704.htm. Posted on December 7, 1999. Official U.S. government statement condemning terrorism, calling upon nations to join in fighting it, and refuting allegations that the U.S. has disproportionately associated followers of Islam with terrorism.

University of Michigan. Documents Center. "Political Science Resources: International Relations." Available online. URL: http://www.lib.umich.edu/libhome/Documents.center/psintl.html. Downloaded on April 27, 2000. This site provides a variety of links to resources on terrorism as well as related topics such as postcolonial history, human rights, international organizations, intelligence, and peace and conflict. There are also links to other university departments and other institutions involved in international affairs studies.

Bibliographies

BOOKS

Alali, A. Oadasuo, and Gary W. Byrd. *Terrorism and the News Media: A Selected, Annotated Bibliography.* Jefferson, N.C.: McFarland, 1994. Contains entries for more than 600 works (print and electronic) dealing with the often symbiotic relationship between terrorism and the media. Entries are divided into three main areas: understanding terrorism, terrorism and the electronic media, and terrorism and the print media.

Babkina, A. M. *Terrorism: An Annotated Bibliography.* Commack, N.Y.: Nova Science Publishers, 1998. This bibliography covers selected books and journal articles from 1993 to 1998. Books are listed in the form of reproduced Library of Congress catalog records, with no annotation other than the occasional summary included in the cataloging. Journal articles are covered in records from the CRS (Congressional Research Service) Public Policy Literature (PPLT) database, and the records include brief notes or summaries.

Bennett, John M., and Laurence Hallewell. *Sendero Luminoso in Context: An Annotated Bibliography.* Lanham, Md.: Scarecrow Press, 2000. A detailed bibliography with sections for general works on revolution and social change and on Peru, various aspects of Peruvian society and economy, periods of modern Peruvian history, and the Sendero Luminoso (Shining Path) group itself.

Lakos, Amos. *Terrorism, 1980–1990: A Bibliography.* Boulder, Colo.: Westview Press, 1991. A comprehensive bibliography. The first sections deal with reference sources and general works, and the remainder is organized by topics or issues (such as legal issues or specific threats such as nuclear) as well as geographical areas.

Mickolus, Edward F. *The Literature of Terrorism.* Reprint ed. Westport, Conn.: Greenwood Press, 1981. This is the beginning of what has become the most comprehensive bibliography series on terrorism (see following entries).

Mickolus, Edward F. *Terrorism, 1980–1987.* Westport, Conn.: Greenwood Press, 1988. A detailed bibliography of materials on terrorism (including analytics for chapters in collections), focusing on the 1980s.

———. *Terrorism, 1988–1991.* Westport, Conn.: Greenwood Press, 1993. Continues the coverage of the preceding work and includes a chronology.

———. *Terrorism, 1992–1995.* Westport, Conn.: Greenwood Press, 1997. Continues the coverage into the 1990s, an eventful decade in the history of terrorism.

Newton, Michael. *Terrorism in the United States and Europe, 1800–1959: An Annotated Bibliography.* New York: Garland, 1988. An extensive annotated bibliography of almost 6,000 early works. Begins with general works and is then organized by country, with the U.S. section further subdivided topically.

Ontiveros, Suzanne R. *Global Terrorism: A Historical Bibliography.* Santa Barbara, Calif.: ABC-CLIO, 1986. Contains abstracts of about 600 articles, extracted from two ABC-CLIO reference databases. Most articles focus on the 1960s and 1970s. Includes chronology.

Prunckun, Henry W., Jr. *Shadow of Death: An Analytic Bibliography on Political Violence, Terrorism, and Low-Intensity Conflict.* Lanham, Md.: Scarecrow Press, 1995. Part I of this handbook presents a brief introduction to terrorism, its definitions, and anatomy. Part II is an annotated bibliography of terrorism broken down alphabetically by topic and by region and country. Publications covered generally range from the 1970s to the early 1990s.

Signorielli, Nancy, and George Gerbner. *Violence and Terror in the Mass Media.* Westport, Conn.: Greenwood Press, 1988. An annotated bibliography developed as part of a UNESCO research project, covering material to spring 1987. The coverage focuses on the impact of portrayal of violence in the media, not just terrorism per se.

INTERNET DOCUMENTS

LSU Law Library. "Terrorism: A Pathfinder and Selective Bibliography." A guide for students and researchers with links for basic legal sources, legal research, subject headings, and bibliography. Available online. URL: http://www.law.lsu.edu/library/biblio/terrsm1.htm. Posted April 21, 1998.

"NCJRS Abstracts Database." Available online. URL: http://www.ncjrs.org/database.htm. This service, provided by the National Criminal Justice Reference Service, is a searchable database that has abstracts for more than 150,000 books and articles on all aspects of criminal justice. This includes thousands of publications relating to terrorism, counterterrorism, and related topics. Some abstracts include links to the full-text document.

Rand Corporation. "Subject Index to Terrorism."

Introductions, Overviews, and Anthologies

BOOKS

Combs, Cynthia C. *Terrorism in the 21st Century.* 2nd ed. Upper Saddle River, N.J.: Prentice-Hall, 2000. An introductory survey geared for college undergraduates. Discusses the anatomy of modern terrorism (the actors and their methods), the organization of national and international counterterrorist agencies, and predictions about future trends. Each discussion concisely presents and assesses the key factors.

Crenshaw, Martha, ed. *Terrorism in Context.* University Park: Pennsylvania State University Press, 1995. A collection of essays that amounts to a broad survey of the history of terrorism and its expression in many regions of the world. The first contributions deal with the origins of the concept of terrorism in early modern Europe and 19th-century anarchism. Later contributions include discussion of left-wing terrorism in Italy and West Germany, the Basque extremists in Spain, Northern Ireland, political violence in Argentina and Peru, and a variety of movements in the Middle East.

Egendorf, Laura K., ed. *Terrorism: Opposing Viewpoints.* San Diego, Calif.: Greenhaven Press, 2000. This collection of periodical articles, interviews, and book excerpts presents pro and con viewpoints on a variety of issues relating to terrorism. Topics discussed include the seriousness of the terrorist threat, motivations and justifications for terrorism, and appropriateness of counterterrorism measures.

Hoffman, Bruce. *Inside Terrorism.* New York: Columbia University Press, 1998. Provides a historical perspective on the development of terrorism from its origins in the French Revolution to anarchist and socialist movements of the 19th century to the nationalism and postcolonialism of the 20th century. The author argues that a new terrorism can be seen in the emergence of groups such as fanatical Islamic and Jewish extremists in the Middle East, the extremist fringe of American militia movements, and apocalyptic sects such as Japan's Aum Shinri Kyo. Argues that this new terrorism is at the same time less tractable and predictable and potentially more dangerous due to these groups' access to weapons of mass destruction and their willingness to use them.

Mullins, W. C. *Sourcebook on Domestic and International Terrorism: An Analysis of Issues, Organizations, Tactics and Responses.* 2nd ed. Springfield, Ill.: Thomas, 1997. A general handbook on terrorism directed to law enforcement personnel. Areas cover include: definitions of terrorism, motivations and psychology of terrorists, dynamics of leadership and organization in terrorist groups, terrorist tactics and weapons, and approaches to counterterrorism.

Schechterman, Bernard, and Martin Slann, eds. *Violence and Terrorism 98/99.* 4th ed. Guilford, Conn.: Dushkin/McGraw Hill, 1998. Fourth in a series of annual editions on the topic of terrorism, this book is a collection of selected journal and periodical articles roughly spanning the 1994–97 period and divided into 10 units: (1) the concept of terrorism; (2) the causes and scope of terrorism; (3) state-sponsored terrorism; (4) revolutionary terrorism and state terrorism used against dissidents; (5) terrorism in America; (6) terrorism and women; (7) terrorism and the media; (8) tactics, strategies, and targets of terrorism; (9) countering terrorism; (10) trends and projections of terrorism.

———. *Violence and Terrorism 99/00.* 5th ed. Guilford, Conn.: Dushkin/McGraw Hill, 1999. The fifth volume in a series of annual editions is organized using the same topical units as the preceding volume. Other than a small amount of introductory material, there is little duplication of coverage with the earlier volume. Most articles included were published from 1996 through 1998.

Simonsen, Clifford E., and Jeremy R. Spindlove. *Terrorism Today: The Past, the Players, the Future.* Upper Saddle River, N.J.: Prentice-Hall, 2000. A survey textbook for college and law enforcement training courses. The first part discusses the definition, history, and typology of terrorism. Part two discusses terrorism in nine geographical regions. The third part discusses counterterrorism and trends for the 21st century.

White, Jonathan R. *Terrorism: An Introduction.* 2nd ed. Belmont, Calif.: West/Wadsworth, 1998. A good introductory textbook covering the nature, scope, and expression of terrorism. Topics covered include definitions and typologies of terrorism, ways in which terrorist groups justify their activities, structure and dynamics of terrorist groups, and regional surveys of terrorism in Latin America, the Middle East, Europe, and the United States. Each regional section includes background about the ideologies, groups, and conflicts as well as differing interpretations by experts.

VIDEOS

"Domestic Terrorism." Princeton, N.J.: Films for the Humanities & Sciences, n. d. Video (VHS) 52 minutes. Explores the motivations of terrorists and the appropriate response of government, including civil liberties considerations.

Theoretical or Analytical Works

BOOKS

Buhite, Russell D. *Lives at Risk: Hostages and Victims in America's Foreign Policy.* Scholarly Resources, 1995. A history of federal responses to terrorism from the Barbary pirates of the early 1800s to today's skyjackers. U.S. approaches have alternated between flexibility and willingness to negotiate and a hard-line military response.

Chasdi, Richard J. *Serenade of Suffering: A Portrait of Middle East Terrorism, 1968–1993.* Lanham, Md.: Lexington Books, 1999. Applies a systematic analysis to the behavior of the various terrorist groups that became prominent in the Middle East during the 1970s and 1980s. Begins with discussion of definitions, typologies, and significant variables. The book then turns to the ideological factors influencing terrorist group behavior, the process of formation and evolution of terrorist groups, and an analysis of the groups' behavior, including choice of targets and methods used.

Chomsky, Noam. *The Culture of Terrorism.* Boston: South End Press, 1988. Although this book is primarily a critique of U.S. foreign policy during the Reagan administration (particularly in Nicaragua), it is of interest to students of terrorism in its forthright insistence that abuses carried out by governments against their own people or people abroad are every bit as much "terrorism" as the actions of guerrillas or others fighting the established power. This theme is seen consistently in many of the author's other works.

Corradi, Juan E., Manuel A. Garreton, and Patricia W. Fagen, eds. *Fear at the Edge: State Terror and Resistance in Latin America.* Berkeley: University of California Press, 1994. A collection of essays that explore the implications of the "culture of fear" under military regimes in Argentina, Chile, Brazil, and Uruguay from the 1960s to the 1980s. The essays, focusing on the individual countries, discuss many aspects including the perpetrators of fear, the "guardians" who protected or abetted them, the victims, the various ways people or groups fought back, literary aspects of the culture, and the possibility for justice and reconciliation.

Follain, John. *Jackal: The Complete Story of the Legendary Terrorist, Carlos the Jackal.* New York: Arcade, 1998. Recounts the life of Ilyich Ramirez Sanchez, better known as "Carlos the Jackal," and murderer of 83 people by his own account. A "freelance terrorist," he carried out attacks on behalf of Muammar al-Qaddafi, Saddam Hussein, Fidel Castro, and the Italian Red Brigade, until he was captured and imprisoned in 1994. The Jackal appears to have been motivated far more by narcissism and hedonism than any consistent ideology.

Gilbert, Paul. *Terrorism, Security, and Nationality.* New York: Routledge, 1995. The author tackles difficult philosophical questions that are often ignored but are necessary for looking objectively at the causes and possible cures for terrorism. These questions revolve around the concepts of national identity and nationalism, the role of the state as seen in various political communities, and the nature of human rights. Principles of political philosophy are applied to assess the justifications given for terrorist and counterterrorist action.

Gordon, Hayim. *Quicksand: Israel, the Intifada, and the Rise of Political Evil in Democracies.* East Lansing: Michigan State University Press, 1994. The author uses the Palestinian uprising (Intifada) and Israeli response as a springboard to exploring the problem of how evil can arise and flourish even in a society that proclaims and appears to implement democratic values. Classic writers on the problem of evil such as Hannah Arendt, Dostoevsky, and Plato are used as relevant touchstones. The author argues against the supposedly detached "postmodern" approach that has no room for a visceral sense of evil.

Grosscup, Beau. *The Newest Explosions of Terrorism: Latest Sites of Terrorism in the 1990s and Beyond.* Far Hills, N.J.: New Horizon Press, 1998. The author argues that the conventional wisdom that sees terrorism diminishing after the end of the Cold War may well be mistaken. Instead, terrorism may be emerging in many new and troubling forms, as shown in recent developments in Europe (including Ireland and Germany), the Middle East, and India, as well as in American right-wing groups who strike out against facilities associated with globalism and the "New World Order." The authoritarian response to terrorism, first evident in the Reagan administration, is also critiqued, as is the limitation of conventional definitions. A "middle view" of terrorism is proposed, in which terrorism is seen as a changing, multifaceted, and permanent challenge.

Guelke, Adrian. *The Age of Terrorism and the International Political System.* New York: I. B. Tauris, 1995. This book focuses on the origin of "the age of terrorism" as a way of thinking about small group violence during the postcolonialist Cold War era of roughly 1960–90. One side of the discussion looks at how the activities of the terrorist groups reflected a transition in world politics, while the other side looks at the characterization of acts as terrorism in the media and by governments during this time. The ending of the Cold War has challenged the established paradigm and points to both instability and some hope for resolving conflicts.

Heymann, Philip B. *Terrorism and America: A Commonsense Strategy for a Democratic Society.* Cambridge, Mass.: MIT Press, 1998. An introduction to the development of policy with regard to terrorism in the United States and other democratic societies. Using shocking incidents such as the 1993 World Trade Center and 1995 Oklahoma City bombings as starting points, the author explores the limits of action against terrorism in a democratic society. Better intelligence-gathering is crucial, particularly with regard to the emerging threats of chemical, biological, and nuclear weapons. But government actions must not compromise liberty to the point where they destroy people's ability to trust their institutions. Foreign and state-sponsored terrorism require somewhat different approaches than domestic terrorism, and military action (such as President Clinton's cruise missile strikes against Afghanistan) is often unsuccessful and counterproductive.

Juergensmeyer, Mark. *Terror in the Mind of God: the Global Rise of Religious Violence.* Berkeley: University of California Press, 2000. A sociologist of religion argues that it is simplistic to say that the appeal of violence or terror is not part of legitimate religion but is only the province of cults or fanatics. Rather, violence can be part of the enactment of "cosmic war"—struggles of ultimate significance that become linked with urgent political and ideological issues and are embodied in religious imagery, so that religion and violence are mysteriously and perhaps inextricably intertwined.

Koonings, Kees, and Dirk Kruijt, eds. *Societies of Fear: The Legacy of Civil War, Violence and Terror in Latin America.* New York: Zed Books, 1999. A detailed study of the uses and development of political violence and terror in Latin America. The introduction discusses the concept of a "society of fear" and how it arose in the development of Latin American nations. Part I looks at civil war and low-intensity conflict in Peru and Guatemala. Part II discusses the long-term consequences of violence in terror, including case studies involving Mexico, Argentina, and Colombia. Part III looks at the prospects for a transition to a democratic society, and the challenges facing such transitions.

Kressel, Neil J. *Mass Hate: The Global Rise of Genocide and Terror.* Perseus Books, 1996. The author, a psychologist specializing in international affairs, addresses the question of why mass terrorism and genocide reached a peak in the 20th century. As case studies, he examines in particular the Nazi Holocaust, genocide in Rwanda, the campaign of rape and torture in Bosnia, and the bombing of the World Trade Center in New York by Islamic extremists. He suggests that while the ideologies underlying acts of terror differ, the psychological process by which leaders manipulate followers into committing them is essentially the same.

Kumamoto, Robert D. *International Terrorism and American Foreign Relations, 1945–1976.* Boston: Northeastern University Press, 1999. Describes how confrontation with three terrorist movements helped shape the approach of American diplomacy toward regional conflicts. The author looks at Jewish extremists' attacks against the British government in Palestine, 1945–48; the revolt of Algerian nationalists against France, 1954–62; and the Palestinian jihad against Israel and American interests, 1968–76. He argues that America's response to terrorism became flexible and moderated as it took into account Cold War alignments, relations with allies, domestic politics, and other concerns.

Leeman, R. W. *Rhetoric of Terrorism and Counterterrorism.* Westport, Conn.: Greenwood, 1991. The author suggests that counterterrorists often ignore the rhetorical agenda of terrorists and the rhetoric of their own public response. This is unfortunate because the message that is sent in condemning terrorism can have different effects depending on whether it is based on moral principles or pragmatism. Case studies from the Reagan and Nixon administrations are used to suggest a rhetorical response to terrorism that promotes democratic values while discouraging further terrorist activity.

Lifton, Robert J. *Destroying the World to Save It: Aum Shinrikyo, Apocalyptic Violence, and the New Global Terrorism.* New York: Henry Holt, 1999. Psychiatrist and award-winning writer Lifton looks at the 1995 Tokyo subway nerve gas attack by the Aum Shinri Kyo cult and suggests that it may be just the tip of an iceberg. He suggests that there may be an emerging, loosely connected network of believers in apocalyptic destruction who may be able to enlist the help of psychologically vulnerable but technologically adept individuals.

Malamud-Goti, Jaime, and Libbet Crandon Malamud. *Game Without End: State Terror and the Politics of Justice.* Norman: University of Oklahoma Press, 1996. Malamud-Goti, asked by Argentine president Raul R. Alfonsin to organize trials of the military for human rights violations, describes the proceedings and their aftermath. He believes the trials may have failed in their purpose of unequivocally condemning the perpetrators and affirming a commitment to democracy.

Nacos, Brigitte L. *Terrorism and the Media: From the Iran Hostage Crisis to the World Trade Center Bombing.* New York: Columbia University Press, 1994. The author argues that terrorists have become adept at exploiting a cycle in which hostage-taking is followed by the media's fixation on the plight of the hostages, which inflames American public opinion and often forces the government to make concessions to the terrorists. Statistics are given to support this correlation. (A 1996 paperback edition has a new preface in which the author also discusses the role of media voices such as talk show hosts in promoting the extreme right-wing ideology that can result in actions such as the Oklahoma City bombing.)

Neuberger, Luisa De Cataldo, and Tiziana Valentini. *Women and Terrorism.* Translated by Leo Hughes. New York: St. Martin's Press, 1996. This Italian work deals with a largely neglected aspect of the terrorism debate: the participation of women in terrorism. Using case studies, the authors point out both the distinctive motivations of female terrorists and the stereotypes that prevent proper consideration of female terrorism by both academic researchers and the criminal justice system. Includes interview and questionnaire transcripts.

Nordstrom, Carolyn, and Joann Martin, eds. *The Paths to Domination, Resistance, and Terror.* Berkeley: University of California Press, 1992. A collection of essays that explore case studies with a focus on the cultural context of sociopolitical violence in the Americas, Europe, the Middle East, and Asia. The authors explore a complex fabric of international, national, and local institutions in terms of the exercise and experience of dominance and of resistance to oppression.

O'Neill, Bard E. *Insurgency and Terrorism: Inside Modern Revolutionary Warfare.* Washington, D.C.: Brassey's, 1990. A systematic account and classification of insurgencies, including their relation to revolutionary and state terror.

Oliverio, Annamarie. *The State of Terror.* Albany: State University of New York Press, 1998. A study of the social construction of concepts of terrorism since Machiavelli, focusing on the conceptualization of terrorism in relation to statecraft. The *Achille Lauro* and TWA 847 hijackings, both of which took place in 1985, are used as case studies.

Pearlstein, Richard M. *The Mind of the Political Terrorist.* Wilmington, Del.: SR Books, 1991. Taking a Freudian approach to his analysis of terrorists belonging to the Weathermen, the Symbionese Liberation Army, the Baader-Meinhof Gang, and the Italian Red Brigades, the author concludes that the terrorists suffer from a "narcissistic rage" that creates both self-destructiveness and violence toward others.

Reich, Walter, ed. *Origins of Terrorism: Psychologies, Ideologies, Theologies, States of Mind.* Washington, D.C.: Woodrow Wilson Center, 1990. The contributors, experts in history, religion, and behavioral science, discuss a variety of worldviews, motivations, states of mind, and goals for terrorism. They begin with the assumption that terrorism is a complex, multidimensional problem and offer diverse approaches to understanding it.

Simon, Jeffrey D. *Terrorist Trap: America's Experience with Terrorism.* Bloomington: Indiana University Press, 1994. A detailed narrative of terrorist incidents and the response of the U.S. government and public, focusing on the 1970s and 1980s. There is a special focus on the role played by the U.S. president in responding to terrorism, and the book includes interviews with former presidents as well as other government officials, terrorists, hostages and victims. The author concludes that terrorism is growing in frequency and the threat of more deadly attacks using sophisticated weapons is real.

Sluka, Jeffrey A., ed. *Death Squad: The Anthropology of State Terror.* Philadelphia: University of Pennsylvania Press, 1999. A collection of papers analyzing the use of state terror, particularly quasi-official death squads, from the perspective of anthropology and the deep roots of popular culture. Areas discussed include Argentina, Spain, Northern Ireland, Punjab and Kashmir, Indonesia, and the Philippines.

Snow, Donald M. *Distant Thunder: Patterns of Conflict in the Developing World.* 2nd ed. Armonk, N.Y.: M. E. Sharpe, 1997. This book provides a broad background on the kinds of conflicts that have erupted throughout the developing world, explaining how they differ from the proxy wars of the Cold War era. The author goes on to look at the dynamics of insurgency and counterinsurgency, internal (civil) war, the role of the narcotics trade, the problems of counterterrorism, and a critique of the so-called New World Order.

Tanter, Raymond. *Rogue Regimes: Terrorism and Proliferation.* New York: St. Martin's Press, 1999. Examines the new landscape of foreign policy in which the polarized world of the Cold War era has been replaced by the challenge of establishing an international legal order in the face of "rogue states" such as Iraq, Iran, Libya, Syria, and North Korea. Such states threaten the legal order and U.S. national security by sponsoring terrorism and producing (or trying to produce) weapons of mass destruction. The relationship between rogue states and terrorist groups (and "freelance" terrorists such as Osama bin Laden) is discussed, as well as policy options for the future.

Tucker, David. *Skirmishes at the Edge of Empire: The United States and International Terrorism.* Westport, Conn.: Praeger, 1997. An analysis of the evolution of U.S. antiterrorism policy, based on interviews with key decision-makers from the Nixon to the Clinton administrations. Includes discussion of both broad strategic principles and tactics for responding to incidents.

Von Tangen Page, Michael. *Prisons, Peace and Terrorism: Penal Policy in the Reduction of Political Violence in Northern Ireland, Italy and the Spanish Basque Country, 1968–97.* New York: St. Martin's Press, 1998. A comparison of the effectiveness of penal systems in handling politically motivated violent offenders in three regions that have intense terrorist conflict. Because the motivations and responses of people who consider themselves to be political prisoners are different from those of conventional criminals, different approaches are required. While longer sentences on the one hand and the use of the "carrot" of parole on the other can be effective, the time may come in a terrorist conflict that concessions made as part of a "peace building" process may be needed to bring resolution to the conflict.

Wieviorka, Michel. *The Making of Terrorism.* Translated by David Gordon White. Chicago: University of Chicago Press, 1993. A comparative analysis of Italian, Peruvian, Basque, and Middle Eastern terrorist groups. The author gathered his evidence through staged confrontations and extensive interviews, using a method called "interventionist sociology." He argues that terrorism at root represents the alienation of the individual from the very ideology he or she professes as motivation.

Zartman, William, ed. *Elusive Peace: Negotiating an End to Civil Wars.* Washington, D.C.: Brookings Institute, 1995. A collection of articles by experts on conflict resolution exploring techniques for bringing about peace through negotiation. Different types of conflicts (such as struggles for succession and struggles for self-determination by ethnic minorities) are discussed, and examples are drawn from Angola, Ethiopia, Lebanon, Sri Lanka, and other countries.

Zulaika, Joseba, and William A. Douglass. *Terror and Taboo: The Follies, Fables, and Faces of Terrorism.* New York: Routledge, 1996. Based on the author's research into the Basque terrorist group ETA and its opponents, this is a study of how language about terrorism is itself a weapon deployed by various players including the government, media, academia, the arts community, and the terrorists themselves. The controlling images and thought patterns involving terrorism are described as portrayed in literature and the media. This book serves as both a look at seldom discussed aspects of terrorism and as a specific study of the Basque situation.

ARTICLES AND PAPERS

Bowman, Robert. "Truth Is, We're Terrorized Because We're Hated." *National Catholic Reporter*, vol. 34, October 2, 1998, p. 17. According to the author, a bishop and former Vietnam combat pilot, the unpleasant truth is not, as President Clinton claims, that the U.S. is attacked by terrorists because it stands for freedom. Rather, it is attacked because it has too often stood for dictatorship and human exploitation. (A number of examples are given, including the installation of the Shah in Iran and a right-wing dictator in Chile.) Terrorism springs from this hatred. To end terrorism, we should offer the world aid to rebuild rather than sending troops or weapons.

Carr, Caleb. "Terrorism as Warfare: The Lessons of Military History." *World Policy Journal*, Winter 1996/97, pp. 1–12. An overview of the use of terror as a military tactic that has been employed throughout history. For example, General Sherman terrorized the civilian population of the South during the Civil War. Terror tactics are pervasive because they have been effective, at least in the short term, but in the long term they may be counterproductive in creating generations of bitterness and resentment, often sowing the seeds of renewed conflict. Rather than launching attacks that result in significant collateral damage to civilians, the U.S. should strike at military targets in nations that continue to sponsor terrorist groups, and possibly launch commando raids against terrorist leaders themselves.

Claridge, David. "State Terrorism? Applying a Definitional Model." *Terrorism and Political Violence*, Autumn 1996, pp. 47–63. Attempts to characterize state terrorism. States that use terrorism as an instrument of repression or social control generally pervert the judicial process, the role of the military, or both. The state uses its monopoly on violence to coerce rather than to protect rights. The author develops a model of state terrorism as similar to standard terrorism even though the actor is different. Death squads in Indonesia are discussed as an example of state terrorism.

Crossette, Barbara. "An Old Scourge of War Becomes Its Latest Crime." *New York Times*, June 14, 1998, pp. 1, 6. Suggests that rape is being used more frequently as a premeditated terror tactic in factional conflicts in Bosnia, Indonesia, Rwanda, and other countries. Rape is often an element in "ethnic cleansing" campaigns, used to instill fear and demoralize. Women's organizations are calling international attention to this trend.

Deutch, John. "Terrorism." *Foreign Policy*, Fall 1997, pp. 10–22. According to a former CIA director, terrorists operate increasingly on a global basis, using sophisticated technology, and are gaining the ability to use weapons of mass destruction as well as "cyber-weapons" to disrupt information systems. There must be better coordination among the FBI, CIA, State Department, and other agencies charged with fighting terrorism. The intelligence community must play an important role. Concerted action is needed, both domestically and internationally. Civil liberties must be respected, but people may need to give up some liberty, as they already do in airports.

Douglas, Susan. "Terror and Bathos." *Progressive*, vol. 60, September 1996, p. 40. Critiques the media coverage and news analysis of the TWA flight 800 crash and the Olympic Park bombing in Atlanta. The media produces supercilious observations, indecent pressure for quick conclusions, and the need to find someone at whom to point the finger.

Eland, Ivan. "Defending Other Nations: The Risk to America's Homeland." *USA Today Magazine*, vol. 127, September 1998, p. 12ff. The author suggests that the risk of terrorist attacks on U.S. soil is proportional to the extent of U.S. interventions in foreign conflicts. With the growing ability of even small terrorist groups to unleash mass destruction in the United States, the nation should limit its foreign military interventions to cases that involve vital national interests.

Hammond, Allen. "Terrorism's Roots." *Christian Science Monitor*, October 7, 1998, p. 11. Economic downturns (as in Indonesia), a growing split between rich and poor both between and within countries, and environmental crises such as loss of fisheries can all spur terrorism. Growing cities with concentrations of poor people are fertile recruiting grounds for terrorist groups.

Hoffman, Bruce. "The Confluence of International and Domestic Trends in Terrorism." *Terrorism and Political Violence*, Issue 9.2, Summer 1997. The author argues that the character of terrorism changed during the 1980s and 1990s. More terrorists today are motivated by religion, and the absolute and compelling nature of religious belief tends to make religious-based terrorists more deadly and less amenable to negotiation than nationalist terrorists. Also, the "new terrorism" typified by the Unabomber and Oklahoma City bombers is amorphous and decentralized but able to use sophisticated means of attack. New terrorists are harder to identify than traditionally organized groups, and as in the case of Aum Shinri Kyo in Japan, they are not interested in taking responsibility for their actions.

Kidder, Rushworth M. "Unmasking Terrorism: Manipulation of the Media." *Christian Science Monitor*, May 16, 1986, pp. 18–20. Terrorism creates painful dilemmas for journalists. Terrorists and their activities are sensational and often genuinely important news, but journalists (both print and broadcast) can be manipulated, as well as threatened, by both terrorists and repressive governments. The author considers whether journalists can develop standards of responsibility as an alternative to censorship.

Klare, Michael T. "Redefining Security: The New Global Schisms." *Current History*, November 1996, pp. 353–358. In the 21st century, conflicts are less likely to arise from national or bloc boundary disputes as in the Cold War. Instead, strife and accompanying extremism and terrorism is likely to be triggered by ethnic conflicts, religion, class division, economic crises, or demographic displacement.

Lindstedt, Martin. "UnCommon Sense." *Southwest Missouri Libertarian*, July/August 1995, n.p. Also available online. URL: http://www.janics.com/~mlindste/swmolb12.html#uncommonsens. From the viewpoint of a libertarian group, a typical justification for violent action against the

U.S. government, based on the language of Thomas Jefferson in the Declaration of Independence and Thomas Paine's *Common Sense.* The present federal government is viewed as even more oppressive than that of the British under King George III, justifying the exercise of the fundamental right of revolution.

Rapoport, David C. "Fertile Ground for Terrorism." *San Diego Union-Tribune*, May 28, 1995, p. G-3. In the wake of the Oklahoma City bombing, the author suggests that terrorism is more likely to arise in democracies than in authoritarian countries because people in democratic societies have freedom of movement, association, and speech, and police powers are circumscribed. At the same time, democracies raise expectations about rights and participation in the political process that are often unfulfilled, leading to frustration, alienation, and violence. But while terrorism may be inevitable in a democracy, terrorists usually can't overthrow the government.

Ross, Jeffrey Ian. "A Model of the Psychological Causes of Oppositional Political Terrorism." *Peace and Conflict: Journal of Peace Psychology*, vol. 2, no. 2, 1996, pp. 129–141. The author develops a psychological model for terrorism. Involvement in terrorism begins with frustration generating aggression in individuals, who go through a process of becoming affiliated with a group that is perceived to fulfill their needs. Once in the group, the individual has opportunities to learn terrorist methods and receives positive reinforcement or punishment. Terrorists are not simply crazy but rationally choose what they see as "cost-effective" ways of carrying out their agenda.

Rumrill, Clark. "Tribal Conflicts: What to Do?" *Christian Science Monitor*, July 17, 1996, p. 19. Conflicts between "tribes" bound together by ethnicity, religion, culture, race, or clan are often volatile and can erupt into terrorist violence. The author provides guidelines for U.S. citizens who must deal with such conflicts. U.S. citizens should avoid taking sides or even appearing to favor one side. Traditional U.S. values of assimilation and egalitarianism can make it hard for U.S. citizens to understand the tribal perspective and the intensity of motivations of tribal conflict. If punitive force is used by peacekeepers, it should be seen as the consequence of behavior, not an attack on any group's identity.

Smith, Sam. "The Semiotics of a Terrorist Bombing." *Insight on the News*, vol. 11, June 5, 1995, p. 34ff. The author is critical of the rhetoric used in the media in the aftermath of the Oklahoma City bombing. Portraying the bombers simply as extreme, apocalyptic, or paranoid does not address the alienation but simply shoves the alienated aside. Understandable skepticism about the manipulative pronouncements of politicians and the media is too easily dismissed as simple paranoia. The author suggests that "the cure is not ridicule or demands for an end to doubt; the cure is to provide answers or some reasonable manifestation of the search for the same."

Vegar, Jose. "Terrorism's New Breed." *Bulletin of the Atomic Scientists*, vol. 54, March–April 1998, p. 50ff. Reports that while the frequency of terrorist attacks has been declining, the number of people killed per attack is increasing. This trend may soon be accelerated by the use of chemical or biological weapons. The author interviews experts, among them Brian Jenkins, who describe motivations that may lead terrorists to use weapons of mass destruction. Two such motives are genocide of a hated racial or ethnic group and religious fanaticism. The article includes a "primer" introducing chemical-biological warfare (CBW).

"The 'War of the Future'." *Nation*, vol. 267, September 21, 1998, p. 6ff. Editorial argues that President Clinton's retaliatory attacks on a Sudanese chemical plant and terrorist bases in Afghanistan associated with Osama bin Laden reflects clumsy Cold War thinking. The United States had supported bin Laden as a useful client who could help to bog down the Soviets in Afghanistan. U.S. citizens need a deeper understanding of how the strategy of terrorism fits into the complex realities of Middle East politics. The United States should be more even-handed in also condemning Israeli tactics and should reach out to moderate Islamic groups.

INTERNET DOCUMENTS

Ganor, Boaz. "Defining Terrorism: Is One Man's Terrorist Another Man's Freedom Fighter?" Available online. URL: http://www.jef.org.il/articles/define.htm. Downloaded on April 27, 2000. This paper explores definitions of terrorism and distinctions between terrorism and guerrilla warfare. It derives a definition of terrorism as the intentional use of, or threat to use violence against civilians or against civilian targets, in order to attain political aims.

"The Islamic Legitimacy of the 'Martyrdom Operations.'" Available online. URL: http://www.counterror.org.il (Click on links "International Terrorism," "Terrorist Organization Profiles; Hamas; suicide bombings"). An article originally from an Australian Islamic periodical presents a justification for "martyrdom" as opposed to suicide. According to the author, the Koran condemns suicide done for base motives such as impatience or desperation, but actions done to further the will of Allah are not suicide even if the actor must die as a result.

Sheehan, Michael A. "Post Millennial Terrorism Review." Available online. URL: http://www.state.gov/www/policy_remarks/2000/000210_sheehan_brookings.html. Speech given on February 10, 2000, at the Brookings Institution, Washington, D.C. The speaker reviews recent terrorist attacks and other developments. He notes that the most active terrorist groups today have few ties to sponsoring states and are developing new sources of funding and recruitment. The new terrorist leaders tend to be more fanatical and less restrained, and they are interested in making a sensational impact, seeking out weapons of mass destruction for the purpose.

REGIONAL DEVELOPMENTS

Northern Ireland

BOOKS

Bell, J. Bowyer. *Back to the Future: The Protestants and a United Ireland.* Dublin, Ireland: Poolbeg, 1996. A detailed study of the Irish Protestants and their worldview and perspective on themselves, their Catholic opponents, and the Irish state.

Bell, J. Bowyer. *The Secret Army: The IRA.* 3rd revised ed. New Brunswick, N.J.: Transaction Publishers, 1997. A detailed history of the Irish Republican movement and the IRA from 1916 to the 1990s, which are described as "the armed struggle transformed" and "the endgame."

Bruce, Steve. *The Edge of the Union: The Ulster Loyalist Political Vision.* New York: Oxford University Press, 1994. The author suggests that the position of the Ulster Unionists is becoming more intractable as they become increasingly isolated in the ongoing dialogue for peace in Northern Ireland. This marginalization and feeling of betrayal, together with the intractably ethnic nature of the conflict, make the prospects for a lasting peace settlement problematic.

Coogan, Tim Pat. *The IRA: A History.* Niwot, Colo.: Roberts Rinehart, 1993. A detailed but readable history of the IRA up to the mid-1990s. It shows the ebb and flow of the organization's influence in relation to key political events, such as the treaty of Irish independence (1922), Nazi overtures during World War II, and the Bloody Sunday massacre in 1972 that revived the dormant IRA in an atmosphere of public outrage against the British. Key leaders and factional struggles within the Republican movement also receive detailed consideration.

Dillon, Martin. *The Dirty War.* New York: Routledge, 1999. A detailed account of the gruesome secret war between the British security forces and the Provisional Irish Republican Army (PIRA) during the 1970s and 1980s. As the PIRA carried out a bombing campaign in the hope of making the country ungovernable, British agencies deployed secret, illegal death squads who hunted down and murdered PIRA operatives. The PIRA responded by rooting out suspected informers, often with a bullet to the head. The implications for the limits of counterterrorism in a democratic society are disturbing.

———. *God and the Gun: The Church and Irish Terrorism.* New York: Routledge, 1998. A journalist who worked for 18 years in Northern Ireland describes the religious roots of the conflict and how historic grievances continue to motivate the violence, explored through interviews with both religious and lay people. He argues that both religious and political leaders have failed in their moral duty to bring an end to the conflict.

———. *The Shankill Butchers.* New York: Routledge, 1999. American edition of an exposé of a northern Ireland loyalist group that brutally murdered Catholics in Belfast. The group, which was affiliated with the paramilitary Ulster Volunteer Force (UVF), was led by Lenny Murphy, whom the author describes as a psychopath and the worst mass murderer in British history. The bitter strife between Protestants and Catholics both helped shape Murphy's rage and gave him cover to carry out his killings in a milieu where the ordinary restraints of law were not present. Murphy was eventually killed by the IRA.

Feldman, Allen. *Formations of Violence: The Narrative of the Body and Political Terror in Northern Ireland.* Chicago: University of Chicago Press, 1991. The author weaves oral histories from participants and victims in the Northern Ireland conflict with analysis of the narratives based on postmodernist principles and the "politics of the body." The historical content is useful even for readers who do not wish to tackle the analysis.

Maguire, Anne, Jim Gallagher, and Cardinal Hume. *Miscarriage of Justice: An Irish Family's Story of Wrongful Conviction as IRA Terrorists.* Niwot, Colo.: Roberts Reinhart Publishers, 1994. The story of an Irish family (also recounted in the 1993 movie *In the Name of the Father*) who were caught between the British authorities and the IRA. Anne Maguire was falsely convicted of involvement with the IRA and spent eight years in prison before being freed by an appeals court.

O'Day, Alan, and Yonah Alexander, eds. *Dimensions of Irish Terrorism.* New York: G. K. Hall, 1994. A collection of 22 scholarly articles on several aspects of Irish terrorism (both Republican and Loyalist or Unionist). Topics include the causes of terrorist violence in Ireland, attitudes of participants, the contending groups, the impact of terrorism on the general society, and the attempts to contain or resolve the underlying crisis.

Sands, Bobby. *Bobby Sands: Writings from Prison.* Boulder, Colo.: Roberts Rinehart, 1997. Sands, the leader of IRA prisoners in Belfast's Long Kesh Prison, describes brutal treatment, prison conditions, and the hunger strike that would eventually kill him and nine other prisoners. Sands became a celebrated martyr-hero to the IRA cause. The book invites the reader to consider whether prisoners who had been convicted of brutal terrorism should themselves be terrorized by the state.

Taylor, Peter. *Behind the Mask: The IRA and Sinn Fein.* TV Books, 1997. A journalist who has spent nearly 30 years covering the "Troubles" in Northern Ireland based this book on his television documentary. He was given extensive and unprecedented access to key figures in the IRA and its political wing, Sinn Féin, thus allowing readers access to the frank opinions of people who have devoted their lives to a violent struggle.

ARTICLES AND PAPERS

MacLeod, Alexander. "A Blast Rips N. Ireland's Grasp on Peace." *Christian Science Monitor*, August 17, 1998, pp. 1, 10. Reports that the British and Irish governments are struggling to preserve a tentative peace agreement in the wake of a deadly bomb attack in Omagh by renegade Irish nationalists. The bombers tricked authorities into evacuating shoppers into the path of the blast.

Paul, Annie Murphy. "Dispatch from Derry." *Psychology Today*, vol. 31, November–December 1998, p. 28ff. While the April 1998 signing of a Northern Ireland peace agreement may be a hopeful sign, the psychological effects of having lived with pervasive violence and death for generations may be harder to overcome than even the political obstacles. The Catholic and Protestant cultural identities are deeply ingrained, as are the ways of keeping distance between the groups. Further, those people who have committed to terrorism and are now being released on amnesty may be unable to adjust to peace.

"Praying for Peace." *Current Events*, vol. 98, September 18, 1998, p. 1ff. On April 10, 1998, Good Friday, Protestant and Catholic leaders signed an agreement brokered by former U.S. Senator George Mitchell. It established a 108-member legislative assembly with both Protestants and Catholics and called for the formation of a council that would allow the Republic of Ireland and Northern Ireland to make joint decisions in areas such as transportation and the environment. On May 22, 1998, the people of both Northern Ireland and the Republic of Ireland ratified the agreement, but on August 15 a powerful car bomb killed 28 people and wounded hundreds in the town of Omagh, Northern Ireland. Among the victims were classmates who had written a poignant poem calling for peace.

Stevenson, Jonathan. "The Shadow of a Gunman." *National Review*, vol. 49, December 31, 1997, p. 26ff. Describes the split in the Irish Republican movement after two cease-fires had been made and broken by the IRA. A dissident group called the 32-County Sovereignty Committee has rejected the Mitchell Principles, which require renunciation of violence, and has left the IRA and Sinn Féin. The author believes that the failure of the mainstream IRA to effectively condemn such sentiment and the persistence of equally intractable Unionist positions make a settlement unlikely. The British seem unwilling to hold firm.

INTERNET DOCUMENTS

"Index of/Politics/INAC" Available online. URL: http://www.etext.org/Politics/INAC/. Downloaded on April 27, 2000. Directory of "e-text" (electronic text) documents relating to Northern Ireland and the Troubles. Click on document titles to read.

"Irish History on the Web." Available online. URL: http://wwwvms.utexas.edu/~jdana/irehist.html. Updated on September 2, 1999. Provides a number of useful links to resources relating to Irish history. Of particular interest for students of terrorism is the page linked under "The North and 'The Troubles.'"

"The Northern Ireland Conflict." Available online. URL: http://cain.ulst.ac.uk/index.html. Updated on April 3, 2000. This site is created by the CAIN (Conflict Archive on the Internet) Web Service. It provides extensive background and links concerning the conflict in Northern Ireland from 1968 to the present. Includes a searchable bibliographic database, glossary, list of acronyms, description of organizations, and much more.

"Sinn Féin." Available online. URL: http://sinnfein.ie/index.html. Downloaded on April 27, 2000. Web site for the political arm of the Irish Republican movement, including background and position papers relating to peace negotiations.

Europe

BOOKS

Chalk, Peter. *West European Terrorism and Counter-Terrorism: The Evolving Dynamic.* New York: St. Martin's Press, 1996. Discusses the development of terrorism in Western Europe since the 1960s and the latest response of the European Union to terrorism, the "Maastricht Third Pillar." The author expresses concerns about the lack of accountability and public participation in the process of developing security and counterterrorism policies. This is part of a comprehensive critique of antiterrorism from a liberal democratic prospective.

Conquest, Robert. *The Great Terror: A Reassessment.* New York: Oxford University Press, 1991. A noted Sovietologist, Conquest used the opportunity brought about by glasnost and the opening of Soviet archives to revise his classic work on Stalin's purges, one of history's worst examples of state terrorism.

ARTICLES AND PAPERS

Berger, Deidre. "Beyond Skinheads, Germany's Far Right Forms a Political Base." *Christian Science Monitor,* March 27, 1998, p. 7. Reports that right-wing parties such as France's National Front, Austria's Freedom Party, and the German League of Free Citizens are growing in power and may create a climate that encourages right-wing terrorism. Their appeal combines nationalism, anti-immigrant sentiment, and racism.

"Chaos in the Caucasus: Islamic Terrorism in Russia." *Economist (U.S.),* vol. 353, October 9, 1999, p. 23. In response to bomb attacks in Moscow, the Russian government has blamed Chechen terrorists and has launched a full military assault on Chechnya. The Russians are trying to prevent the perception that they are anti-Muslim in general, and historic Russian ties with nations such as Iran may be helping them maintain good relations with the Muslim world.

Daly, Emma. "Basques Take Political Tack." *Christian Science Monitor,* February 19, 1999. Available online. URL: http://www.csmonitor.com/durable/1999/02/19/p8s1.htm. Reports on the possible transition of the Basque independence movement from terrorism to political activity. Basques on both sides of the Spain-France border are uniting into a political organization. A truce seems to be holding, though the unwillingness of the Spanish government to engage in talks with the Basque groups is creating frustration.

Gessen, Masha. "Moscow Dispatch: The Clampdown." *New Republic,* October 4, 1999, p. 18. Reports that in the aftermath of three bomb explosions which killed more than 200 people in Moscow, the response of Russian authorities has been confused and ineffective. At the same time, random police sweeps and a curtailment of civil liberties suggest that Russia's democracy is not mature enough to cope with terrorism.

Hoffman, Bruce. "Is Europe Soft on Terrorism?" *Foreign Policy,* Summer 1999, p. 62. The failure of Germany and Italy to prosecute or extradite Turkish Kurdish terrorist Abdullah Ocalan has led to renewed charges that Europe is soft on terrorism. Critics hearken back to the 1970s, when terrorism was rampant and European governments implicitly agreed not to prosecute terrorist groups as long as they did not attack their nations directly. The author suggests that U.S. citizens, who view the war against terrorism as a global effort, misunderstand European nations, which focus on preventing terrorism within their own borders. United Europe has in fact been quite effective in regional cooperation against terrorist threats, and in prosecuting domestic terrorists. The arrest of Kurdistan Workers' Party (PKK) leader Abdullah Ocalan by the Turkish government in February 1999 led to renewed threats of violence, particularly against foreign tourists in Turkey.

"Terror Returns?" *Economist (U.S.)*, vol. 351, May 29, 1999, p. 50. Reports speculation following the killing of an adviser to the Italian government that the Red Brigades terrorists, active during the 1970s, may have returned. It is unclear how large the new group using the old name may be, and whether any of the old terrorists are part of it. The manifesto issued following the killing does echo language used by earlier leftist writings, but conspiracy theories abound as to the real nature of the killers.

INTERNET DOCUMENTS

"Basque Nationalism: History and Historical Documents of Euskadi Ta Askatasuna." Available online. URL: http://www.contrast.org/mirrors/ehj/html/eta.html. Downloaded on April 27, 2000. Provides background on the goals and activities of the Basque ETA terrorist group, including interviews and peace proposals.

Middle East

BOOKS

Appleby, R. Scott, ed. *Spokesmen for the Despised:Fundamentalist Leaders of the Middle East.* Chicago: University of Chicago Press, 1997. This collection of essays sponsored by the Fundamentalist Project of the American Academy of Arts and Sciences broadly explores a variety of fundamentalist Islamic, Jewish, and Christian movements in the Middle East. Through profiles of groups and their leaders, the authors look at both the relationship between the movements and their general religious background, and the interplay between fundamentalism and social and political forces in the region.

Bell, J. Bowyer, ed. *Terror out of Zion: The Fight for Israeli Independence.* New Brunswick, N.J.: Transaction Publishers, 1996. A definitive work on the 1943–48 period during which two Jewish extremist groups, the Irgun and the Lehi, conducted a terrorist campaign against the British occupation and then fought against Arabs who had attacked the nascent Jewish state.

Annotated Bibliography

Bodansky, Yossef. *Bin Laden: The Man Who Declared War on America.* Rocklin, Calif.: Forum, 1999. A biography of the enigmatic Saudi millionaire who entered American consciousness at the end of the 1990s as the leading organizer and financier of international terrorism. To unravel his story, the author provides extensive context about Islamic extremists and their often violent struggle against what they see as the cultural imperialism of the West. He suggests that rather than being an independent mastermind, bin Laden is an agent who carries out a broader agenda, possibly directed by the Pakistani government's ISI intelligence service.

Cooley, John K. *Unholy Wars: Afghanistan, America, and International Terrorism.* Sterling, Va.: Pluto Press, 1999. Details how the U.S. support for Islamic freedom fighters against the Soviet occupiers in Afghanistan later backfired as the people the United States helped train (including the now-notorious Osama bin Laden) turned their weapons and expertise against the West after defeating the Soviets. The result was a wave of destabilization in nations such as in Egypt and Algeria, the conflict in Chechnya, the rise of the Taliban, and terrorist attacks on the United States itself, notably the World Trade Center bombing.

Davis, Joyce M. *Between Jihad and Salaam: Profiles in Islam.* New York: St. Martin's Press, 1999. A collection of 17 interviews with influential figures in the Muslim world, including Anwar Haddam of Algeria's Islamic Salvation Front, Hassan al Turabi, considered by some to be a spiritual successor to Ayatollah Khomeini, Muntassir al Sayat, of a violent jihad faction in Egypt, and as well as moderate or liberal leaders such as former Pakistani ambassador to the United States Abida Hussain. Valuable for providing access to the words of people not often heard directly in the West.

Harris, William W. *Faces of Lebanon: Sects, Wars, and Global Extensions.* Princeton, N.J.: Marcus Wiener, 1996. Because Lebanon has been an arena for much terrorist and counterterrorist activity, this overview of Lebanese history is useful for the student of terrorism. Part 1 is an overview of the religious, ethnic, and other groups whose complex interrelationships have driven much of the country's history. Part 2 covers that history from the beginning of the French mandate in 1920 to the end of the civil war in 1989. Part 3 covers the tumultuous struggle leading to the Ta'if agreement and events up to 1996.

Jaber, Hala. *Hezbollah: Born with a Vengeance.* New York: Columbia University Press, 1997. Vividly describes the secretive world of Hezbollah, viewed by many as the prototypical Islamic extremist movement. Explores the evolution of the organization since 1982 and its relationship with Syria and Iran. A prevailing theme is the tremendous devotion Hezbollah followers have to the cause, up to and including martyrdom.

Jenco, Lawrence Martin. *Bound to Forgive: The Pilgrimage to Reconciliation of a Beirut Hostage.* Notre Dame, Ind.: Ave Maria Press, 1995. The author describes his kidnapping by Lebanese Shi'ite Muslim extremists and his 19 months of captivity. He emphasizes his spiritual journey in coming to terms with his captors and captivity, its meaning, and his possible fate.

Karawan, Ibrahim A. *The Islamist Impasse.* New York: Oxford University Press, 1997. In this short study the author explains the structure of Islamist movements and the strategies that states have taken in countering or restraining the influence of Islamists. The perspective is then broadened to look at regional political balances and at the response from the West. The conclusion is that the ineffectiveness of self-proclaimed Islamist states and the relatively successful strategies of moderate states have resulted in the only limited effectiveness for the Islamic movement.

Katz, Samuel M. *The Hunt for the Engineer: How Israeli Agents Tracked the Hamas Master Bomber.* New York: Fromm International, 1999. A vivid inside account of how Israeli Shin Bet agents played an extended cat-and-mouse game with the Hamas bomb-maker Yehiya Ayash. They eventually succeeded in blowing him up with a booby-trapped cell phone.

Norval, Morgan. *Triumph of Disorder: Islamic Fundamentalism, the New Face of War.* Bend, Oreg.: Sligo Press, 1998. Because much of the terrorism in the Middle East as well as that taking place in Africa, Central and South Asia, and the United States is perpetrated by fundamentalist Islamic extremists, this discussion of their worldview and attitude toward the West is useful to the student of terrorism. The author argues that this kind of culturally motivated terrorism and warfare has not been effectively addressed by institutions geared to defending the nation-state against competing nation-states. Terrorism must thus be considered in the context of an overall shift from traditional nation-states to new forms of organization.

O'Ballance, Edgar. *Islamic Fundamentalist Terrorism, 1979–1995: The Iranian Connection.* New York: New York University Press, 1997. Describes the development of the international strategy and tactics of terrorism by the Ayatollah Khomeini and his followers after their 1979 takeover in Iran. They developed an extensive international network with links to embassies, safe houses, weapons caches, and other infrastructure to support terrorist groups.

Olson, Robert W., ed. *The Kurdish Nationalist Movement in the 1990s: Its Impact on Turkey and the Middle East.* Lexington: University Press of Kentucky, 1997. Contains nine studies of the continuing conflict between Kurdish nationalists and the Turkish government, a conflict that is little known in the West but has potentially explosive effects in neighboring countries of the Middle East.

Rapaport, Era. *Letters from Tel Mond Prison: An Israeli Settler Defends His Act of Terror.* New York: Free Press, 1996. The odyssey of a U.S.-born Jew who became involved as a social worker with the movement for Jewish settlement on the West Bank. He describes how he came to see violence as necessary for countering the violence of the PLO. In 1982, he planted a bomb under the car of a PLO official in retaliation for the killing of six Jewish students by a PLO sniper. He lived as a fugitive for five years, and then returned to Israel, where he was tried and imprisoned.

Reeve, Simon. *The New Jackals: Ramzi Yousef, Osama bin Laden and the Future of Terrorism.* Boston: Northeastern University Press, 1999. A dramatic account of the FBI investigation that uncovered Ramzi Yousef as the mastermind of the 1993 bombing of the World Trade Center in New York City, and then revealed Osama bin Laden, a Saudi millionaire, as the instigator and funder of the attack and many other acts of terrorism. The account is based on extensive interrogation files and interviews with senior FBI agents. The author suggests that the sophisticated terrorism exemplified by Youssef and bin Laden may soon lead to terrorist attacks using weapons of mass destruction.

Sutherland, Tom, and Jean Sutherland. *At Your Own Risk: An American Chronicle of Crisis and Captivity in the Middle East.* Golden, Colo.: Fulcrum, 1996. College dean Tom Sutherland and his wife chronicle his six-and-a-half years of captivity at the hands of the Islamic Jihad in Beirut, Lebanon, along with Terry Anderson and Terry Waite. He faced grinding boredom more than imminent threats. Meanwhile, his wife worked tirelessly to prod American officials to work for his release.

ARTICLES AND PAPERS

Al-Ashmawy, Sai'd. "Islam's Real Agenda." *Reader's Digest,* January 1996, pp. 156–160. According to the author, Islam is at its heart a religion of tolerance and brotherhood, and embraces Jews and Christians as fellow believers in God. The true jihad is a struggle for spirituality. Rabble-rousing extremists and corrupt governments are barriers to the true fulfillment of Islam, which requires democracy and celebrates diversity.

Bright, Martin. "The Demonisation of Islam." *New Statesman,* vol. 127, September 4, 1998, p. 20ff. Anti-Muslim hysteria reflected in a proposal to create a crime of "incitement" to terrorist acts is not serving Britain well. Muslim dissidents have genuine grievances and London's large Muslim community should be allowed a variety of free expression as long as its members do not actually resort to violence.

Davis, Douglas. "Iranian Terror: At Rafsanjani's Door." *Jerusalem Post International Edition,* July 13, 1996, pp. 8–9. Details the Iranian network that gathers intelligence and carries out terrorist actions overseas. Recommends ways of reducing the ability of this network to operate abroad, such as by downsizing Iranian embassies and reducing cultural and commercial contacts. (An apparent trend toward liberalization in Iran at the end of the 1990s may be changing this situation somewhat.)

"Dozen Arrested in Alleged Terrorist Plot Against Christian Targets." CNN.com December 13, 1999. Available online. URL: http://www.cnn.com (search). Reports that terrorists associated with Osama bin Laden were being arrested in a number of Middle Eastern countries because of suspicion that they were planning terror attacks against Christian tourists visiting holy sites over the Christmas holidays.

Emerson, Stephen. "Islamic Terror: From the Midwest to the Mideast." *Wall Street Journal*, August 28, 1995, p. A12. A description and diagram of the Hamas terror network, its penetration into the heart of the United States, and the activities leading up to the World Trade Center bombing. These activities include those of Mousa Abu Marzuk, founding leader of Hamas and a key figure in terrorist planning.

Farley, Christopher John. "Going Without a Prayer: An Inside Look at How the FBI and CIA Nabbed an Infamous Suspect after a Global, Four-Year Manhunt." *Time*, vol. 149, June 30, 1997, p. 34ff. Reports on the hunt for and arrest of Mir Aimal Kansi, accused of a 1993 shooting attack that killed two people and injured three outside CIA headquarters in Langley, Virginia. Includes a description of Kansi's background, conflicting reports on his personality, and the roles played by the White House and the Pakistani government.

Fields-Meyer, Thomas. "United in Grief: Sharing the Same Land but Worlds Apart, Two Families—One Israeli, One Palestinian—Long for Peace After Each Loses a Child to an Act of Rage." *People Weekly*, vol. 48, July 7, 1997, p. 38ff. Explores the way two families on opposite sides of the Arab-Israeli conflict are coping with the loss of children to violence. The diary of young Bat-Chen, found after her death, speaks poignantly of love and war far beyond her years. Helmi Shousha, an 11-year-old Palestinian killed by a security guard at a Jewish settlement, provides a bone marrow transplant for his ailing sister.

Fisk, Robert. "Talks with Osama bin Laden: How an Afghan 'Freedom Fighter' Became 'America's Public Enemy Number One.'" *Nation*, vol. 267, September 21, 1998, p. 24ff. A British correspondent who has extensively interviewed Osama bin Laden describes the Saudi millionaire's roots in the war against Russia in Afghanistan. He says that bin Laden is isolated and has a distorted view of America—but that President Clinton, in turn, made a mistake by vilifying him and raising him to the exalted status of "Public Enemy Number One."

Fried, Joseph P. "Sheikh and 9 Followers Guilty of a Conspiracy of Terrorism." *New York Times*, October 2, 1995, pp. A1, A11. Reports the conviction of Sheikh Omar Abdel Rahman and nine other militant Muslims for a conspiracy to carry out a terrorist campaign of bombings against the United States and the United Nations, in an attempt to force U.S. officials to stop supporting Israel and Egypt. Includes backgrounds of all 10 conspirators.

Gellman, Barton, and Laura Blumenfeld. "Portrait of an Assassin." *Washington Post National Weekly Edition*, November 20–26, 1995, p. 9. Portrait of Yigel Amir, who assassinated Israeli prime minister Yitzhak Rabin. It is disturbing to many Israelis that Amir came from an Orthodox upbringing and used careful reasoning from the Torah to justify killing Rabin, who had decided to give up Israeli control of the West Bank. Amir's rejection by his fiancée may have triggered the final deed.

"Hamas Terrorist Mastermind Dies in Gaza Blast." *Near East Report*, January 15, 1996, pp. 1, 7. Reports the reaction to the death of Yehiya Ayyash ("the Engineer"), the Palestinian master bomb maker long sought by Israel. He had equipped suicide bombers who had killed dozens of bus passengers in Israel. The article also includes a chart of the organization of the Gaza Muslim Brotherhood and the "10 principles of faith" of Hamas.

Johnston, David. "Evidence Is Seen Linking Bin Laden to Algerian Group." *New York Times*, January 27, 2000. Available online. URL: www.nytimes.com (search). Reports that investigators have uncovered links between Osama bin Laden and a group of Algerians and others accused of plotting a terrorist attack in the United States. One of the accused being held in Senegal, Mohambedou Ould Slahi (a citizen of Mauritania), is the brother of one of bin Laden's key lieutenants. Border agents in Port Angeles, Washington, discovered Ahmed Ressam, an Algerian, smuggling a bomb and detonators over the border from Canada.

Katz, Lee Michael. "Financial Records Lifting Veil on bin Laden Network." *USA Today*, October 1, 1998, pp. 1A–2A. U.S. intelligence agencies are "following the money" to uncover terrorist mastermind Osama bin Laden's financial dealings. Bin Laden is believed to have sponsored the 1998 bombing attacks on U.S. embassies in Kenya and Tanzania, as well as the 1993 World Trade Center bombing in New York. Running a major terrorist network is expensive, and the secretive bin Laden may be vulnerable to intelligence work and computer snooping that will uncover his accounts.

Loeb, Vernon. "The Man Who Pulls the Terrorists' Strings." A portrait of Osama bin Laden, who is widely regarded as the most effective terrorist mastermind of the 1990s. Using his personal fortune and ties to thousands of veteran Islamic fighters in Afghanistan, bin Laden has built an extensive network and has withstood U.S. attempts to neutralize him, including a cruise missile attack on terrorist bases in Afghanistan. Bin Laden is attempting to unite the Islamic world under anti-Western regimes.

Mackenzie, Richard. "The Succession: the Price of Neglecting Afghanistan." *New Republic*, vol. 219, September 14, 1998, p. 23ff. The author suggests that much of the trouble the United States and the West have had with Islamic terrorism is the result of America having neglected Afghanistan once the Soviet invaders had been defeated. The United States gave no aid to Afghani political forces who were trying to set up a moderate government. In the early 1990s, some Afghans tried to warn the United States that terrorist bases were being set up Afghanistan, but they were ignored. Meanwhile, the U.S. oil company Unocal, seeking new profits, courted the Taliban.

Marcus, Amy Dockser, et al. "Crackdown on Terror has Muslim Militants Trying New Strategies." *Wall Street Journal*, August 19, 1997, pp. A1, A8. In response to the perceived failure of the terror campaign to create fundamentalist Islamic states, some extremist groups are turning to mainstream politics and legal action. In Lebanon, Hezbollah is no longer calling for establishment of an Islamic state but is seeking social reforms and government aid for residents in the Bekaa Valley.

McCarthy, Andrew C. "Prosecuting the New York Sheikh." *Middle East Quarterly*, March 1997. Available online. URL: http://www.counterror.org.il/ (link from Terrorist Organization Profiles: Al Gama'a al-Islamiyya) The U.S. attorney who led the successful prosecution of Sheikh Umar Abdel Rahman for the World Trade Center bombing and related conspiracies describes the background of Rahman's group and the transplanting of a jihad onto American soil. Includes chronology.

Miller, Judith. "Even a Jihad Has Its Rules." *New York Times*, vol. 147, August 29, 1998, p. A13ff. Islamic terrorists often use doctrines of their faith to justify terrorism as part of a jihad (holy war) against Israel, the United States, and other enemies. But according to Peter J. Awn, professor of religion and Middle Eastern studies at Columbia University, Islam provides the jihad only as a last resort. It is to be declared only by legitimate leaders of the state or top religious leaders, not self-appointed leaders such as Osama bin Laden. The killing of noncombatants (including women and children) is forbidden.

Morris, Nomi. "Terror in the Temple." *Maclean's*, vol. 110, December 1, 1997, p. 38ff. Describes the aftermath of the terrorist attack that killed 58 tourists in the Temple of Queen Hatshepsut in Luxor, Egypt. The attack undermined the impression that secularist Egyptian president Hosni Mubarak was winning the battle against Islamic terrorists such as the Islamic Group, which claimed responsibility for the attack.

Nelan, Bruce W. "The Dark Side of Islam." *Time*, vol. 142, October 4, 1993, p. 62ff. The author suggests that lack of a basic distinction between church and state, theology and politics in Islamic doctrine is the well-spring from which volatile fundamentalist movements arise. The drive to govern by Sharia—Islamic law—pits passionate, often violent fundamentalists against every secular government in the Islamic world. Fundamentalism also offers an answer to people who are alienated by the economic and cultural change of the modern world.

Newman, Richard J. "America Fights Back: Clinton Raises the Stakes in the War Against Terrorism." *U.S. News & World Report*, vol. 125, August 31, 1998, p. 38ff. Describes President Clinton's decision, in the midst of his domestic problems, to launch cruise missile attacks against terrorist targets in Sudan and Afghanistan to retaliate for the bombings of U.S. embassies in Kenya and Tanzania. The missile attacks may have killed some of bin Laden's associates in Afghanistan as well as damaging his infrastructure. It is unclear whether bin Laden's operation has been permanently crippled. Meanwhile, some domestic critics accused the president of using the military action to distract the public from his pending impeachment.

Peterson, Scott. "Is Yemen a Conduit for Global Terrorism?" *Christian Science Monitor*, March 31, 2000, p. 1. Reports that Ali Abdullah Saleh, president of Yemen, has vowed to no longer allow his country to be a convenient recruiting and staging area for terrorist groups and arms smugglers, but international observers remain skeptical. In their upcoming meeting, President Clinton will press Saleh to make good on this promise, while offering cooperation and development aid.

Pipes, Daniel. "The Paranoid Style in Mideast Politics: From the Gulf War to Somalia, Fear of a Sinister Uncle Sam." *Washington Post*, November 6, 1994, pp. c01ff. Reports that interventions such as those in Haiti and Somalia that are considered to be humanitarian efforts by Americans are often viewed in the Islamic world as being part of an agenda of cultural imperialism. Many other events are interpreted in this way. For example, the Cairo population conference in September 1993 was seen by Islamic militants as a Western effort to undermine Islam by cutting Muslim population growth.

Prusher, Ilene R. "Arafat's Forces Charged with Strong-Arm Tactics." *Christian Science Monitor*, August 31, 1998, p. 8. A human rights group reports that corrupt officials of the newly formed Palestine Authority are using imprisonment and torture to extract "taxes" for their own use. Hanan Ashwari, one of Yasir Arafat's leading officials, has resigned to protest the lack of reform and accountability in the new government.

Prusher, Ilene R. "Budget Weddings by Hamas." *Christian Science Monitor*, July 27, 1998, pp. 1, 7. The Islamic extremist group Hamas, better known in the West for terrorist attacks, has begun promoting its public image by sponsoring low-cost weddings for Palestinians. Hamas has provided a variety of other social services in what it sees as a culture war against decadent Western practices.

Said, Edward W. "Declaring War on Islam: The Legacy of Sharm el Sheikh." *Progressive*, vol. 60, May 1996, p. 30ff. The author argues that while the United States and Israel have decried Islamic terrorism, they have refused to come to terms with their arrogant colonialist policy that echoes the actions of British imperialists in India in the 19th century. The sweeping of all opposition under the rubric of "Islamic fundamentalism" has denied and frustrated the legitimate aspirations of the Arab peoples.

Sprinzak, Ehud. "How Israel Misjudges Hamas and Its Terrorism," *Washingtion Post*, vol. 120, October 19, 1997, p. C1. The author argues that Hamas, which has primarily targeted the Israeli military and settlers during the Intifada (1987–93), resorted to suicide attacks on buses within Israel only after it had been provoked by Israel. Two provocations were in February 1994 when Baruch Goldstein massacred 29 Palestinians at prayer in the Tomb of the Patriarchs in Hebron, Israel, and in 1996 when Israeli agents assassinated Hamas master bomb maker Yehiyah Ayash. Hamas, therefore, seems to be motivated more by revenge for specific provocations than by a policy of terror bombings per se.

Vistica, Gregory L., and Daniel Klaidman. "Tracking Terror: Inside the FBI and CIA's Joint Battle to Roll up Osama bin Laden's International Network." *Newsweek*, vol. 132, October 19, 1998, p. 46. Reports on the joint FBI-CIA effort to uncover and stop Osama bin Laden's worldwide terrorist operations. The agencies' joint Counter Terrorism Center keeps tabs on the world's terrorist threats. The leads, breaks, and methodology of the investigation that led to the arrest of suspects in the 1993 World Trade Center bombing are described, as well as the investigation following the bombing of American embassies in Africa in 1998. The agents have now launched a war of attrition on bin Laden's organization and its infrastructure.

Watson, Russell, Gregory L. Vistica, and Christopher Dickey. "Saddam + Bin Laden?" *Newsweek*, January 11, 1999, p. 34. Offers speculation that Osama bin Laden may be joining forces with Saddam Hussein. Such a "marriage made in hell" would enable Saddam to rebuild his foreign intelligence networking by using bin Laden's terrorist connections, while gaining expertise in terrorist operations. Saddam, in turn, could provide bin Laden with resources such as biological weapons.

Yeranian, Edward Alan. "US-Style Culture Erodes Lebanon's 'Party of God'" *Christian Science Monitor*, April 2, 1996, p. 7. The Iranian-backed Hezbollah extremist group seems to be losing its grip on Lebanon. One reason is the nation's gradual economic recovery. Hezbollah has responded by becoming a source of social services for the poor, but it can no longer dictate cultural life in the face of the growing influence of American culture.

Zuckerman, Mortimer B. "After the Hebron Massacre." *U.S. News and World Report*, March 14, 1994, pp. 79–80. In the wake of the massacre of

29 Muslims by fanatic Zionist Baruch Goldstein, the author looks at the larger phenomenon of Zionism. Zionists believe that God has given the land to the Jews, and it cannot be shared with the Palestinians. Only a small number of Zionists are willing to resort to violence. Goldstein's deed was emphatically condemned by virtually all Israeli leaders and by the public. The author points out that Arab societies have not similarly condemned the terrorists in their ranks.

INTERNET DOCUMENTS

Bin Laden, Osama, and John Miller. "Talking with Terror's Banker." *ABC News* transcript. Available online. URL: http://more.abcnews.go.com/sections/world/dailynews/terror_980609.html. Posted August 20, 1998. In an interview, Osama bin Laden defends the violent struggle (jihad) against the United States and its allies. He says that his goal is to "purify Muslim land of all non-believers" and claims that events show that America lacks the will to fight a protracted war.

Emergency Response and Research Institute. "Usama Bin Laden Page." Available online. URL: http://www.emergency.com/1999/bnldn-pg. Updated April 3, 2000. Provides brief background on the terrorist leader and links to a variety of recent articles about his activities and the efforts to apprehend him.

"Islamic Resistance Support Association." Available online. URL: http://www.moqawama.org/page2/main.htm. Updated April 8, 2000. This site provides a variety of reports and statements from anti-Israel sources in and concerning Lebanon. It thus provides background on the motivations and beliefs for extremist and terrorist groups that have attacked Israel.

Shahar, Yael. "Osama bin Ladin: Marketing Terrorism." Available online. URL: http://www.ict.org.il/default.htm (linked under Al-Qa'ida). Describes multimillionaire terrorist Osama bin Laden as representing "the terrorist as entrepreneur"—applying entrepreneurial planning, management, and marketing principles to delivering the "product" of terrorism.

Steinberg, Matti. "The Radical Worldview of the Abu-Nidal Faction." *The Jerusalem Quarterly*, October 1, 1988. Available online. URL: http://www.ict.org.il/default.htm (link under Terrorist Organization Profiles—Fatah Revolutionary Council—Abu Nidal Group). A detailed discussion of the religious ideology behind Abu Nidal, based on the organization's official publications and interviews with leaders. The author suggests that the guiding principle of Abu Nidal was not self-determination for Palestinians, but Arab unity.

VIDEOS

"The Fundamental Question." Falls Church, Va.: Landmark Media, 1995. Video (VHS). 65 minutes. Describes the rise of Islamic fundamentalism throughout the world and the controversies it has engendered in many countries. Includes pro and con statements.

"International Terrorism." Princeton, N.J.: Films for the Humanities & Sciences, n. d. Video (VHS). 52 minutes. A case study in the terrorist challenge to democracy that looks at the terrorist activities of Palestinians and Islamic fundamentalists.

Africa

BOOKS

Ciment, James. *Algeria: The Fundamentalist Challenge.* New York: Facts On File, 1997. Comprehensive background to the conflict that arose in Algeria in 1992 when the government refused to recognize an election won by fundamentalist political groups. The ensuing conflict has involved both terrorist atrocities by fundamentalist extremists and severe repression from the government.

Crenshaw, Martha, Alan O'Day, and Yonah Alexander, eds. *Terrorism in Africa.* New York: G. K. Hall, 1997. A collection of essays dealing with the causes and development of terrorism in Africa. Topics discussed include the 1976 Entebbe aircraft hijacking and rescue, the development of guerrilla insurgencies (including the Mau Mau rebellion of the 1950s), and a variety of contributions dealing with South African topics including the relationship between apartheid, terrorism, and the legal system.

Human Rights Watch. *Angola Unravels: The Rise and Fall of the Lusaka Peace Process.* New York: Human Rights Watch, 1999. Reports on the breakdown of peace negotiations and the resumption of an all-out war between the government and UNITA (National Union for the Total Independence of Angola), an anticommunist rebel group. Failure to enforce a UN embargo on arms and oil transfers has enabled both sides to rebuild their military capability.

Vines, Alex. *Renamo: Terrorism in Mozambique.* Bloomington: Indiana University Press, 1991. Discusses the chaotic situation in the late 1980s as RENAMO, an anticommunist guerrilla movement backed by South Africa, engaged a marxist government backed by the Soviets. As the South Africans disengaged and underwent their own radical transformation and the Soviet Union disintegrated, the situation became chaotic. It thus serves as a case study in what happens to a guerrilla or terrorist group when its old enemy disappears and the society begins to focus on building democracy.

Annotated Bibliography

Articles and Papers

Donnelly, John. "Algerian Massacres Outrage the World." *Miami Herald*, October 19, 1997, pp. A1, A18. Describes horrific massacres in the continuing war between the Algerian army and radical Islamic factions. In a 1997 attack, factionalist raiders broke into homes and killed 214 men, women, and children, slitting their throats while the army stood by. Although the army is beginning to respond more effectively, no end to the conflict is in sight.

Kaplan, David E. "On Terrorism's Trail." *U.S. News & World Report*, November 23, 1998, p. 30. Reports on the painstaking forensic and intelligence investigation by the FBI following the 1998 bombings of U.S. embassies in Kenya and Tanzania. A massive force of 375 FBI agents and experts poured into East Africa, but the real break came from questioning a man arrested while carrying a phony passport.

Peterson, Scott. "How Reporters Cheat Assassins in Algeria's War with Islamists." *Christian Science Monitor*, July 24, 1997, p. 8. The conflict in Algeria typifies the dilemma faced by journalists. On the one hand, terrorists sometimes target them as representatives of the establishment. On the other hand, authorities want to control all information and sometimes censor, expel, or even arrest journalists. The ability of a journalist to present an independent point of view often comes into question.

Stone, Andrea. "Staggering Carnage Overwhelms Rescuers: Nairobi Scene Evokes Comparisons to Oklahoma City Blast in 1995." *USA Today*, August 10, 1998, p. A6. Reports on the nearly simultaneous terrorist bomb attacks on the U.S. embassies in Nairobi, Kenya, and Dar es Salaam, Tanzania. Diagrams show the sequence of events and the extent of the damage. Differences in construction of the two embassy buildings may account for the lower casualties in Tanzania.

Internet Documents

USA Today. "Embassy Bombings." Available online. URL: http://www.usatoday.com/news/world/bomb000.htm. Updated on August 7, 1999. Page of links to *USA Today* stories about the bombings of the U.S. embassies in Kenya and Tanzania.

Videos

"The Terrorist and the Superpower." Alexandria, Va.: PBS Video, 1999. Video (VHS). 60 minutes. An account of the bombings of the U.S. embassies in Kenya and Tanzania. Includes a profile of Osama bin Laden, terrorist financier and suspected organizer of the attacks.

Asia

BOOKS

Chandler, David P. *The Tragedy of Cambodian History: Politics, War, and Revolution Since 1945.* New Haven, Conn.: Yale University Press, 1993. Drawing on his experience as a foreign affairs officer, interviews, and historical archives, the author unfolds in great detail the tragic history of Cambodia from the postcolonial years through the bloody excesses of the Pol Pot regime, up to 1979.

Da Cunha, Derek, ed. *Southeast Asian Affairs 1998.* New York: St. Martin's Press, 1998. In the 25th in a series of annual volumes, the authors provide overviews of conflicts and political developments in countries such as Cambodia, Indonesia, Malaysia, Myanmar (Burma), the Philippines, Singapore, Thailand, and Vietnam, as well as an analysis of regional developments.

ARTICLES AND PAPERS

Bonner, Raymond. "Tamil Guerrillas in Sri Lanka: How They Build Their Arsenal." *New York Times,* March 7, 1998, pp. A1, A5. The activities of the Tamil Tigers, who are waging a bloody insurrection in Sri Lanka (formerly Ceylon), are given as an example of how easy it is for terrorists, revolutionaries, and paramilitary groups to tap into a worldwide, largely unregulated, market in small arms. Even heavier weapons such as grenade and missile launchers are readily available. The Tamil Tigers recently bought a large amount of explosives in Ukraine.

Cargata, Warren, et al. "Reprisal in East Timor." *Maclean's,* September 20, 1999, p. 30. Reports on the violence following East Timor's vote to secede from Indonesia. Pro-Jakarta militias engaged in an orgy of burning and looting, driving 200,000 people out of the province. The UN had failed to prepare, despite clear warnings of possible violence.

Dawkins, William. "The Japanese Sect That Is Preparing for Armageddon." *Financial Times,* May 13–14, 1995, pp. 1–2. A portrait of the Japanese cult Aum Shinri Kyo and its leader, Shoko Asahara. Police are gathering evidence linking the nerve gas attack on the Tokyo subway to the cult. The motive for the attack appears to be the fulfillment of a vision of the end of the world. The attack is a sinister example of what terrorists can now do with chemical weapons.

Desmond, Edward W. "Under Arrest—Finally." *Time,* vol. 145, May 29, 1995, p. 43. Reports on the circumstances leading up to the arrest of Shoko

Asahara, leader of the Aum Shinri Kyo cult. The police had been sweeping through the cult's extensive complexes for months, arresting followers and seizing evidence. A big break came with the confession of Masami Tsuchiya, who manufactured the sarin gas used in the Tokyo subway attack.

Mydans, Seth. "Pol Pot, Brutal Dictator Who Forced Cambodians to Killing Fields, Dies at 73." *New York Times*, April 17, 1988, p. 12. Obituary of Pol Pot, the Khmer Rouge leader who perpetrated state terrorism on a massive scale in Cambodia after his takeover of the country in 1975. His attempt to create a radical change in society through a return to rural life resulted in the death of millions of Cambodians directly or through starvation or exposure.

Sims, Calvyn. "Poison Gas Group in Japan Distances Itself from Guru." *New York Times*, January 19, 2000. Available online. URL: http://www.nytimes.com (search). Reports that the religious cult Aum Shinri Kyo says that Shoko Asahara, on trial for masterminding the 1995 nerve gas attack on the Tokyo subway, will no longer be the group's leader, although they will continue to follow his teachings. The group claims to be "renewing" itself but is not taking any responsibility for the attack.

"Southern Terror: Philippines." *Economist (U.S.)*, vol. 335, May 13, 1995, p. 37ff. Reports that Muslim separatist terrorists are robbing and burning towns in the southern island of Mindanao. New radical groups may be reviving the bitter fighting between Christians and Muslims that wracked the island during the 1970s. The Philippine government has asked the governments of Vietnam and Japan for help in cutting off supplies to the terrorist groups.

Latin America

BOOKS

Archdiocese of Guatemala. Human Rights Office. Recovery of the Historical Memory Project. *Guatemala: Never Again!* Maryknoll, N.Y.: Orbis Books, 1999. Described by the publisher as being "like a Holocaust Museum for the people of Guatemala," this is an English translation and one-volume abridgement of a massive report on the human rights abuses in Guatemala during the 1980s and continuing today. This detailed account delves not only into the physical events but the social use of terror, the profound psychological effects of brutality and fear, the methodology used by the state terrorists, historical context for the conflict, and attempts at resistance and renewal.

Giraldo, Javier. *Colombia: The Genocidal Democracy.* Monroe, Me.: Common Courage Press, 1996. The author, a Jesuit priest who heads the Colombian Intercongregational Commission on Justice and Peace, describes his nation's internal turmoil. His organization estimates that more than 60,000 Colombians were killed between 1988 and 1995 by paramilitary forces loosely connected with the army. The United States has supported the Colombian government as part of a war on drugs and terrorism, but Giraldo suggests that the paramilitary death squads and drug leaders often work together and that counterterrorism is carried out by means of terror.

Human Rights Watch. *Colombia's Killer Networks: The Military-Paramilitary Partnership and the United States.* New York: Human Rights Watch, 1996. Report details the organizers of paramilitary violence in Colombia during the 1980s who in the 1990s became largely assimilated into the Colombian military. The supposedly "unofficial" paramilitary operatives in reality worked closely with the military authorities, particularly in intelligence-gathering and surveillance efforts. Military commanders directed paramilitary fighters in attacks on political opposition figures. Despite Colombia's poor human rights record, U.S. officials worked closely with the military in their building of intelligence networks.

Human Rights Watch. *Torture and Political Persecution in Peru.* New York: Human Rights Watch, 1997. Reports that while the insurgency in Peru has wound down now that the Fujimori administration has largely defeated the rebels, the military continues to use torture against opponents, and the legal system and legislature have failed to enact effective safeguards for human rights. Meanwhile, Shining Path and MRTA insurgents continue to torture and kill opponents.

Human Rights Watch. *War Without Quarter: Colombia and International Humanitarian Law.* New York: Human Rights Watch, 1998. An update on affairs in Colombia, where the brutal war between the military and insurgents continues, although the election of a new president and the creation of a broad-based peace movement offer some help for negotiating settlements.

Marchak, M. Patricia, and William Marchant. *God's Assassins: State Terrorism in Argentina in the 1970s.* McGill–Queen's University Press, 1999. Tells the story of state terrorism in Argentina through interviews with participants on all sides, including military officers, guerrillas, journalists, union organizers, and religious workers. The interviews are amplified by additional documentation and contemporary media accounts. The failure of the Catholic Church to take a stand against the terror is examined.

O'Shaughnessy, Hugh. *Pinochet: The Politics of Torture.* New York: New York University Press, 2000. A veteran journalist uses interviews and eyewitness accounts to explore the case of Augusto Pinochet, whose widespread use of state terrorism in Chile led after his retirement to his arrest by

Spain on charges of torturing and murdering Spanish citizens. The general's life is examined from his early career to his rise to power, his regime, and his later arrest, internment, and eventual return to Chile for health reasons. Finally, the complex maneuverings and legal implications of Pinochet's case are detailed.

Stanley, William Deane. *Protection Racket State: Elite Politics, Military Extortion, and Civil War in El Salvador.* Philadelphia: Temple University Press, 1996. Discusses the development of state terrorism and repression in El Salvador and its relationship to the civil war, the breakdown of social institutions, eventual mass murder, and reform.

Verbitsky, Horacio. *The Flight: Confessions of an Argentine Dirty Warrior.* New York: New Press, 1996. The author describes the state terrorism in Argentina during the 1970s, telling the story of Francisco Silingo, a junior naval officer who was enlisted by his superiors, who told him that brutal measures against dissidents were necessary to preserve the country. Victims, who became known as "the disappeared," were kidnapped, tortured, and often thrown, still living, into the sea from military aircraft.

ARTICLES AND PAPERS

Dettmer, Jamie. "Colombia Implodes." *Insight on the News*, vol. 15, September 13, 1999, p. 8. Colombia's democracy is under severe strain. The overall economy is weak, drug production has increased, and leftist guerrillas allied with the drug lords threaten to bring chaos to the country. U.S. "drug czar" General Barry McCaffrey proposes $1 billion in U.S. aid for the Colombian government to fight the terrorists. Republicans accuse the Clinton administration of having dithered for too long, while other critics worry that the aid is too narrowly focused on counternarcotics as opposed to counterinsurgency efforts.

Lewis, Anthony. "The Price of Truth." *New York Times*, August 4, 1997, p. 7. Reports that in the last 10 years 173 Latin American journalists have been murdered—not during wars, but in the course of doing their ordinary job of uncovering facts that powerful interests sometimes want to remain concealed. In nearly all the cases the authorities have been unwilling or unable to solve the crimes. Even democratization has failed to create an environment where information can flow freely.

Reyes, Gerardo. "Blood, Freedom in Peru, Sudden Assault Ends Four-Month Hostage Crisis. How Daring Rescue Was Carried Out." *Miami Herald*, April 23, 1997, p. 1Aff. Describes the successful assault by Peruvian troops on the Japanese ambassador's residence in Lima, where 72 hostages were being held by Tupac Amaru rebels. All the rebels and one hostage died; the rest of the hostages were rescued.

Vogel, Thomas T., Jr., and Matt Moffett. "Latin Leftists Make a Noisy Comeback: But with Scant Support, Radicals Seem Anachronistic." *Wall Street Journal*, January 2, 1997, p. 8. Describes the limited resurgence of leftist guerrilla activity seen in such groups as Mexico's Zapatistas and Peru's Tupac Amaru. But leftists still seem to be flailing about after the collapse of world communism. Leftist groups that have tried to enter mainstream politics have done poorly at the ballot box. In some countries, such as Colombia, leftist groups have turned to running criminal enterprises.

"Who Planted the Bombs?" *Economist (US)*, vol. 344, September 13, 1997, p. 34ff. Reports that the Cuban government has blamed the United States for a series of firebomb attacks in Havana aimed at the tourist trade. A Salvadoran tourist was arrested by Cuban authorities and confessed to some of the bombings. Cuban exiles in Miami are divided over the use of bombing tactics, and the possible involvement of exiles in the bombings is being investigated by the FBI.

Zarate, Cecilia. "Human Rights Abuses in Colombia: An Interview with Javier Giraldo." *America*, vol. 178, April 4, 1998, p. 20ff. Giraldo, a Jesuit priest and founder of a religious coalition for peace and justice, puts most of the blame for Colombia's violence on the government. He says the military has had a free hand to attack all dissidents as threats to national security and has encouraged clandestine paramilitary groups and death squads. Government attempts to investigate violations of human rights have been ineffective.

VIDEOS

"Terror and Counter-Terror: Can Democracy Survive?" Princeton, N.J.: Films for the Humanities & Sciences, n. d. Video (VHS). 52 minutes. Uses the battle between the Peruvian government and the Shining Path (Sendero Luminoso) guerrillas as a case study in the effects of terrorism and counterterrorist response on democratic institutions.

United States and Canada

BOOKS

Barkun, Michael. *Religion and the Racist Right: The Origins of the Christian Identity Movement.* Chapel Hill: University of North Carolina Press, 1996. A study and exposé of the small but virulent Christian Identity movement. The author traces the origin of its white supremacist theology to an obscure 19th-century doctrine called British-Israelism and explains links between Christian Identity and such contemporary groups such as Aryan Nations, Posse Comitatus, and the Ku Klux Klan.

Dees, Morris. *Gathering Storm: America's Militia Threat.* New York: HarperCollins, 1997. Describes the activities of right-wing extremists and the threat they pose to U.S. society. Dees' associates at the Southern Poverty Law Center have been investigating right-wing extremist and hate groups for many years, and the text includes descriptions of beliefs and practices from informants inside some of the more radical groups.

Dwyer, Jim, et al. *Two Seconds Under the World: Terror Comes to America: The Conspiracy Behind the World Trade Center Bombing.* New York: Crown Publishers, 1994. A vivid and suspenseful account of the World Trade Center bombing in 1993, including a moment-by-moment scenario of reconstructed events surrounding the explosion, accounts by survivors, and questions about the FBI investigation and whether authorities could have prevented the attack by responding to information they had received earlier.

George, John, and Laird M. Wilcox. *American Extremists: Militias, Supremacists, Klansmen, Communists & Others.* Buffalo, N.Y.: Prometheus Books, 1996. Based on extensive interviews and study of extremist literature, the authors survey a number of groups on the U.S. political fringe, some of which have engaged in terrorist activities. While not condoning violence, the authors are somewhat sympathetic to the grievances of antigovernment groups and raise questions about abuse of power and civil liberties. They believe that such questions have often been ignored in recent years because most of today's radical groups are on the Right rather than the Left.

Hamm, Mark S. *Apocalypse in Oklahoma: Waco and Ruby Ridge Revenged.* Boston: Northeastern University Press, 1997. The author, a professor of criminology at Indiana State University, suggests that three principal elements contributed to the Oklahoma City Bombing: the right-wing, conspiracy-based ideology of the perpetrators (Timothy McVeigh and Terry Nichols), McVeigh's psychological problems and drug-induced delusions, and the government's botched and deadly raids at Ruby Ridge and Waco, which created the perpetrators' focus on vengeance.

Irving, Clive, ed. *In Their Name: Dedicated to the Brave and the Innocent, Oklahoma City, April 1995.* New York: Random House, 1995. The "official memorial volume" detailing the events, victims, rescue efforts, and survivors' accounts of the Oklahoma City bombing.

Jones, Stephen and Peter Israel. *Others Unknown: The Oklahoma City Bombing Conspiracy.* New York: Public Affairs, 1998. Stephen Jones, the appointed chief defense counsel for convicted bomber Timothy McVeigh, describes how he investigated the possibility, acknowledged by the grand jury indictment, that "others unknown" may have been involved in the bombing. He points out evidence such as a leg found in the rubble that did not belong to any of the known victims and the possibility that Terry Nichols may have worked with Muslim terrorists from the Philippines to build the bomb. He claims that the government was trying to hide evidence that would have revealed it had ignored danger signs and perhaps could have stopped the attack.

Kight, Marsha, compiler. *Forever Changed: Remembering Oklahoma City, April 19, 1995*. Amherst, N.Y.: Prometheus Books, 1998. A collection of 80 accounts by survivors of the worst domestic terrorist attack in U.S. history. A moving account of the physical and emotional sufferings of the victims as they struggled to rebuild their lives.

Mizell, Louis R. Jr., and James Grady. *Target U.S.A.: The Inside Story of the New Terrorist War.* New York: John Wiley & Sons, 1998. A former intelligence agent highlights the many ways in which terrorists have penetrated deep into the heart of the United States, including a group of Libyan terrorists who set up a secret training camp in Colorado. The author uses anecdotes and detailed evidence from interrogation reports to paint a picture of the nation's vulnerability to terrorist attack.

Serrano, Richard A. *One of Ours: Timothy McVeigh and the Oklahoma City Bombing*. New York: Norton, 1998. A *Los Angeles Times* reporter who covered the Oklahoma City story from the bombing to conviction explores McVeigh's life, looking for clues as to what led him to the extremes of violence. A troubled childhood, career disappointments, and the hardening of antigovernment rhetoric following Ruby Ridge and Waco all played a part.

Smith, Brent L. *Terrorism in America: Pipe Bombs and Pipe Dreams.* Albany: State University of New York Press, 1994. A discussion of developments in U.S. terrorism during the 1980s. The motivations and goals of the terrorists (usually lone individuals or very small groups) are discussed, as well as the government's escalation of its response as the attacks grew more widespread. While right-wing terrorism predominates, leftist, single-issue, and internationally inspired terrorism is also discussed.

Snow, Robert L. *The Militia Threat: Terrorists Among Us.* New York: Plenum Press, 1999. A police captain describes the beliefs, culture, training, and tactics of right-wing militia groups in the United States. He argues that they represent a simmering cauldron of hate and potential terrorist threats and appears to discount any diversity or positive motivations in the movement.

Stern, Kenneth. *A Force Upon the Plain: The American Militia Movement and the Politics of Hate.* Norman, Okla.: University of Oklahoma Press, 1997. An even-handed, detailed, fact-based examination of the motivations and activities of the modern right-wing militia and Patriot movement. The relationship between militias and white supremacist, neo-Nazi, Christian Identity, and other groups is also examined.

ARTICLES AND PAPERS

Anti-Defamation League. "ADL Special Report: Armed Militias and Vigilante Justice." *Anti-Defamation League Special Report*, 1997, pp. 1–6. A report by the Anti-Defamation League (ADL) detailing incidents of violence by right-wing U.S. extremists, including robberies and bombings. According to the report, some militias, "common law" groups that set up their own "courts," and Christian Identity and other racist groups seem to be cooperating on a significant scale.

Bragg, Rick. "Abortion Clinic Hit by 2 Bombs; Six Are Injured." *New York Times*, January 17, 1997, pp. A1, A9. Reports two bomb attacks on an Atlanta abortion clinic. The second bomb, apparently timed to go off after people had responded to the first, injured six people, including investigators and reporters. President Clinton and leaders of women's groups condemned the attack, while responses from antiabortion groups were mixed.

Brooke, James. "For Radical Freemen, All the Courts Are Stages." *The New York Times*, vol. 146, March 26, 1997, p. A18. Describes the legal antics of the Freemen, who believe that all courts above the local level are illegitimate and noisily object to any attempt to try them for their fraudulent financial instruments. Typically, the Freemen issue bogus securities that are "backed" by judgments enacted by their own "common law courts."

Bunker, Robert J. "Street Gangs—Future Paramilitary Groups?" *Police Chief*, June 1996, pp. 54–58. Suggests that the background and influences on U.S. inner-city youth gang members is strikingly similar to that of teenage soldiers of warring paramilitary groups in places such as Beirut, Lebanon. The nonhierarchical, "adaptive" structure of street gangs is also similar to that of emerging paramilitary and terrorist groups, and it is possible that street gangs may evolve into a threat to U.S. domestic security.

"The Future of Terror: On Guard, America Is the Dominant Nation Entering the New Century—and Top Target for Extremists." *Newsweek*, vol. 135, January 10, 2000, p. 34. Despite the quiet New Year's holiday, FBI officials believe that a loose network of Islamic extremists is planning future terrorist attacks in the United States. Precisely because the United States is the world's most powerful nation and owns—and is dependent on—the world's best technology, it is uniquely vulnerable to terrorist attack. Attacks can come from a number of directions, including the new generation of terrorists in the Armed Islamic Group and the still-active bin Laden network.

Gelertner, David. "How I Survived the Unabomber." *Time*, vol. 150, September 22, 1997, p. 82ff. Review of Gelertner's book *Drawing Life: Sur-*

viving the Unabomber. The author, a computer scientist, recalls the mail bomb attack and his struggle with severe injuries, pain, and depression in the aftermath. Gelertner went on to help the FBI paint an exhaustive picture of the terrorist—while clever surgery and devices restore the use of his mangled right hand.

Jenkins, Philip. "Home-Grown Terror." *American Heritage,* vol. 46, September 1995, p. 38ff. The Oklahoma City bombing has called U.S. attention to right-wing terrorism, but the militia, racist groups, and other extreme right-wing groups have a long history that goes back to the similar movements in the 19th century. The Ku Klux Klan has its origins in Reconstruction, and the 1930s saw a flourishing of anti-Semitic and fascist groups, often in religious guise (an example was Father Charles E. Coughlin's Christian Front). Another influence on the modern far right is William L. Pierce, whose pseudonymous racist fantasy *The Turner Diaries* inspired the terrorist group called the Order. The author suggests that prosecutors of modern terrorist groups should avoid sweeping rhetoric that could create political martyrs and new terrorist recruits, and instead, concentrate on proving specific crimes.

Johnston, David. "Bomber Manifesto Is Found in Cabin, Law Officials Say." *New York Times,* April 13, 1996, pp. 1, 8. Reports on the finding of evidence in Theodore Kaczynski's Montana cabin linking him to the Unabomber attacks. Includes excerpts from a letter sent by Kaczynski to the media, offering to cease the bombings if his "manifesto" were published in a national periodical.

Kaplan, David E., and Mike Tharp. "Terrorism Threats at Home: Two Years after Oklahoma City, Violent Sects Abound." *U.S. News & World Report,* December 29, 1997, vol. 123, p. 22ff. Investigators opened 900 domestic terrorism investigations in 1997, as compared to 100 in 1995. Heightened security consciousness following the 1995 Oklahoma City bombing may be partly responsible for the increase in cases, and there is an ongoing crackdown on a shadowy underground of white supremacists, neo-Nazis, and the most violent fringe of the militia movement. Neo-Nazi skinheads appear to be the most virulent threat. The terrorists have responded to the crackdown by breaking into tiny, decentralized cells, making it hard to gather intelligence.

Lacayo, Richard. "A Moment of Silence." *Time,* vol. 145, May 8, 1995, p. 42ff. In the aftermath of the Oklahoma City bombing, U.S. citizens should reflect on whether dissent, a solid U.S. virtue, has ripened into bitter paranoia for a fringe minority. Discusses the rhetoric of talk shows, President Clinton, and his Republican rivals. There are some signs that extremists are backing away from their more radical views.

"Reporting on Domestic Terrorism Against Women's Health Clinics." *Anti-Abortion Violence Watch,* March 1998, pp. 1–2. Summarizes attacks on women's health clinics by antiabortion terrorists. An unusual bomb design links a Birmingham, Alabama, clinic attack with an earlier clinic bombing and with the 1996 Olympic Park bombing in Atlanta. Eric Robert Rudolf is charged with and sought for these crimes.

Ross, Jeffrey Ian. "The Structure of Canadian Terrorism." *Peace Review*, vol. 7, no. 3/4, 1995, pp. 355–361. A history and survey of right-wing extremist organizations in Canada. Historically, the Ku Klux Klan and other U.S. racist groups have been able to establish some offshoots in Canada. Anticommunism and resentment of immigrants, as well as economic dislocation, have fueled extreme right-wing sentiment. In general, Canadian right-wing extremism and terrorism have been more urban-centered and smaller in scope than their U.S. counterparts.

Rothschild, Matthew. "Fury and Fun." *Progressive*, vol. 59, July 1995, p. 4. An editorialist strongly disagrees with what he calls the facile idea that the right wing of today has anything in common with the leftist rebels of the 1960s. Instead, today's Right hearkens back to the white supremacist and nativist movements of the late 19th century. The author denies that the modern right wing learned its hatred of the government or its protest tactics from the earlier leftists.

Russakoff, Dale, and Serge F. Kovaleski. "Two Angry Men." *Washington Post National Weekly Edition*, July 24–30, 1995, pp. 6–11. Portraits of Timothy J. McVeigh and Terry Nichols, who would be convicted of the Oklahoma City bombing. Describes their childhoods, McVeigh's fascination with guns and his army career, and Nichols's desperate struggle with debt. For McVeigh, the Ruby Ridge and Waco incidents became the final justification for violent action. Also includes a chart explaining decisions that the jury had to make before sentencing McVeigh to death.

Scarf, Maggie. "The Mind of the Unabomber: Narcissism and Its Discontents." *The New Republic*, vol. 214, June 10, 1996, p. 20ff. Presents a psychiatric profile of Theodore Kaczynski, the Unabomber, based on theories from psychiatrist Carl P. Malmquist's new book *Homicide: a Psychiatric Perspective*. The author suggests that Kaczynski fit the profile for "Narcissistic Personality Disorder." According to the American Psychiatric Association's *Diagnostic and Statistical Manual of Mental Disorders*, this condition is characterized by a "pervasive pattern of grandiosity (in fantasy or behavior), need for admiration, and lack of empathy beginning by early adulthood and present in a variety of contexts . . . an overinflated sense of uniqueness, self-importance and personal entitlement."

Seipel, Tracy. "The Trial of Theodore Kaczynski: Home-Grown Terrorist?" *Miami Herald*, November 9, 1997, pp. A1, A8. Profiles Theodore Kaczynski, who would be convicted of the Unabomber killings. He is portrayed as a brilliant but socially maladjusted student who withdrew from the world at the start of his professional career, then methodically planned the attacks that killed three and injured 23. The article includes a summary of the Unabomber attacks.

Smolowe, Jill. "Hidden in Plain Sight." *People Weekly*, vol. 52, July 26, 1999, p. 88ff. Recounts the story of Kathleen Soliah, former member of the Symbionese Liberation Army who created a new life as a wife and a mother while remaining a fugitive for 23 years. She lived a typical suburban life, married to a physician and raising three daughters. She was active in community affairs. She was caught when the FBI followed a tip called in by a viewer of the "America's Most Wanted" television program.

"Terror at the Olympics." *U.S. News & World Report*, August 5, 1996, pp. 24–27. Initial reports of the bomb attack at Centennial Olympic Park in Atlanta, during the 1996 summer games. Responses from officials and the public reflect fear, confusion, dismay, and resolve. Includes a map and diagram of the site.

"A Violent Priesthood." *Christian Century*, vol. 116, September 8, 1999, p. 842. An interpretation of scripture called the Phineas Priesthood is being increasingly used by white supremacists to justify killing people they view as the enemies of God and the United States. Convicted bank robber Walter Eliyah Thody claims that killing and theft are justified when involved in spiritual warfare. Buford O'Neal Furrow, accused of a shooting spree in a Jewish community center in Los Angeles, expresses similar views. Antiabortion terrorist Paul Hill had also written an essay calling for "Phineas actions." The name "Phineas" refers to the Old Testament's Book of Numbers, in which it is written that Phineas killed an Israelite and his "heathen" wife for violating God's prohibition against intermarriage.

INTERNET DOCUMENTS

CNN Interactive. "Oklahoma City Bombing Trials." Available online. URL: http://cnn.com/US/9703/okc.trial/. Downloaded on April 27, 2000. Archive page of resources and background material on the trials of Timothy McVeigh and Terry Nichols. Includes coverage of the bombing, background on the convicted bombers, trial transcripts, and story behind the reporting.

CNN Interactive. "The Olympic Park Bombing." Available online. URL: http://cnn.com/US/9707/olympic.park.bombing/. Downloaded on April 27, 2000. Archive page of resources and background material on the Olympic Park bombing. Includes the story of Richard Jewell, the park security guard who was falsely accused of the bombing, and later evidence linking the attacks to Eric Robert Rudolph.

Gorka, Sebestyen L. v. "Militias and Millenarians: A Preliminary Typology." Available online. URL: http://www.terrorism.com/documents/

GorkaTRC.pdf. Downloaded on April 27, 2000. A discussion paper for the Terrorism Research Center. Although the title is formidably academic, the discussion brings out important characteristics that distinguish traditional (Cold War–era) political terrorist groups, millenarian (apocalyptic) terrorist cults, and militias. The motivations and capabilities of, and appropriate responses to, these types of group are quite different.

Pitcavage, Mark, compiler. "Militia Watchdog." Available online. URL: http://www.militia-watchdog.org/. Updated on March 7, 2000. This site is "devoted to monitoring far right extremism in the United States." It includes news reports on militia activities, background information about militia and patriot groups, and an FAQ ("frequently asked questions" section) on the subject.

VIDEOS

"Jihad in America." Alexandria, Va.: PBS Video, 1994. Video (VHS). 60 minutes. Reports on an investigation of the activities of fundamentalist Islamic radicals in the United States.

KEY ISSUES

Counterterrorism

BOOKS

Bevelacqua, Armando, and Richard Stilp. *Terrorism Handbook for Operational Responders.* Albany, N.Y.: Delmar Publishers, 1998. A concise guide for police, paramedics, firefighters, and other persons who may have to walk into a terrorist situation and deal with the effects of the attack or the demands of the attackers. Coordination of police and firefighting efforts is essential for effectiveness under adverse conditions.

Buck, George. *Preparing for Terrorism: An Emergency Services Guide.* Albany, N.Y.: Delmar Publishers, 1997. A textbook for emergency services personnel. Covers preparing and planning for terrorist attacks, including evaluation of existing plans and procedures. Includes procedures for responding to incidents and minimizing casualties for responders.

Clutterbuck, Richard. *Terrorism in an Unstable World.* New York: Routledge, 1994. Looks at counterterrorist strategies in the light of the post–cold war world. The author focuses on two main issues: new technologies, such as those for identification and searching of airport passengers, that offer enhanced security but may threaten civil liberties; and the possible expanded role for UN and other international peacekeeping forces in fighting terrorism and resolving conflicts.

Coulson, Danny O., and Elaine Shannon. *No Heroes: Inside the FBI's Secret Counter-Terror Force.* New York: Pocket Books, 1999. Coulson, the FBI agent who founded the bureau's Hostage Rescue Team, recounts his years of pursuing criminals and terrorists, including right-wing extremists and Middle Eastern bombers. He gives a vivid insider's account of events such as the Ruby Ridge and Waco incidents and the World Trade Center and Oklahoma City bombings. While acknowledging mistakes (particularly with regard to Ruby Ridge and Waco) and problems of bureaucracy and politicization in the agency, he takes an uncompromising position in favor of law enforcement.

Decker, Ronald Ray. *Bomb Threat Management.* Boston: Butterworth-Heinemann, 1998. The author, an attorney and security consultant, provides procedures and tools for security personnel to use when confronted by bomb threats. Gives examples of forms for evaluating threats, procedures for reacting to incidents, and recovering from the effects of an explosion.

Kushner, Harvey W., ed. *The Future of Terrorism: Violence in the New Millennium.* Thousand Oaks, Calif.: Sage Publications, 1998. An overview of the current status and emerging trends in terrorism. Part 1 deals with foreign terrorism, mainly of Islamic origin. Part 2 deals with U.S. domestic terrorism, including hate crimes and militant antigovernment groups. Part 3 gives legislative, law enforcement, and technological recommendations for fighting terrorism. Part 4 looks at future terror threats including weapons of mass destruction and the use of the Internet for terror attacks.

Lesser, Ian O., ed. *Countering the New Terrorism.* Santa Monica, Calif.: Rand Corporation, 1999. The authors characterize a "new terrrorism" in which emerging groups with new sponsors, motives, agendas, and weapons have made the traditional Cold War analysis of terrorist conflict largely obsolete. The new terrorists are more loosely organized and flexible than the traditional groups and are gaining access to weapons of far greater lethality than mere bombs and guns.

Moses, Russell Leigh. *Freeing the Hostages: Reexamining U.S.–Iranian Negotiations and Soviet Policy, 1979–1981.* Pittsburgh, Pa.: University of Pittsburgh Press, 1996. A detailed analysis of the conflicting agendas of the United States, Iran, and the Soviet Union during the hostage crisis. Iranian leader Ayatollah Khomeini used the events to strike out at both the United States, which had backed the Shah, and the Soviets, who were invading Afghanistan. The author uses extensive documentary sources from both the Carter administration and the Soviet media.

Netanyahu, Binyamin. *Fighting Terrorism: How Democracies Can Defeat Domestic and International Terrorism.* New York: Farrar, Straus & Giroux, 1995. The leader of Israel's Likud Party (and Israeli prime minister 1996–99) presents a 10-point plan to combat terrorism, focusing mainly on putting pressure on the Islamic states that have sponsored terrorism against Israel. He also compares Islamic fundamentalism as a source of terrorism in the Middle East to the rise of right-wing militia groups in the United States as challenges to democracy and advocates curtailment of some civil liberties.

Picco, Giandomenico. *Man Without a Gun: One Diplomat's Secret Struggle to Free Hostages, Fight Terrorism, and End a War.* New York: Times Books, 1999. The vivid and suspenseful account of a top-level UN diplomat's participation in negotiations to end the Soviet-Afghani and Iran-Iraq wars, and in particular, his direct and harrowing encounters with Hezbollah terrorists in Beirut, Lebanon, where he negotiated for the freedom of hostages. One of the best accounts "from on the ground."

Rich, Paul B., and Richard Stubbs, eds. *The Counter-Insurgent State: Guerrilla Warfare and State Building in the Twentieth Century.* New York: St. Martin's Press, 1997. A collection of papers dealing with the relationship between political development, insurgency, and counterinsurgency in various parts of the world. Areas covered are the Philippines, Malaysia, Sri Lanka, Algeria, Mozambique, Peru, Northern Ireland, and Afghanistan. Overall, authors suggest that governments that are able to respond to insurgency by creating broad-based programs of social and economic reform are more likely to be able to contain insurgent violence.

Rogan, Randall G., Mitchell R. Hammer, and Clinton R. Van Zandt, eds. *Dynamic Processes of Crisis Negotiation.* Westport, Conn.: Praeger Publications, 1997. A collection of articles on the theory and practice of crisis (hostage) negotiation from a behavioral science standpoint. Negotiation policy is an important part of counterterrorist strategy.

Thomas, Gerry S. *Business Handbook on Terrorism, Security and Survival: A Proactive Guide for Personal Security in Today's Business Environment.* West Newbury, Vt.: Vance Books, 1994. The author of this handbook, who has 30 years' experience in military intelligence, warns that U.S. businesspersons are increasingly being targeted by terrorists, both at home and abroad. He recommends procedures and equipment for residential security and for protection from both terrorism and civil disorder while traveling, including checklists and summaries of regional terrorist threats.

Wallis, Rodney. *Combating Air Terrorism.* Washington, D.C.: Brassey's, 1993. Describes the need for international cooperation in preventing bombing, skyjacking, and other crimes of terrorism against aviation. The author suggests further steps that can be taken to improve security and incident response.

Ward, Richard H., and Cindy S. Moors, eds. *Terrorism and the New World Disorder.* Chicago: University of Illinois at Chicago, 1998. A collection of articles by law enforcement experts with a variety of local, national, and international criminal justice perspectives. Part 1 deals with worldwide trends in the motivation of terrorists and the nature of their potential targets. Part 2 examines intelligence-gathering by law enforcement agencies such as Chicago's Terrorist Task Force. Part 3 deals with a variety of incidents including the Oklahoma City bombing, threats to aviation, terrorism by organized crime and drug groups, and other motivations such as religion, left-wing politics, ecology, and nationalism, such as in Northern Ireland. Part 4 deals with the threat of biological terrorism and law enforcement tactics.

ARTICLES AND PAPERS

Akasie, Jay. "Thwarting Terrorists." *Forbes*, vol. 162, p. 184ff. Describes how business executives who spend time abroad are receiving specialized training in dealing with terrorist attacks and kidnappings. A course given by International Training, Inc., is described. Among other things, the executives learn how to be aware of their environment and driving techniques for evading terrrorists.

Bamford, James. "Our Best Spies Are in Space." *New York Times*, vol. 147, August 20, 1998, p. A23. Because close-knit, highly committed terrorist groups are hard for U.S. intelligence agencies to penetrate on the ground, the National Security Agency's spy satellite and computer surveillance facilities are vital to the counterterrorist effort. But the agency's biggest challenge is not in gathering data, but in sifting through the tremendous amount of information it receives.

Bryson-Alderman, Jason. "Achilles Heel: Why Our Top Political Leaders Are Easy Targets for Terrorists." *Washington Monthly*, vol. 30, October 1998, p. 17ff. The killing of two security guards at the U.S. capitol building by a mentally disturbed gunman highlights the U.S. government's actual vulnerability to terrorism. The cars of congress members are unguarded and could be easily tampered with by terrorists. Out of deference to congresspersons, security staff seldom inspect cars. Similarly, members of congressional staffs are usually "waved through" security entrances after a perfunctory flashing of ID. Congressional staffs should accept some inconvenience and start taking security seriously.

Caryl, Christian. "The Very Long Arm of American Law." *U.S. News & World Report*, vol. 123, June 7, 1997, p. 49ff. Describes the FBI's work at the International Law Enforcement Academy in Budapest, Hungary. The FBI is training police officers from Hungary and other former Eastern bloc countries to handle crime scenes and evidence-gathering, deal with the media, and respect legal rights. Officers trained in modern police techniques will be more effective against burgeoning organized crime in the former Soviet world, as well as the continuing threat of terrorist attacks.

"Corporate Security: Risk Returns." *Economist (U.S.)*, vol. 353, November 20, 1999, p. 78. Describes risks to companies who get involved with business in dangerous places such as Chechnya. In addition to terrorist attack, companies may face threats from criminals, litigation for failure to protect employees, and loss of reputation. To protect themselves, large corporations are developing or hiring the necessary expertise. The security industry, drawing on former police and government security agents, is flourishing.

Deutch, John. "Fighting Foreign Terrorism: The Integrated Efforts of the Law Enforcement Community." *Vital Speeches of the Day*, October 1, 1996, pp. 738–40. Author John Deutch, CIA director at the time, says that U.S. counterterrorism agencies are cooperating more closely than ever before. Meetings have been held between CIA chiefs of station and FBI legal attachés in many countries. The Counter-Terrorist Center (CTC), established in 1986 to coordinate the antiterrorism efforts of the U.S. intelligence community, has achieved great strides in identifying and countering terrorist networks such as that of Hezbollah. Includes chart of U.S. counterterrorism agencies.

Fultz, Keith O. "Status of Aviation Security Efforts with a Focus on the National Safe Skies Alliance and Passenger Profiling Criteria." Testimony before the U.S. House of Representatives Committee on Transportation and Infrastructure, Subcommittee on Aviation, May 14, 1998. Available in Egendorf, Laura K., ed. *Terrorism: Opposing Viewpoints.* San Diego, Calif.: Greenhaven Press, 2000, p. 148–55. Testimony on the status of improved airport security measures in the United States. Such measures include computerized passenger screening, improved explosives detection devices, matching of passengers to their bags, assessment of airport security vulnerabilities, and better training for security personnel.

Gleick, Elizabeth. "No Barrier to Mayhem." *Time*, vol. 148, July 29, 1996, p. 42ff. Suggests that while U.S. airports have been able to stop the hijacking threat through the use of metal detectors and other security measures, the bombing threat has increased. The sophisticated plastic explosives available to terrorists are not easy to detect. Technology aside, in too many airports basic security procedures are not being properly followed. Five years after the 1988 airplane bombing over Lockerbie, Scotland, federal inspectors reported that the Federal Aviation Agency (FAA) had done little to improve security and that in tests agents were able to enter secure areas 15 out of 20 times. Some bags checked at the curb do not go through the X-ray procedure, and bags are not being matched to passengers.

Hahn, Robert W. "The Cost of Airport Security Measures." *Consumers' Research Magazine*, vol. 80, July 1997, p. 15ff. Argues that implementing security measures proposed by the Clinton administration following the crash of TWA flight 800 (which was not caused by terrorists) will cost billions of dollars and could cause extensive delays at airports. New detection technologies are very expensive, while matching baggage to passengers could cause hours of delays if a passenger fails to board. Automated passenger profiling could save time and money by identifying which bags should be further scrutinized but has been challenged by the American Civil Liberties Union (ACLU) as being discriminatory.

Hahn, Robert W. "The Cost of Antiterrorist Rhetoric." *Regulation*, vol. 19, no. 4, 1996, n.p. Also available online. URL: http://www.cato.org/pubs/regulation/reg19n4e.html. Argues that proposed tightened airport security measures are likely to be costly, and the cost is far out of proportion to the small number of lives that might be saved. Delays caused by more detailed passenger and baggage screening are the biggest cost factor.

Hoffman, Bruce. "Responding to Terrorism Across the Technological Spectrum." *Terrorism and Political Violence*, Autumn 1994, pp. 366–90. The growing power and sophistication of military weapons has not carried over to the terrorist's arsenal. Terrorists still rely mainly on guns and relatively small and primitive bombs, apparently preferring simplicity and reliability over destructive power. However terrorist groups continue to become more "professional" and effective even as a greater variety of "amateurs" enter the field.

Howard, Michael. "Combatting Crime & Terrorism." *Vital Speeches of the Day*, October 1, 1996, pp. 741–43. An address by the British secretary of state for the home department. Howard summarizes international antiterrorist measures. Areas discussed include agency cooperation between the United States and Britain, legal cooperation and extradition, the use of asset forfeiture laws against money launderers working for terrorist groups, and the fight against drugs.

Jensen, Holger. "United States Should Take Cue from Terrorists Themselves." *Denver Rocky Mountain News*, August 25, 1998, n.p. (Also available online through paid Electric Library service, http://archives.insidedenver.com/.) The efforts of the Clinton administration to retaliate against terrorists have been largely ineffective. The Soviets and the Israeli Mossad agency deterred terrorists by going directly after them and killing them. The U.S. rejects assassination as uncivilized, but its military actions (such as cruise missile attacks on terrorist training camps) have had little effect on terrorist leaders.

Johnson, Larry C. "The Fall of Terrorism." *Security Management*, April 1997, p. 26. Contrary to both official statements and popular perception, terrorism has actually declined since the mid-1980s. Compared to a similar period in 1985–86, in 1995–96 there were fewer incidents, fewer casualties, fewer groups involved, and fewer countries sponsoring terrorists. This decline is due to better international coordination of antiterrorism efforts, additional resources given to law enforcement, and the fall of the Soviet Union.

Levitin, Howard. "Preparing for Terrorism: What Every Manager Needs to Know." *Public Management*, vol. 80, December 1998, p. 4ff. City managers must learn to view their communities as potential targets for terrorists, visualize potential weaknesses, and devise a step-by-step plan to deal with the threats. Responders must be trained in how to protect themselves before they can help citizens effectively. All public facilities must be reviewed for security. Employees at all levels need to know how to respond to various situations. A "universal plan" that can address considerations common to a number of different kinds of disasters and threats and that can be tailored to specific situations is more cost-effective than creating a complete, separate plan for each kind of situation.

Lucier, James P. "We Are What We Eat—and that Makes the United States Vulnerable." *Insight on the News*, vol. 14, November 16, 1998, p. 6. Experts at a conference of the National Consortium for Genomic Resources Management and Services (GenCon) have pointed out that the United States food supply is extremely vulnerable to accidental or intentional contamination. Because the U.S. has about a five-day local food supply, any attack that either disrupted food shipment or contaminated the food (such as with disease pathogens) could cause hoarding and severe economic losses. Attacks on crops and food animals could also destroy markets for U.S. food exports.

Methvin, Eugene H. "Hide and Seek: America's Impressive Record of Catching Terrorists Is Helping Keep their Activities to a Minimum." *National Review*, vol. 49, December 8, 1997, p. 37ff. Reports that federal agents are achieving greater success in catching and prosecuting terrorists. For example, Aimal Kansi, the sniper who killed two people and wounded three others outside CIA headquarters in Langley, Virginia, in 1993, was apprehended through a combination of forensic evidence, a $2 million reward, and a raid on his apartment in Pakistan. He was convicted of capital murder by a Virginia jury. The reduction in the average number of terrorist acts against U.S. citizens from 616 a year in 1984–88 to 389 a year from 1992–95 reflects this aggressive approach.

Morrocco, John D. "Hardening Concepts Tested to Counter Terrorist Blasts." *Aviation Week & Space Technology*, vol. 146, June 2, 1997, p. 44ff.

Reports on British tests of ways to "harden" aircraft interiors and compartments so that they can contain bomb blasts and prevent the plane from being destroyed.

Otero, Juan. "Commission Report Finds Federal Efforts Against Domestic Terrorism 'Inadequate'." *Nation's Cities Weekly*, vol. 22, July 26, 1999, p. 5. The Bipartisan Commission to Assess the Organization of the Federal Government to Combat the Proliferation of Weapons of Mass Destruction concludes that the United States needs a single agency to monitor the threat of weapons of mass destruction and report to the president. There are too many congressional committees with overlapping responsibilities.

Perry, Collin. "Bomb Squad." *Reader's Digest*, vol. 151, July 1997, p. 94ff. An interview with Detective Joe Paul of the Los Angeles Police Department's bomb squad. He explains the challenges faced by a modern bomb squad. Bombings have increased in number and sophistication, making planning and operations more complex.

Stiefel, Chana Freiman. "Science Strikes Back at Terrorism." *Science World*, vol. 53, November 1, 1996, p. 8ff. Discusses possible and emerging technologies for detecting weapons and explosives in airports and on planes. These include a wand that can "sniff" vapors from chemical explosives, an X-ray machine called the CTX 5000 that creates three-dimensional images like those in a hospital CAT scanner, and a device that uses high-energy X-rays to take "chemical fingerprints" of luggage contents. The chief obstacle to adopting these technologies, as one might expect, is cost.

Weiner, Tim. "Peering into Unknown, U.S. Agents Monitor Millennium Trouble Spots." *New York Times*, December 18, 1999. Available online. URL: http://www.nytimes.com (search). Reports on heightened security plans of the FBI and other government agencies as they prepare for possible terrorism during the turn of the new millennium. (Very little happened.)

Wilson, Jim. "Blowing Up a 747: A Dramatic Test Proves That Simple Improvements Can Checkmate Bomb-Wielding Terrorists." *Popular Mechanics*, vol. 174, October 1997, p. 56ff. The British Civil Administration has tested an improved aircraft cargo container that can hold in the force of a bomb exploding inside, protecting the plane carrying it. The container is made from material similar to that used in bulletproof vests.

INTERNET DOCUMENTS

Armond, Paul de. "Rock, Paper, Scissors: Counter-terrorism, anti-terrorism, and terrorism." Available online. URL: http://www.nwcitizen.com/publicgood/reports/rockpaperscissors/. Posted 1997. The author distinguishes between antiterrorism, which is a broad political strategy of combating terrorism through strengthening democracy, and counterterrorism, which is a military response that treats the fight against terrorism as a low-intensity military conflict. The circumstances under which antiterrorist and counterterrorist options are available vary with the nature of the terrorist threat and the structure of the target state. Responses to right-wing and millenarian terrorism in the contemporary United States are used as an example.

Terrorism Research Center. "Counterterrorist Organization Profiles." Available online. URL: http://www.terrorism.com/terrorism/CTgroups.html. Downloaded on April 27, 2000. Offers descriptions of counterterrorist, special operations, and hostage rescue/response units around the world, with additional links.

United States Department of State. "Democracy, Human Rights, and Labor." Available online. URL: http://www.state.gov/www/global/human_rights/index.html. Downloaded on April 27, 2000. This is the main page for the State Department's Bureau of Democracy, Human Rights, and Labor Affairs. It includes news items and reports including a link to the annual reports on human rights, which are organized by region and then by country. Significant human rights abuses are described and characterized.

United States Department of State. Bureau of Diplomatic Security, and the Overseas Security Advisory Council. "Personal Security Guidelines for the American Business Traveler Overseas." Brochure.

VIDEOS

"Incident in the Mediterranean." Alexandria, Va.: PBS Video, 1987. Video (VHS). 2 cassettes, 120 minutes. Two-part exploration of the decision-making process for dealing with a terrorist hostage crisis, using a hypothetical plane-hijacking scenario.

"Managing the Terrorism Events: The Oklahoma Experience." Springfield, Va.: National Audiovisual Center, 1996. Video (VHS). 120 minutes. Uses coverage of the initial response to the Oklahoma City bombing to explain the procedures to be followed by disaster response, medical, and law enforcement personnel in dealing with a major terrorist attack.

"Medical Response to Terrorism." Washington, D.C.: U.S. Veterans Administration, 1996. Interviews with experts on the different forms of terrorist incidents (explosions, chemical, biological, and psychological) give basic advice for health care professionals and planners.

"Search for the Master Terrorist: The Hunt for the Jackal." Princeton, N.J.: Films for the Humanities & Sciences, n. d. Video (VHS). 90 minutes. A narrative of the long and suspenseful hunt for one of the world's most notorious terrorists, "Carlos the Jackal" (Ilyich Ramirez Sanchez), who was captured in 1994.

Legal Issues

BOOKS

Chadwick, Elizabeth. *Self-Determination, Terrorism, and the International Humanitarian Law of Armed Conflict.* Boston, Mass.: M. Nijhoff, 1996. Focuses on terrorism conducted as part of a popular struggle for self-determination, a complex area that often blurs the distinction between terrorism and guerrilla war. Discusses the problem of applying international humanitarian law to such actions and the broader question of the strategy behind such terrorism and the failure of states to deter it.

Dempsey, James X., and David Cole. *Terrorism & the Constitution: Sacrificing Civil Liberties in the Name of National Security.* Los Angeles: First Amendment Foundation, 1999. Discusses the impact of federal counterterrorist laws and policies on civil liberties. Parts I and II discuss the implications of FBI investigations and actions during the 1980s and early 1990s against groups such as Amnesty International, Earth First!, and U.S. supporters of left-wing insurgencies in Central America, as well as the agency's attempt to enlist the aid of librarians in tracking potential terrorists. Part III is devoted to the Antiterrorism and Effective Death Penalty Act of 1996, discussing its core provisions and their implications.

Higgins, Rosalyn, and Maurice Flory. *Terrorism and International Law.* New York: Routledge, 1997. A comprehensive collection of documents, including laws and treaties, reflecting the response of the British, French, and international legal systems to terrorism. Includes discussion of the extent and existing limitations of international cooperation against terrorism.

Reisman, M., and Chris T. Antoniou. *The Laws of War: A Comprehensive Collection of Primary Documents on International Laws Governing Armed Conflict.* New York: Vintage Books, 1994. Because terrorist acts often arise during wars (particularly civil war and ethnic conflicts), this useful collection of sources on the law of armed conflict is also relevant to the student of terrorism.

ARTICLES AND PAPERS

Beown, Andrew. "The Price of Liberty." *New Statesman*, vol. 128, February 19, 1999, p. 41ff. A case in which a jury awarded $100 million to people who were threatened when publishers of an extremist antiabortion web site called the Nuremberg Files posted their names and addresses raises issues of free speech, as does a British site called Hansard Report containing Northern Irish Protestant leader Ian Paisley's list of Republicans accused of murdering Protestants in 1975. The author believes the threats to those listed are quite real, but the alternative of censorship is even worse.

Berg, Terrence. "Human Rights for Terrorists Beyond the Water's Edge." *America*, vol. 180, January 16, 1999, p. 14. The author, a federal prosecutor, argues that it is ironic and unfair that accused terrorists who have been arrested have legal rights and protections, but people abroad who are suspected of being terrorists can be bombed or attacked by missiles without any evidence that the targets really are guilty of terrorism. Surely some evidence should be identified before resorting to retaliatory military force.

Cole, David. "Terrorist Scare." *Nation*, vol. 268, April 19, 1999, p. 26. A Justice Department committee created during the Reagan administration and charged with identifying and deporting Palestinians with expired visas in an attempt to reduce terrorist infiltration into the United States has met legal rebuffs because of its failure to distinguish between "activists" who may share certain political sentiments and people actually involved in terrorist groups.

———. "Terrorizing the Constitution." *Nation*, March 25, 1996. Available online. URL: http://www.thenation.com/issue/960325/0325cole.htm. Discusses the politics of antiterrorism in the wake of the Oklahoma City bombing. Suggests that much of the talk about the "new terrorism" is hyperbole, and that the serious restrictions on civil liberties contained in the 1996 antiterrorism legislation are too high price to pay for what is actually only a small risk of terrorist attack.

Eland, Ivan. "Preserving Civil Liberties in an Age of Terrorism." *Issues in Science and Technology*, vol. 15, Fall 1998, p. 23ff. The author, director of defense policy studies at the Cato Institute, a libertarian think tank, disputes Secretary of Defense William Cohen's suggestion that U.S. citizens may have to consider a new balance between civil liberties and the government's ability to get intelligence about terrorist activities. He suggests that the nature of new weapons such as biological agents will make it hard even for expanded intelligence networks to gain information, and that law enforcement agencies have a tendency to use threats as an excuse to abuse their powers. The most effective way to diminish terrorism is to reevaluate U.S. foreign policy and minimize the kind of interventions in foreign affairs that are most likely to provoke terrorist attacks.

Finder, Joseph. "Tap Dance: Hooray for Wiretaps!" *New Republic*, vol. 215, September 16, 1996, p. 14ff. Argues that the American Civil Liberties Union (ACLU) and other libertarians were wrong in their successful campaign to remove "roving wiretap" authorization from the 1996 Antiterrorism bill. Roving wiretaps would have allowed authorities to get a single warrant to tap a suspect's communications regardless of the phone line used. The expense of monitoring wiretaps and the legal sanctions for their misuse provide adequate assurance that authorities would not abuse such warrants.

Freeh, Louis J. "What Can Be Done About Terrorism?" *USA Today Magazine*, January 1996, pp. 24–26. In response to the Oklahoma City bombing, FBI director Louis J. Freeh argues that his agency must have access to court-ordered wiretaps, which are threatened by the availability of encryption programs. Wiretaps are sometimes needed to uncover planned terrorist actions. (The government has advocated that encryption programs provide a "back door" or escrowed key to allow law enforcement officials to decrypt material that has been seized through a search warrant.)

Kopel, David B., and Joseph Olson. "Bipartisan Reign of Terror." *Liberty*, July 1996. Available online. URL: http://www.libertysoft.com/liberty/features/54kopel.html. Discusses the elements of the 1996 Antiterrorism and Effective Death Penalty Act as proposed by the administration and as passed. While a broad coalition of civil liberties groups were able to remove some of the most intrusive provisions, the final bill compromises basic rights of association, privacy, and due process.

"Get Personal." *New Republic*, vol. 219, September 14, 1998, p. 11ff. Argues that Executive Order 123333, signed by President Ford in 1976 and prohibiting the U.S. government from engaging in assassination of foreign leaders, has led to an absurd situation where the U.S. can destroy a factory used by terrorists, killing or injuring bystanders, but cannot intentionally target the terrorist leader himself. The order, while motivated by an idealistic desire not to fall to the moral level of the terrorist, fails to acknowledge the nature of the terrorist and the threat he poses.

"Is Profiling Discriminatory?" *Current Events*, vol. 97, January 30, 1998, p. 3. Among the measures proposed by a commission led by Vice President Al Gore following the crash of TWA flight 800 is CAPS (Computer Assisted Passenger Screening), a computerized profiling system that "scores" characteristics of airline passengers and identifies airline passengers who should be subject to additional scrutiny. The American Civil Liberties Union (ACLU), concerned that the secret profiling system could discriminate against passengers on the basis of ethnic background or other criteria, set up a web form to gather information about who was being stopped. The ACLU argues that because the criteria used are secret, it is difficult to tell if passengers' rights are being protected. The Federal Aviation Administration (FAA), however, claims the system will help catch terrorists and save lives.

Levy, Steven. "The Senate's Bomb Scare." *Newsweek*, vol. 128, August 12, 1996, p. 48. In the perennial conflict between security and freedom of speech, Democratic senator Dianne Feinstein of California has proposed an amendment that would make it illegal for web sites to carry information that could be used by bomb makers, such as the classic *Anarchist's Cookbook* or its modern descendants.

Lewis, Neil A. "Arab-Americans Protest 'Profiling' at Airports." *New York Times*, August 11, 1997, p. A10. Profiling of members of certain groups, such as Arab-Americans, who are supposedly associated with terrorism, raises civil liberties issues. When challenged, the airlines claim that they are just following Federal Aviation Administration (FAA) guidelines, but the FAA claims that the airlines are misinterpreting them. A new computerized screening system is supposed to avoid use of ethnicity as a criterion for picking out passengers for extra scrutiny.

Loundy, David. "Constitution Protects All Modes of Speech." *Chicago Daily Law Bulletin*, May 11, 1995, p. 6. Available online. URL: http://www.leepfrog.com/E-Law/CDLB/Terrorism.html. A technology-law columnist argues that while there are legitimate concerns about terrorists communicating knowledge of bomb-making or other plans for mayhem, electronic modes of speech such as e-mail or online bulletin boards enjoy the same First Amendment protections as do traditional mail or print media.

Meyers, Nechemia. "Tolerance vs. Terrorism?" *World & I*, July 1997, pp. 58–63. Compares the responses of democracies to extremist or hate speech. The United States and Israel give priority to freedom of speech, while Germany completely outlaws expressions of neo-Nazi ideology. Sometimes, as in the Waco incident, the media has compromised antiterrorist activities. The media must avoid becoming an amplifier for extremist ideas, but in some circumstances, such as with the Unabomber, providing a platform for a terrorist might help authorities identify him.

Rosen, Jeffrey. "Shell Game." *New Republic*, May 13, 1996, n.p. Also available online. Search at http://www.thenewrepublic.com/. The author argues that the Effective Death Penalty and Public Safety Act of 1996 (also called the Antiterrorism and Public Safety Act) will do little to fight terrorists. It will, however, erode the appeals rights of defendants and extend federal jurisdiction to thousands of crimes previously tried by the states.

Rubin, Amy Magaro. "U.S. Tests a New System to Track Foreign Students." *Chronicle of Higher Education*, vol. 44, September 19, 1997, p. A49ff. The Immigration and Naturalization Service is testing a new program that will closely track foreign students attending U.S. universities and colleges. Students will be photographed, fingerprinted, and issued bar-coded identification cards. Detailed computer files will be maintained for each student. Officials on some campuses, however, are objecting to the scheme as being too heavy-handed and intrusive.

Schweitzer, Glenn E., and Carole C. Dorsch. "Superterrorism: Searching for Long-Term Solutions." *Futurist*, vol. 33, June–July 1999, p. 40ff. An emerging "superterrorism" will use sophisticated weapons, including chemical and biological agents, and techniques such as computer hacking to cause mass casualties and cripple infrastructure. To make U.S. citizens willing to accept compromises on their liberty that may be needed in crisis situations, government and law enforcement agencies must reform and regain the peoples' trust. There must be much closer coordination between managers of vital vulnerable facilities and security agencies, and the public must be enlisted so they will be alert for suspicious circumstances. NATO must put counterterrorism high on its agenda so it can use its military power and resources when needed.

"Stand Up for Civil Liberties." *New Statesman*, vol. 127, August 28, 1998, p. 4. An editorial opposes proposals by British prime minister Tony Blair to extend conspiracy laws to cover the planning of terrorist actions to be taken overseas and to allow testimony of a single police officer to be sufficient proof of a person's belonging to an illegal organization. Such laws are likely to be imposed arbitrarily depending on attitudes toward the people or groups in question and may lead to arrests that exacerbate rather than improve the Northern Ireland peace process as it recovers from the Omagh bombing.

INTERNET DOCUMENTS

Electronic Privacy Information Center. "Critical Infrastructure Protection and the Endangerment of Civil Liberties: An Assessment of the President's Commission on Critical Infrastructure Protection (PCCIP)." Available online. URL: http://www.epic.org/security/infowar/epic-cip.html. A 1998 report discussing the Clinton administration's Commission on Critical Infrastructure Protection, which was created to assess vulnerabilities to terrorist attack in water, transportation, communications, and other areas. According to the author, the commission's recommendations regarding computer security, eavesdropping, encryption, and related areas pose a threat to privacy and other civil liberties.

Hecksher, Beth. "In the Interest of National Security: Secret Evidence Used to Detain, Deport Muslims." ABC News Online. February 11, 2000. Available online. URL: http://www.abcnews.go.com/sections/us/DailyNews/secretevidence000210.html. Part one of a two-part feature on the use of provisions of the 1996 Antiterrorism and Effective Death Penalty Act that allows the Immigration and Naturalization Service to detain or deport immigrants based on secret evidence of terrorist ties. The case of Hany Mahmoud Kiareldeen, held on secret evidence that he was involved with a group making death threats against Attorney General Janet Reno, is given as an example.

Israeli Supreme Court. "Judgement on the Interrogation Methods Applied by the GSS." Available online. URL: http://www.derechos.org/human-rights/mena/doc/torture.html. Posted September 6, 1999. Decision by the Israeli Supreme Court, which declared that interrogators of terrorist suspects could not be given the right to use physical means (such as violent shaking or forcing suspects to sit in a painful position), even when trying to get information about a pending bomb attack.

Kopel, David, and Joseph Olson. "Preventing a Reign of Terror: Civil Liberties Implications of Terrorism Legislation." Independence Institute. Originally published in the *Oklahoma City Law Review*, Summer/Fall 1996. Available online. URL: http://i2i.org/SuptDocs/Crime/Preventing_a_Reign_of_Terror.htm. The authors discuss a range of antiterrorist legislation proposed in the wake of the Oklahoma City bombings in 1995. They suggest that there are serious threats to civil liberties involved in the expansion of federal power and measures that threaten rights under the First, Second, Fourth, Fifth, and Fourteenth Amendments. Proper implementation of existing federal powers can provide adequate security against terrorism.

Obote-Odora, Alex. "Defining International Terrorism." *E-Law* (Murdoch University Electronic Journal of Law, vol. 6, March 1999. Available online. URL: http://www.murdoch.edu.au/elaw/issues/v6n1/obote-odora61.html. Develops a definition of terrorism in the light of international legal standards. The author points out that many experts feel the broad term "terrorism" is not helpful or appropriate in work for the United Nations or international legal bodies, who generally prefer to deal with specific types of crimes.

Ruppe, David. "Terrorism and the Constitution." ABC News Online. February 14, 2000. Available online. URL: http://www.abcnews.go.com/sections/us/DailyNews/terrorism000216.html. Part two of a feature on the use of secret evidence to detain or deport immigrants. Opponents of the practice cite freedom of association and speech, while government officials insist that the ability to use such evidence is a powerful and needed weapon against terrorism.

VIDEOS

"Allies and Extradition." Alexandria, Va.: PBS Video, 1987. Video (VHS). 60 minutes. If "one person's terrorist is another person's freedom fighter," then how should the United States decide whether to extradite a person accused of terrorism in an allied country such as Great Britain? This video explores that question.

"Protecting a Free Society." Alexandria, Va.: PBS Video, 1987. Video (VHS). 60 minutes. Looks at procedures for investigating terrorist activities and apprehending perpetrators, in the light of constitutional rights.

SPECIFIC TYPES OF TERRORISM

Weapons of Mass Destruction (General)

BOOKS

Brackett, D. W. *Holy Terror: Armageddon in Tokyo.* New York: Weatherhill, 1996. The author, a foreign correspondent specializing in Asia, looks at the Aum Shinri Kyo cult and its activities, which he characterizes as "ultraterrorism"—terrorism using weapons of mass destruction. He argues that terrorism based on religious fanaticism is a growing threat, particularly coupled with the ability to produce weapons such as nerve gas. He suggests that the United States must develop a comprehensive intelligence and response system to cope with the threat.

Falkenrath, Richard A., Robert D. Newman, and Bradley A. Thayer. *America's Achilles' Heel: Nuclear, Biological, and Chemical Terrorism and Covert Attack.* Cambridge, Mass.: MIT Press, 1998. The authors assess current and future capabilities of terrorists to deliver weapons of mass destruction in the United States and consider appropriate policies for gathering intelligence and reaction to specific threats. They suggest that the threat of attacks through chemical, biological, and even nuclear weapons has been underestimated, but a careful, multipronged approach to counterterrorism can mitigate the danger.

Hurley, Jennifer A. *Weapons of Mass Destruction: Opposing Viewpoints.* San Diego, Calif.: Greenhaven Press, 1999. Although written for high school students, this anthology of pro and con articles provides a useful introduction to the threat of use of weapons of mass destruction by terrorists and rogue states, and proposals for countering the threat.

Laqueur, Walter. *The New Terrorism: Fanaticism and the Arms of Mass Destruction.* New York: Oxford University Press, 1999. The author, one of the foremost experts on terrorism, argues that terrorism is taking a new and dangerous form. Traditional terrorist groups, motivated by coherent ideology or nationalism, are giving way to tiny, idiosyncratic groups driven by fanaticism, apocalyptic visions, or the desire for simple vengeance. At the same time, weapons of mass destruction (chemical, biological, even nuclear) are becoming more available, and the complex information systems at the heart of the modern economy have also become vulnerable to "cyberterrorism."

Schweitzer, Glenn E., and Carole C. Dorsch. *Superterrorism: Assassins, Mobsters and Weapons of Mass Destruction.* New York: Plenum Press, 1998. A somewhat sensational account of the threat of biological, chemical, and nuclear weapons getting into the hands of terrorists or criminals. Includes many interviews with diplomats, law enforcement and intelligence agents, and other experts.

Stern, Jessica. *The Ultimate Terrorists.* Cambridge, Mass.: Harvard University Press, 1999. Despite its ominous title, this introduction calmly and concisely places in perspective the threat of terrorism using weapons of mass destruction. The author suggests the threat is real and the effects of a chemical or biological attack could be grave, especially when the effects of panic are added to the initial damage. However, there are a variety of commonsense approaches that can minimize the threat.

ARTICLES AND PAPERS

Landay, Jonathan S. "Antiterror Effort Up, Evan as Threat Wanes." *Christian Science Monitor*, May 14, 1998, p. 3. Although the number of terrorist attacks fell by nearly two-thirds between 1987 and 1996, the Clinton administration plans to spend a record $7 billion on antiterrorism in 1997, up from $5 billion in 1996. Administration officials say that threats using new chemical, biological, and other weapons justify maintaining an increased effort.

Landay, Jonathan S. "Clinton's Antiterrorism Chief Marshals His Troops." *Christian Science Monitor*, July 1, 1998, p. 4. Interview with Richard Clarke, appointed by President Clinton to coordinate efforts to protect the United States from terrorism. Clarke will focus on preventing chemical, biological, and computer-based attacks. He points to the need to coordinate state public health agencies and local hospitals in order to deal with the massive casualties that might be caused by a biological attack.

Sprinzak, Ehud. "The Great Superterrorism Scare." *Foreign Policy*, Fall 1998, p. 110. In a detailed analysis of the risks, the author argues that the apocalyptic scenarios of terrorist attacks with weapons of mass destruction may seem compelling but can lead to bad policy. The high costs and limited effectiveness of countermeasures may actually help terrorists by weakening the state. The overestimation of the threat of "superterrorism" rests on two premises: that the means of mass destruction are readily available, and that the world has become a chaotic place where unpredictable groups abound. The means may be there, but in reality, what has been learned from decades of studying terrorist behavior suggests that terrorists in general are quite predictable. Such attacks would not meet the goals of most terrorists and the retaliation would impose unacceptable costs. A more limited approach to counterrorism emphasizing good intelligence, law enforcement, and a clear doctrine of deterrence would be more appropriate.

Webster, William. "Can We Stop the Super-Terrorist?" *Reader's Digest*, January 1997, pp. 93–96. Wiliam Webster, FBI director (1978–87) and CIA director (1987–91) gives recommendations for stopping the "super-terrorists" who threaten to unleash mass destruction through chemical, biological, or nuclear attack in the near future. He urges closer monitoring of extremist or hate groups, improving response and hostage rescue teams, and the use of rewards to obtain information on past or planned terrorist acts.

Chemical and Biological Terrorism

Books

Burke, Robert. *Counter-Terrorism for Emergency Responders.* Boca Raton, Fla.: Lewis Publishers, 2000. A handbook for paramedics, police, firefighters, and others who are first on the scene and may have to deal with an increasing number of chemical or biological terrorist attacks. The book provides step-by-step procedures for assessing and containing a situation and for aiding victims.

Cole, Leonard A. *The Eleventh Plague: The Politics of Biological and Chemical Warfare.* New York: W.H. Freeman, 1997. Discusses recent developments in biological and chemical warfare, particularly as they emerged in the Persian Gulf War with Iraq in 1991 and the terrorist nerve gas attack on a Tokyo subway in 1995. The author suggests that difficulties in detecting and preventing use of chemical and biological agents by rogue states or terrorist groups will prove to be formidable. The book ends with discussion of a proposal to minimize the threat through a multilayered web of detection, defensive efforts, and active response.

Graves, Barbara, ed. *Chem-Bio: Frequently Asked Questions.* Tempest Publishing, 1998. An introduction to biological and chemical agents that may be used by terrorists, including details on detection, delivery methods, effects, treatment of victims, and decontamination procedures. The book is particularly designed for critical incident first responders, such as paramedics, police, and firefighters.

Potomac Institute for Policy Studies. Counter Biological Terrorism Panel. *Countering Biological Terrorism in the U.S.* Dobbs Ferry, N.Y.: Oceana Publications, 1999. An evaluation by both military and civilian experts of U.S. readiness to cope with potential biological terrorist attacks. Current programs within the Department of Defense designed to detect and respond to such attacks are evaluated.

Venzke, Ben N., ed. *First Responder Chem-Bio Handbook.* Tempest Publishing, 1998. A succinct, practical guide to dealing with chemical or biological attacks. Topics include assessment, treatment, decontamination, and precautions for workers on the scene.

Annotated Bibliography

ARTICLES AND PAPERS

Danitz, Tiffany. "Terrorism's New Theater." *Insight*, January 26, 1998, p. 8ff. Biological agents such as anthrax and botulin toxin are increasingly available to and deliverable by terrorists and rogue nations such as Saddam Hussein's Iraq. Indeed, such agents can be created at home using readily available materials. The U.S. military is inoculating its troops against anthrax, but civilians will remain unprotected.

Gunby, Phil. "RAID Teams to Respond to Terrorism Threat." *JAMA, the Journal of the American Medical Association*, vol. 279, June 17, 1998, p. 1855. Describes how National Guard and other military reserve units will be forming RAID (Rapid Assessment and Initial Detection) teams in each of the 10 FEMA (Federal Emergency Management Agency) regions. The teams can intervene rapidly in case of chemical or biological attack. Each team will have access to specialists in decontamination, security, and medical response procedures. After an attack, the team would assess the damage, perform triage and begin to treat casualties, try to determine the precise agent used in the attack, and assess the need for additional help. The program is expected to phase in over the next five years.

Holloway, Harry C., et al. "The threat of biological weapons: prophylaxis and mitigation of psychological and social consequences." *JAMA, the Journal of the American Medical Association*, vol. 278, August 6, 1997, p. 425ff. Explores the psychological and social consequences of a biological attack. Panic, post-traumatic stress disorder, depression, and survivor guilt are all likely psychological effects. The invisible nature of the microbial threat increases fear. Social consequences might include a breakdown of institutions and loss of trust and cooperation. Psychiatric casualties among survivors must be promptly treated.

Kaplan, David E. "Anthrax Attack Is Said to Be Thwarted by FBI." *U.S. News & World Report*, vol. 124, March 2, 1998, p. 32. Reports how the FBI was alerted by a scientist that white supremacist and microbiologist Larry Wayne Harris wanted to use his laboratory to test anthrax cultures. The FBI arrested Harris and an accomplice, finding 40 petri dishes thought to contain anthrax or other pathogens.

———. "Terrorism's Next Wave: Nerve Gas and Germs Are the New Weapons of Choice." *U.S. News & World Report*, vol. 123, November 17, 1997, p. 26ff. A vivid account of the threat of chemical and biological attack. It begins with the discovery by an IRS investigator that right-wing "common law" movement extremist James Dalton Bell had stockpiled noxious chemicals and was plotting revenge for his troubles with the Internal Revenue Service. A variety of other incidents are described briefly, and the author notes that the FBI currently has 50 open investigations of possible attacks with chemical, biological, or radiological agents.

Paige, Sean. "At the Eleventh Hour." *Insight on the News*, vol. 14, January 26, 1998, p. 8ff. The United States is belatedly starting to take the threat of chemical and biological attack seriously. During the Persian Gulf War, Israel had to quickly develop massive civil defense plans against gas attacks, and European countries have also done some stockpiling of equipment and training of first responders. In 1996, the U.S. Congress established the Domestic Preparedness Program (DPP) to train cadres of trainers who in turn will train the first responders. As a backup to the civilian program, the U.S. Marine Corps has a new Chemical/Biological Incident Response Force, or CBIRF, and the U.S. Army Reserve and National Guard also have chemical defense units.

Simon, Jeffrey D. "Biological Terrorism: Preparing to Meet the Threat." *JAMA, the Journal of the American Medical Association*, vol. 278, August 6, 1997, p. 428ff. The inability to prevent a certain number of conventional terrorist attacks suggests that biological terrorist attacks on the United States will happen soon or later. Physicians and hospitals must prepare for them by studying the pathogens and toxins likely to be used (such as anthrax spores, botulin toxin, or ricin). The attack would most likely be carried out by an aerosol spray into a crowded area or perhaps through an air circulation system. Because there is no reliable detection or defense against such an attack, the focus should be on preparing first responders, other authorities, and the military to respond effectively. Dealing with mental health and stress problems of responders is also an important issue.

Tucker, Jonathan B. "National Health and Medical Services Response to Incidents of Chemical and Biological Terrorism." *JAMA, the Journal of the American Medical Association*, vol. 278, August 6, 1997, p. 362ff. A critique of current plans for federal agencies to provide specialized teams and equipment in response to a chemical or biological attack that overwhelms local resources, and to provide training through the Domestic Preparedness Program. The roles of the various agencies and programs are detailed. Response to a hoax anthrax attack on the Washington, D.C., office of the Jewish service organization B'nai B'rith was inappropriate and indicates the need for further training. (People exposed to the possible agent were quarantined in the building—they should have been moved to another location and observed rather than subject to possible continuing exposure.) A series of recommendations for improved planning, preparation, and integration of efforts is given.

Tucker, Jonathan B., and Amy Sands. "An Unlikely Threat." *Bulletin of the Atomic Scientists*, vol. 55, July 1999, p. 46. The authors suggest that the hype by both media and government leaders about the seriousness of the threat of chemical or biological terrorism may be unwarranted. A detailed study by the authors at the Center for Nonproliferation Studies at the

Monterey Institute of International Studies in Monterey, California, states that there have been no really significant chemical or biological terrorist attacks on U.S. soil and only one actual fatality. Yet government planners seeking big budget increases for fighting terrorism have played up worst-case scenarios, and such attacks have become a staple of movie thrillers. The authors' studies indicate that conventional political terrorists are unlikely to use weapons they view as unreliable or likely to cause massive governmental retaliation, but that terrorists motivated by fanatical or apocalyptic ideas may be more likely to embrace such weapons.

INTERNET DOCUMENTS

"Firefighting: Terrorism." Available online. URL: http://www.about.com (click on jobs/careers, then firefighting). Downloaded on April 27, 2000. Links to information about biological and chemical weapons and terrorist attacks, as well as general resources on terrorism.

Tucker, Jonathan B. "Historical Trends Related to Bioterrorism: An Empirical Analysis." *Emerging Infectious Diseases* Special Issue. vol. 5, July–August 1999. Available online. URL: http://www.cdc.gov/ncidod/EID/vol5no4/tucker.htm. An analysis of a database from the Chemical and Biological Weapons Nonproliferation Project at the Monterey Institute's Center for Nonproliferation Studies. A total of 415 incidents from 1900 to January 31, 1999, are classified according to materials used (chemical, biological, radiological), type of event (conspiracy to acquire, possession, threat, hoax, etc.), type of terrorist organization involved, motivation, and other factors. In general, motivation seems to have shifted from protest to separatist sentiment, retaliation, revenge, or apocalyptic prophecy. Symbolic buildings and the general population are more likely to be targeted.

Nuclear Terrorism

BOOKS

Allison, Graham T., ed. *Avoiding Nuclear Anarchy: Containing the Threat of Loose Russian Nuclear Weapons and Fissile Material.* Cambridge, Mass.: MIT Press, 1996. (CSIA Studies in International Security, No. 12). The contributing authors suggest ways to deal with the danger of nuclear weapons (or weapons materials) "leaking" out of Russia, where lack of regulation and oversight, combined with opportunism, may result in terrorist groups or rogue states obtaining nuclear capability with Russian help. They warn that current U.S. policies in this area are inadequate.

Lee, Rensselaer W. *Smuggling Armageddon: The Nuclear Black Market in the Former Soviet Union and Europe*. New York: St. Martin's Press, 1998. The author, an associate with the Foreign Policy Research Institute, investigates and documents the potential and actual illegal movement of nuclear material in Russia. Desperate economic conditions, chaos, and opportunism combine to create a worrisome situation. While many reports of nuclear smuggling turn out to be bogus or unsubstantiated, the possibility that organized crime or terrorists could gain access to some of the former Soviet Union's huge stockpile of nuclear materials or even warheads cannot be dismissed. Efforts by the U.S. and other governments to cope with the threat are incomplete and poorly coordinated.

ARTICLES AND PAPERS

Deutch, John M. "Combating the Threat of Nuclear Diversion." *USA Today Magazine*, vol. 125, January 1997, p. 36ff. The then CIA director explains the difficulties involved in preventing terrorists from gaining access to nuclear materials in the post–Cold War environment. Economic difficulties in the former Soviet Union increase the opportunities for illicit deals, and technology relevant to building nuclear weapons is widely diffused through the global market. The current status of nuclear efforts in Iran, Iraq, North Korea, Syria, Libya, and other nations is summarized. Terrorist groups may be able to kill people by dispersing radioactive material even without a nuclear explosion, and the Japanese Aum Shinri Kyo cult in their nerve gas attack demonstrated the ability of a terrorist group to develop sophisticated technical capabilities.

Nuckolls, John H. "Post–Cold War Nuclear Dangers: Proliferation and Terrorism." *Science*, vol. 267, February 24, 1995, p. 1112ff. A summary of the nuclear dangers facing the post–Cold War world. The large amount of now surplus nuclear material in dismantled Cold War arsenals is a potential target for black marketers and terrorists. More countries are gaining the ability to acquire or build nuclear weapons and may be motivated to use them in a sufficiently desperate situation. Nuclear expertise is now more readily available as many nuclear scientists and engineers in the former Soviet Union look for work. U.S. programs to monitor nuclear proliferation are described. Recommendations from the Nonproliferation Program Review Committee to prevent nuclear terrorism include building self-destruct devices into all nuclear weapons, having a "hot line" with Russian experts available to help disarm weapons, and creating "Red Teams" to probe security weaknesses. The article includes citations to statements and reports from government officials.

Nunn, Sam. "The New Terror: Nutcakes with Nukes." *New Perspectives Quarterly*, Winter 1996, vol. 13, n.p. The author, at the time ranking minority member of the Armed Services Committee of the United States Senate, warns that the Clinton administration has become overly fixated on exotic terrorist threats such as the nerve gas used in the Tokyo subway, even though such attacks have not been replicated and chemical and biological weapons are difficult to deliver effectively, due to weather, concentration, and other factors. Authorities should focus more on countering terrorists' most reliable weapon, the car or truck bomb, which has been used to destroy a Marine Corps barracks, embassies, the federal building in Oklahoma City, and other targets.

VIDEO

"The Terror Trade—Buying the Bomb." New York: Filmakers Library, 1989. Video (VHS), 55 minutes. Reports on attempts to buy nuclear material on the black market. Includes an interview with a Belgian arms dealer who arranged the sale of nuclear materials to countries seeking to develop nuclear weapons. Includes discussion by Senator John Glenn and former president Jimmy Carter.

Ecoterrorism and Animal Rights

BOOKS

Arnold, Ron. *Ecoterror: The Violent Agenda to Save Nature: The World of the Unabomber.* Bellevue, Wash.: Free Enterprise Press, 1997. The author describes the radical ecological agenda of ecoterrorists such as Earth First!, the Earth Liberation Front, and the Unabomber (whom he considers an ecoterrorist). Some reviewers suggest the author paints "deep ecologists" with too broad a brush.

ARTICLES AND PAPERS

Knickerbocker, Brad. "Animal Activists Get Violent." *Christian Science Monitor,* August 29, 1997, p. 5. A profile of radical animal rights groups, some of which have destroyed animal facilities or "liberated" animals from captivity. One of the most radical and active of such groups is the Animal Liberation Front (ALF).

———. "Concerns Rise as Ecoterrorists Expand Aim: Biotech Reasearch and Fur Farms Are the Latest Targets of Fringe Groups on the Far Left." *Christian Science Monitor,* April 3, 2000, p. 3. An update on developments in ecoterrorism. Ecoterrorists are adding genetic research facilities to their target list. Recent victims include a genetics facility (funded by the Monsanto Corporation) at the University of Michigan, a genetic-engineering project at the University of Minnesota, a Boise Cascade Corporation office in Monmouth, Oregon, and a genetic seed test orchard in British Columbia.

Markels, Alex, and Scott Willoughby. "BACKFIRE: Environmentalists Had Forged an Unusual Coalition with Locals and Animal Rights Activists to Oppose Vail's Growth—Until Ecoterrorists Torched the Mountain." *Mother Jones*, vol. 24, March 1999, p. 60. In the worst ecoterrorist attack in the United States, arsonists linked to the Animal Liberation Front caused $12 million worth of damage to ski resorts in Vail, Colorado. Activists who had built a coalition opposing further expansion of the ski industry on Vail Mountain suddenly found themselves on the defensive as they faced suspicion and outrage from thousands of people who worked in the ski and tourist industry.

Wells, Janet. "Animal Activists Raise the Stakes in Eco-Attacks." *San Francisco Chronicle*, April 21, 2000, pp. A1, A19. Reports on a number of recent attacks by members of the Animal Liberation Front (ALF) in California. The group, which is loosely organized into small cells, apparently maintains communication through a number of web sites. Spokesperson David Barbarash says the group's main objective is to use property damage to cause financial hardship, thus encouraging targets to stop abusing animals for research.

Cyberterrorism

Books

Center for Strategic & International Studies. *Cybercrime, Cyberterrorism, Cyberwarfare: Averting an Electronic Waterloo.* Washington, D.C.: CSIS Press, 1998. Summary available online: URL: http://www.csis.org/pubs/cyberfor.html Report by a task force on the vulnerability of U.S. information systems to hackers and terrorist attack, with recommendations for countering the threat. The United States must develop a comprehensive plan that understands the nature of the information revolution, identifies and secures government functions, understands the needs of the private sector, and provides oversight for the military's use of information warfare.

Articles and Papers

"Clinton Outlines Anti-Terrorism Plan." *InfoWorld*, vol. 21, January 25, 1999, p. 5. Describes President Clinton's new initiative to combat computer-based terrorism. He proposes that $1.46 billion be spent on research, improved detection systems, hiring additional government computer experts, and cooperation between government and the private sector.

Devost, Matthew G., Brian K. Houghton, and Neil Allen Pollard. "Information Terrorism: Political Violence in the Information Age." *Terrorism and Political Violence*, vol. 9, Spring 1997, n.p. The dependence of developed nations on information systems makes information warfare increasingly important. Information warfare techniques used by terrorist groups could cause direct damage, by causing plane crashes, for example, or cause indirect damage by paralyzing transportation, power, or banking systems. The need to strengthen information security while protecting civil liberties poses a difficult challenge.

Laqueur, Walter. "Postmodern Terrorism." *Foreign Affairs*, September/October 1996, n.p. An analyst with the Center for Strategic and International Studies and author of numerous books on terrorism, Laqueur points to the vulnerability implied in modern society's dependence on extensive information systems, most of which are now becoming available via the Internet. "Infoterrorism" and "cyberwarfare" are becoming a reality, and if terrorist groups recruit capable hackers, they could cause economic paralysis by shutting down banking or credit card systems.

Levy, Stephen, and Brad Stone. "Hunting the Hackers." *Newsweek*, vol. 135, February 21, 2000, p. 38. Describes the "denial of service" attacks by hackers who paralyzed major e-commerce sites such as Yahoo! and eBay. While the hackers were not linked to terrorist groups, the attack underscores the vulnerability of the "new economy" to cyberattack.

Maglitta, Joseph E. "Cyberterrorism Is a Serious Threat." *Computerworld*, April 19, 1999, p. 35. The 1999 Melissa virus scare (in which a virus was spread through e-mail attachments) should serve the useful purpose of alerting business managers, the military, and government officials to the very real threat of cyberterrorism. Although Congress recently appropriated $1.4 billion to combat information terrorism, many people in key positions are still not taking the threat seriously. One obstacle is the reluctance of companies to share information about attacks out of fear of legal liability or frightening away customers.

Maier, Timothy W. "Is U.S. Ready for Cyberwarfare?" *Insight on the News*, vol. 15, April 5, 1999, p. 18. Despite increasing evidence that a variety of hostile nations such as Iraq, Syria, Iran, and Libya have already attempted to break into U.S. computers, the United States is not well prepared for such attacks. While some figures (such as "250,000 hacker attempts on the Pentagon in 1995") are greatly inflated, there is evidence of real attacks.

Sher, Hanan. "www.terror." *Jerusalem Report*, June 8, 1998, pp. 32–41. An introduction to the terrifying possibilities of information warfare. By using computer viruses or other hacker techniques, terrorists or enemy governments could cripple the infrastructure of advanced technological societies such as the United States or Israel that depend on information systems for the basic necessities of modern life—air transport, banking, phones, power, even water. Doctored computer chips could be used for spying or for crippling weapons systems.

Whitelaw, Kevin. "Terrorists on the Web: Electronic 'Safe Haven': Guerrillas Use Guns, Bombs, and Home Pages." *U.S. News & World Report*, vol. 124, June 22, 1998, p. 46. Although most observers focus on the potential of terrorist groups to attack computer systems, the other side of the story is the growing extent to which such groups are using the information superhighway to spread their message and coordinate their efforts. ELN in Colombia, the Zapatistas in Mexico, and Hezbollah in Lebanon all have extensive web sites. Trying to force such groups off the Internet would violate the freedom of expression that is at the heart of the new medium. Example web addresses are included.

INTERNET DOCUMENTS

Borland, John, and William Church. "Analyzing the Threat of Cyberterrorism." *Techweb News*. Available online. URL: http://www.techweb.com (search news index). Posted September 23, 1998. In an interview with John Borland, William Church, managing director of a company that monitors computer infrastructure problems, says that while individual hackers and crackers have attacked or exploited information systems, sometimes for criminal purposes, terrorist groups have not yet adopted such techniques. Terrorists generally put their trust in weapons they understand, such as bombs. Most terrorists also prefer weapons that cause direct, sensational damage.

Mosquera, Mary. "Clinton Seeks More Funds for Cyberterrorism." *Techweb News*. Available online. URL: http://www.techweb.com (search news index). Posted January 22, 1999. As part of a package of antiterrorism proposals, President Clinton wants the U.S. to spend about $515 million on protecting the U.S. computer infrastructure from terrorist threats. Proposed measures include new software that can identify attacks such as "trojan horse" programs (a program that can be surreptitiously placed in a computer system and that can steal secret information, such as users' passwords), as well as expanding a computer-alert system that warns users about attacks. A "Cyber Corps" would recruit more computer experts to help the government protect its computer systems. Privacy advocates such as David Banisar of the Electronic Privacy Information Center warn that the proposals would lead to diminished privacy and urge that the government relax controls on encryption software that can be used to protect data from spies.

CHAPTER 9

ORGANIZATIONS AND AGENCIES

Following are listings for organizations and agencies involved with terrorism-related issues. These include government agencies, academic research institutes, and civil liberties and human rights organizations.

American Civil Liberties Union (ACLU)
URL: http://www.aclu.org
E-mail: aclu@aclu.org
Phone: (212) 549-2500
125 Broad Street, 18th Floor
New York, NY 10004-2400
Founded in 1920, the ACLU conducts extensive litigation on constitutional issues including privacy and free speech. This focus often brings the group into conflict with much antiterrorism legislation.

Amnesty International
URL: http://www.amnesty.org (international)
URL: http://www.aiusa.org (U.S.)
E-mail: admin-us@aiusa.org
Phone: (202) 544-0200
Washington Office
600 Pennsylvania Avenue, SE
5th Floor
Washington, DC 20003
This worldwide human rights group publicizes human rights abuses around the world and seeks to mobilize world opinion against oppressive governments. Since human rights abuses are often related to terrorism and counterterrorism, this organization's reports and other resources can be quite useful.

Anti-Defamation League (ADL)
URL: http://www.adl.org
E-mail: webmaster@adl.org
Anti-Defamation League
823 United Nations Plaza
New York, NY 10017
Based on its focus on combating anti-Semitism and the numerous terrorist attacks on Jews, the ADL generally takes a strong position in support of antiterrorism legislation. For example, the group filed an amicus brief supporting the government in *Humanitarian Law*

Project v. Reno, arguing that provisions of the 1996 Antiterrorism and Effective Death Penalty Act prohibiting U.S. citizens from giving any kind of aid to government-designated terrorist groups was reasonable and necessary because there is no way to separate "peaceful" aid from aid that furthers a group's violent agenda. The ADL has a web page at http://www.adl.org/frames/front_terrorism_up.html called "Terrorism Update." It provides periodic reports on international and domestic terrorism.

Center for Democracy and Technology
URL: http://www.cdt.org
E-mail: webmaster@cdt.org
Phone: (202) 637-9800
1634 I Street NW, Suite 1100
Washington, DC 20006
Civil liberties group that works to "promote democratic values and constitutional liberties in the digital age." Has a "Counter-Terrorism Issues Page" at http://www.cdt.org/policy/terrorism/ that includes links to news about legislation relating to terrorism, particularly wiretapping and computer surveillance.

Centre for the Study of Terrorism and Political Violence (St Andrews University)
URL: http://www.st-and.ac.uk/academic/intrel/research/cstpv/
E-mail: CSTPV@st-andrews.ac.uk
Phone: 44 (0)1334 462938
Department of International Relations
University of St Andrews
St Andrews
KY16 9AL
Scotland
A Scottish academic research center that provides an extensive database and links at its web site.

Derechos Human Rights
URL: http://www.derechos.org/
E-mail: hr@derechos.org
Phone: (510) 483-4005
P.O. Box 43299
Oakland, CA 94624-0299
Described as "the first Internet-based human rights organization," Derechos publicizes, investigates, and works to end human rights abuses around the world. Its regional pages (such as the one for Africa) provide useful reports and links to human rights issues by country.

Electronic Frontier Foundation (EFF)
URL: http://www.eff.org
E-mail: ask@eff.org
Phone: (415) 436-9333
1550 Bryant Street, Suite 725
San Francisco, CA 94103-4832
Organization formed in 1990 to maintain and enhance intellectual freedom, privacy, and other values of civil liberties and democracy in networked communications. It publicizes and campaigns against antiterrorism legislation that it considers repressive or threatening

to privacy. The group publishes newsletters, Internet guidebooks, and other documents; provides mailing lists and other online forums; and hosts a large electronic document archive.

Electronic Privacy Information Center (EPIC)
URL: http://www.epic.org
E-mail: info@epic.org
Phone: (202) 544-9240
666 Pennsylvania Avenue, SE
Suite 301
Washington, DC 20003
EPIC was established in 1994 to focus public attention on emerging privacy issues relating to the national information infrastructure. Some of these issues, such as the Clipper Chip and the Digital Telephony proposal, have arisen from antiterrorism legislation. The organization publishes the *EPIC Alert* newsletter and leads campaigns on privacy issues.

First Amendment Foundation
URL: http://www.floridafaf.org/
E-mail: foi@vashti.net
Phone: (800) 337-3518
336 East College Avenue
Tallahassee, FL 32301
Florida-based organization that seeks to strengthen First Amendment rights and to educate the public about their importance. It has expressed serious concerns about the 1996 Antiterrorism and Effective Death Penalty Act, and published a book in 1999 titled *Terrorism & The Constitution*, which detailed concerns about the legislation and reviewed the history of abuses of the rights of dissident groups and immigrants by the FBI and other federal agencies.

Human Rights Watch
URL: http://www.hrw.org/
E-mail: hrwnyc@hrw.org
Phone: (212) 290-4700
350 Fifth Avenue, 34th Floor
New York, NY 10118-3299
A group dedicated to investigating and publicizing human rights violations around the world and working for reforms that strengthen human rights. Its web site offers access by region and country to reports on human right abuses, as well as offering the group's annual World Report and an extensive catalog of publications.

Humanitarian Law Project
URL: http://hlp.home.igc.org
Phone: (310) 836-6316
8124 West Third Street, Suite 105
Los Angeles, CA 90048
Supports legal protection for international humanitarian efforts. Became involved with the debate and subsequent litigation over the Antiterrorism Act of 1996, because the law includes a provision prohibiting U.S. citizens from giving humanitarian aid to or through groups that the federal government has designated as terrorist. In 1998, the project filed a suit, *Humanitarian Law Project v. Reno*, seeking to overturn that provision.

International Association for Counterterrorism & Security Professionals
URL: http://www.iacsp.com/
P.O. Box 10265
Arlington, VA 22210
An organization for professionals involved with security and counterterrorism issues. Has two member publications, the *Journal of Counterterrorism & Security* and the *Counterterrorism & Security Report.* Pages on the web site include Terrorism Watch, which summarizes recent news developments, Terror Info Bank, and an archive of selected articles from the organization's publications.

International Policy Institute for Counter-Terrorism
URL: http://www.ict.org.il/
E-mail: services@ict.org.il
Fax: 972-9-9513073
ICT
Interdisciplinary Center Herzlia
P.O. Box 167
Herzlia, 46150
Israel
A research institute and think tank in Herzliya, Israel, primarily concerned with developing public policy and strategies to deal with terrorism as a global issue. Offers publications and holds conferences. The web site includes news updates and background data about terrorist groups and attacks.

McGill University
Seminar on Terrorism and Political Violence
URL: http://www.arts.mcgill.ca/programs/polisci/marrett/marrett1.html
E-mail:cyr6@musica.mcgill.ca
Phone: (514) 398-4800
Department of Political Science
McGill University
855 Sherbrooke Street West
Montréal, Québec
Canada
Conducts annual seminar series. The topic for the 1999–2000 seminar series is "Into a New Millennium: War, Peace and International Institutions in the 21st Century."

National Committee Against Repressive Legislation
E-mail: kgage@igc.apc.org
Phone: (202) 529-4225
NCARL Washington Office
3321 12th Street NE, 3rd Floor
Washington, DC 20017
ATTN: Kit Gage, Washington Representative
A civil liberties group that specializes in fighting legislation that would restrict rights of speech or political expression. It is frequently involved in the debate over new counterterrorism legislation such as the 1996 Antiterrorism Act.

Southern Poverty Law Center
URL: http:/www.splcenter.org
400 Washington Avenue
Montgomery, AL 36104
This organization monitors the activities of Ku Klux Klan and other hate groups as well as Patriot groups and militias. Its projects have included Klanwatch (founded

in 1981) and the Militia Task Force (1995). The home page for the Intelligence Project, which monitors hate groups, is at URL: http://www.splcenter.org/intelligenceproject/ip-index.html. The organization also publishes the quarterly *Intelligence Report* available at the web site, and it also conducts tolerance education.

Terrorism Research Center
http://www.terrorism.com/welcome.htm
E-mail: TRC@terrorism.com
An independent organization conducting research and providing public information on terrorism and related issues. The organization's web site provides extensive resource links.

United States Department of Health and Human Services
Centers for Disease Control and Prevention
Bioterrorism Preparedness and Response Network
URL: http://www.bt.cdc.gov/
Phone: (800) 311-3435
The Centers for Disease Control and Prevention has, like many other federal agencies, undertaken new initiatives to assess and deal with the threat of biological terrorism. Its Bioterrorism Preparedness and Response web page includes links to background information, news, official statements, and emergency services. Procedures for notification in case of actual or threatened biological attacks are outlined.

United States Department of Justice
Federal Bureau of Investigation (FBI)
URL: http://www.fbi.gov
Phone: (202) 324-5520
935 Pennsylvania Avenue, NW
Washington, DC 20535
The FBI investigates incidences of terrorism and compiles data on domestic terrorism.

United States Department of Justice
Domestic Preparedness Office
URL: http://www.ndpo.gov/
E-mail: ndpo@leo.gov
Phone: (202) 324-9026
Fax: (202) 324-2224
This office, formed in 1998 by agreement of the Department of Justice and other federal agencies, is charged with coordinating the federal efforts to prepare for and respond to attacks using weapons of mass destruction against U.S. targets, presumably by terrorists.

United States Department of State
URL: http://www.state.gov/www/ind.html
E-mail: publicaffairs@panet.us-state.gov
Phone: (202) 647-6675
Bureau of Public Affairs
Room 6808
Washington, DC 20520-6810
The U.S. State Department provides a variety of resources dealing with foreign affairs, including annual reports on human rights

abuses and terrorism. The above web site provides an index to these resources.

United States Department of State
Office of the Coordinator for Antiterrorism
URL: http://www.state.gov/www/global/terrorism/index.html
E-mail: secretary@state.gov
Phone: (202) 647-6575
Public Information
Bureau of Public Affairs, Room 6808
U.S. Department of State
Washington, DC 20520

This office coordinates antiterrorism efforts with foreign governments and provides reports and advisories to the general public. It is a good source of official information.

PART III

APPENDICES

APPENDIX A

ACRONYMS FOR TERRORIST GROUPS

The following acronyms are commonly used for various terrorist or related groups. (This is a somewhat larger selection of groups than those profiled in Chapter 2.)

AD Action Directe (France)
AIM American Indian Movement
ALF Animal Liberation Front (United States)
ALF Arab Liberation Front (part of the PLO) (Middle East)
ANC African National Congress (South Africa)
ANO Abu Nidal Organization (Middle East)
ANYOLP Arab National Youth Organization for the Liberation of Palestine (Middle East)
ASALA Armenian Secret Army for the Liberation of Armenia (Armenia)
BLA Black Liberation Army (United States)
BR Brigate Rosse, Red Brigades (Italy)
BSO Black September Organization (Middle East)
CSA The Covenant, the Sword, and the Arm of the Lord (United States)
DFLP Democratic Front for the Liberation of Palestine (Middle East)
ELF Earth Liberation Front (assumed to be same as Animal Liberation Front) (United States)
ELF Eritrean Liberation Front (or Eritrean People's Liberation Front) (Eritrea/Ethiopia)
ELN Ejército de Liberación Nacional (National Liberation Army) (used by a Colombian and a Bolivian group)
ETA Euzkadita Azkatasuna (Basque Fatherland and Liberty) (Spain)—also ETA-M (militant) and ETA-PM (moderate)

FAL Frente Argentino de Liberación (Argentine Liberation Front) (Argentina)
FAL Fuerzas Armadas de Liberación (Armed Forces of Liberation) (member of FMLN, El Salvador)
FALN Fuerzas Armadas de Liberación Nacional (Armed Forces of National Liberation) (Puerto Rico)
FARC Fuerzas Armadas Revolucionarios de Colombia (Armed Revolutionary Forces of Colombia) (Colombia)
FIS Jabha al Islamiyah li-Inqadh (Islamic Salvation Front) (Algeria)
FLN Front de Libération National (National Liberation Front) (Algeria)
FLQ Front de Libération du Québec (Quebec Liberation Front) (Canada)
FMLN Frente Farabundo Martí de Liberación Nacional (Farabundo Martí National Liberation Front) (El Salvador)
FNLC Front de la Libération Nationale de la Corse (Corsican Liberation Front) (Corsica)
FRC Fatah Revolutionary Council (Abu Nidal Organization; Middle East)
FRELIMO Mozambican Liberation Front (Mozambique)
FRP-LZ Fuerzas Revolucionarios Populares Lorenzo Zelaya (Lorenzo Zelaya Popular Revolutionary Forces) (Honduras)
FSLN Frente Sandinista de Liberación Nacional (Sandinista National Liberation Front) (Nicaragua)
GBR Bandero Roja (Red Flag) (Venezuela)
GIA Groupe Islamique Armée (Armed Islamic Group) (Algeria)
GRAPO Grupo de Resistencia Antifascista, Primero de Octubre (First of October Antifascist Resistance Group) (Spain)
HUM Harakat ul-Mujahadeen (Pakistan, India)
IG Al Gama'at al-Islamaya, Islamic Group (Middle East)
IRA Irish Republican Army (Northern Ireland)
IWW Industrial Workers of the World (United States)
JDL Jewish Defense League (United States and Israel)
JRA Japanese Red Army, also ARJ (Japan)
KKK Ku Klux Klan (United States)
LEHI Lohame Herut Israel, also called Stern Gang (Israel)
LTTE Liberation Tigers of Tamil Eelam, or Tamil Tigers (Sri Lanka)
LVF Loyalist Volunteer Force (Ireland)
M-19 Movimiento 19 de Abril (April 19th Movement) (Colombia)
MIR Movimiento de la Izquerda Revolucionaria (Movement of the Revolutionary Left) (Chile, Peru, and Venezuela)
MLF Moro Liberation Front (Philippines)

Appendix A

MLN	Movimiento de Liberación Nacional (National Liberation Movement)—Tupamaros (Uruguay)
MNR	Mozambique National Resistance (later, RENAMO) (Mozambique)
MPL	Cinchoneros Popular Liberation Movement (Honduras)
MR-8	Movimiento Revolucionario do Octobre 8 (Revolutionary Movement of October 8) (Brazil)
MRTA	Movimiento Revolucionario Tupac Amaru (Tupac Amaru Revolutionary Movement) (Peru)
NAYLP	National Arab Youth for the Liberation of Palestine (Middle East)
NORAID	Irish Northern Aid Committee (Northern Ireland, United States)
NPA	New Peoples' Army (Philippines)
NSWPP	National Socialist White People's Party (neo-Nazi, United States)
NWLF	New World Liberation Front (United States)
OAS	Organization Armée Secrete (Secret Army Organization) (Algeria)
PDFLP	Democratic Front for the Liberation of Palestine (Middle East)
PFLP	Popular Front for the Liberation of Palestine (Middle East)
PFLP-GC	Popular Front for the Liberation of Palestine-General Command (Middle East)
PIRA	Provisional Wing, Irish Republican Army (Northern Ireland)
PKK	Partiya Karkaran Kurdistan, Kurdistan Workers' Party (Turkey)
PLF	Palestine Liberation Front (Middle East)
PLO	Palestine Liberation Organization (Middle East)
PSF	Popular Struggle Front (Middle East)
RAF	Rote Armee Faktion (Red Army Faction) (Germany)
RENAMO	Resistência Nacional Moçambicana (Mozambique National Resistance) or MNR (Mozambique)
RZ	Revolutionaere Zellen (Red Cells) (Germany)
SL	Sendero Luminoso (Shining Path) (Peru)
SLA	Symbionese Liberation Army (United States)
UDA	Ulster Defense Association (Northern Ireland)
UFF	Ulster Freedom Fighters (Nothern Ireland)
UFF	United Freedom Front (United States)
UNITA	União Nacional para a Independência Total de Angola (National Union for the Total Independence of Angola) (Angola)
WAR	White Aryan Resistance (United States)
UVF	Ulster Volunteer Force (Northern Ireland)
ZAF	Zapata Armed Front (Mexico)
ZAPU	Zimbabwe African Peoples' Union (Rhodesia/Zimbabwe)

APPENDIX B

STATISTICS ON TERRORISM

Most of the following statistics are excerpted from the Department of State publication *Patterns of Global Terrorism 1999*. This publication may be browsed online at http://www.state.gov/www/global/terrorism/1999report/ 1999index.ht ml.

International Terrorist Attacks

TOTAL TERRORIST ATTACKS, 1980–99

The graph "Total International Terrorist Attacks, 1980–99" indicates the total number of terrorist attacks worldwide from 1980 through 1999. The number of attacks peaked in the late 1980s and the overall trend in the 1990s was downward, although 1999 shows an upward spike.

Appendix B

TOTAL INTERNATIONAL TERRORIST ATTACKS, 1980–1999

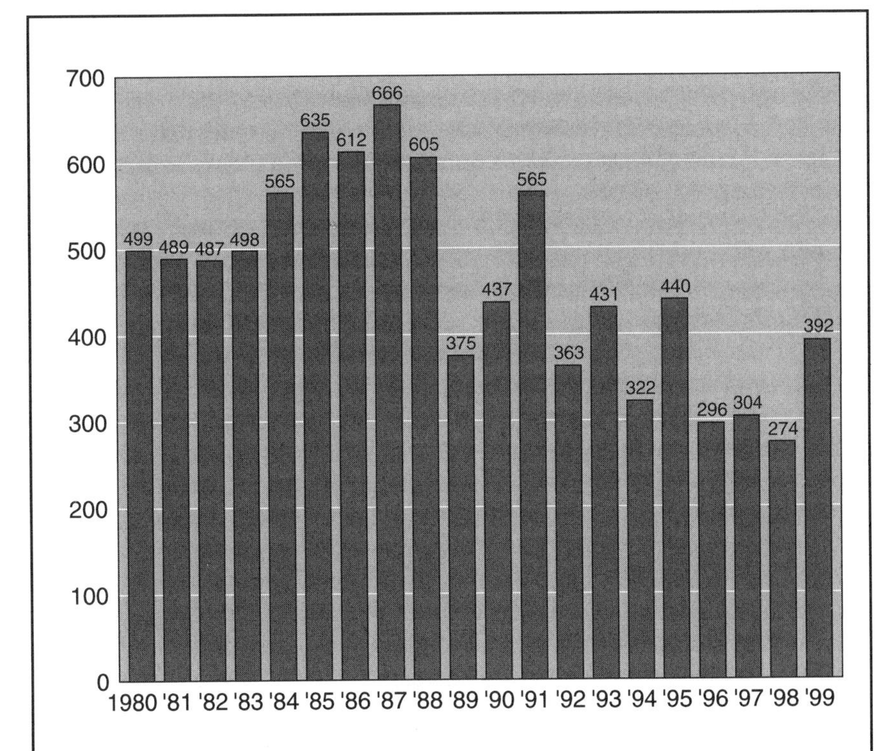

Note: The criteria for counting terrorist attacks have been revised over the years, so this chart cannot be compared directly with ones published earlier. See Appendix C of *Patterns of Global Terrorism 1999* for further details.

Source: U.S. Department of State. *Patterns of Global Terrorism 1999.*
URL: http://www.state.gov/www/global/terrorism/1999report/1999index.html.

FREQUENCY OF ATTACKS BY REGION, 1994–99

The graph "Total International Attacks by Region, 1994–99" breaks down the total number of international terrorist attacks by region for the years 1994–99. (The high total for western Europe predominately reflects activity in Northern Ireland.)

TOTAL INTERNATIONAL ATTACKS BY REGION, 1994–1999

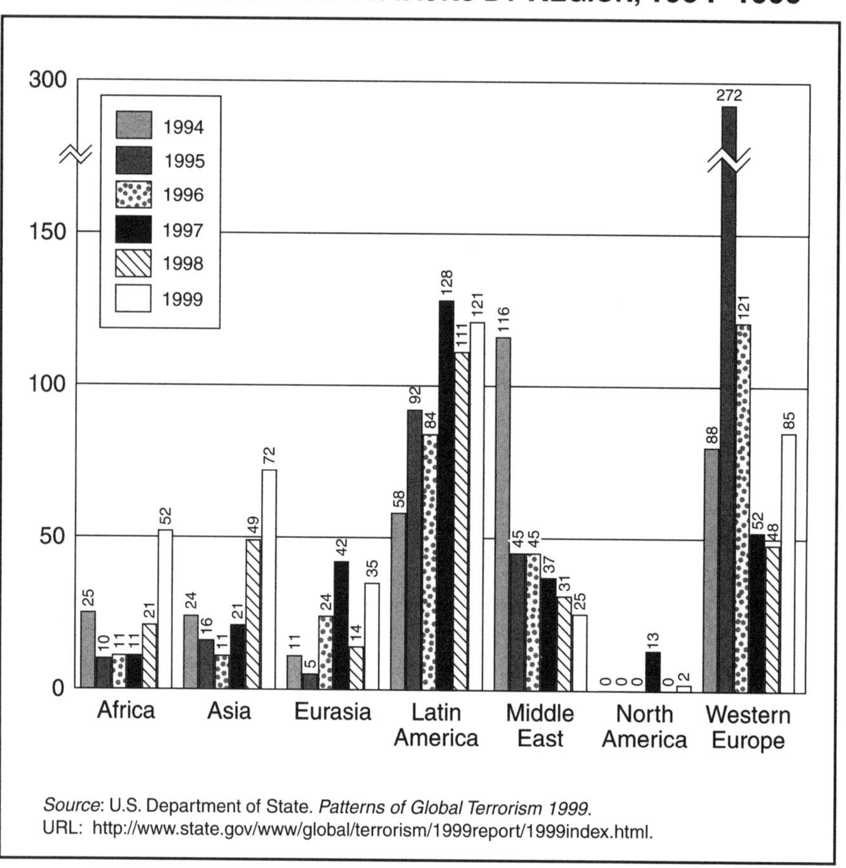

Source: U.S. Department of State. *Patterns of Global Terrorism 1999.*
URL: http://www.state.gov/www/global/terrorism/1999report/1999index.html.

SEVERITY OF TERRORISM BY REGION, 1994–99

The graph "Total International Casualties by Region, 1994–99" breaks down the casualties caused by international terrorist attacks by region for the years 1994–99. (Note the "scale break" marks indicating some of the higher figures are not drawn to scale.) It is hard to draw conclusions from this data because just a few incidents or situations can cause disproportionate numbers of casualties. If one excludes the two "spikes" in Africa (caused

TOTAL INTERNATIONAL CASUALTIES BY REGION, 1994–1999

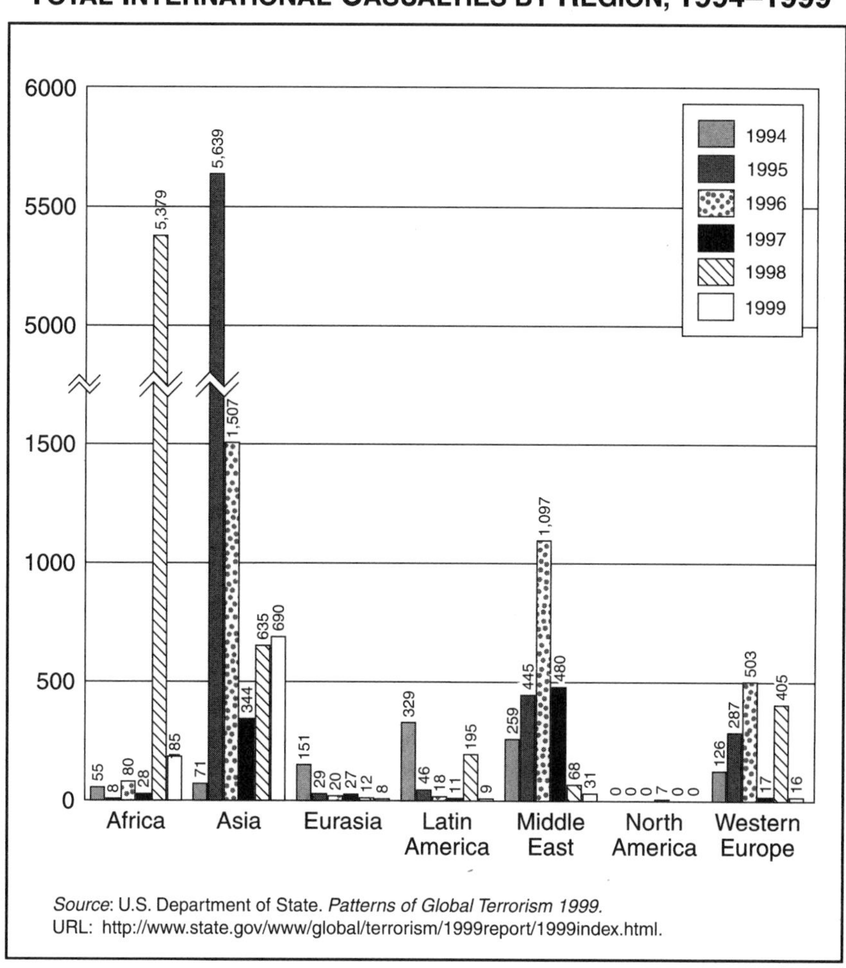

Source: U.S. Department of State. *Patterns of Global Terrorism 1999.*
URL: http://www.state.gov/www/global/terrorism/1999report/1999index.html.

by the bombings of two U.S. embassies in 1998) and Asia in 1995, the Middle East tends to have the most casualties, followed by western Europe (which is primarily accounted for by Northern Ireland). In most years there are actually very few victims of international terrorism (that is, terrorism not of domestic origin) in the United States.

ATTACKS AGAINST U.S. CITIZENS OR FACILITIES

ATTACKS ON AMERICANS BY REGION (1999)

The pie chart "Total Anti–U.S. Attacks by Region, 1999" breaks down attacks on U.S. citizens and facilities in 1999 by region. As has been generally true, by far the largest number of such attacks occurred in Latin America.

TOTAL ANTI-U.S. ATTACKS BY REGION, 1999

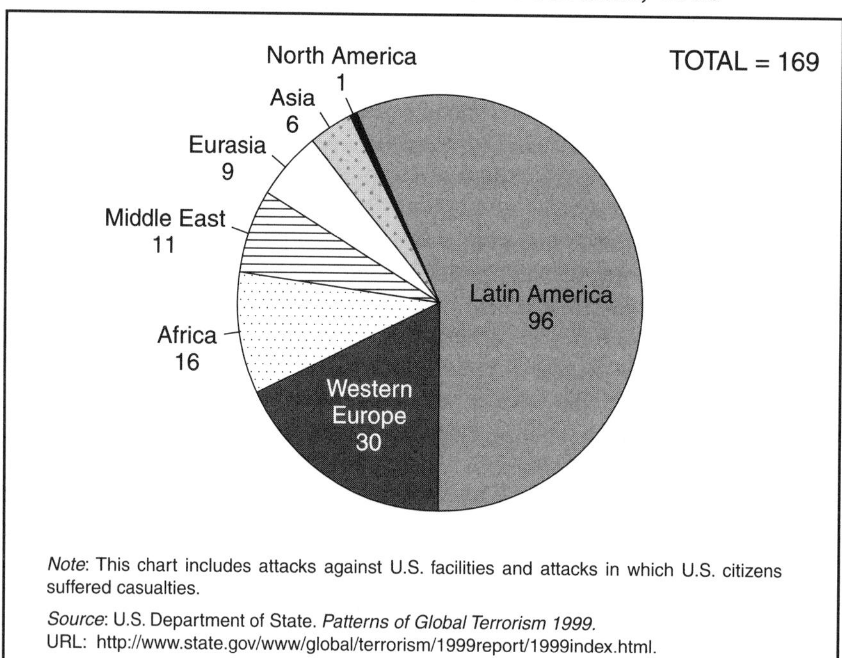

Note: This chart includes attacks against U.S. facilities and attacks in which U.S. citizens suffered casualties.

Source: U.S. Department of State. *Patterns of Global Terrorism 1999.*
URL: http://www.state.gov/www/global/terrorism/1999report/1999index.html.

Types of Terrorist Attacks (1999)

The pie chart "Total Anti–U.S. Attacks by Type of Event, 1999" breaks down the attacks against U.S. citizens and facilities by type. Clearly, the bomb remains the weapon of choice.

TOTAL ANTI-U.S. ATTACKS BY TYPE OF EVENT, 1999

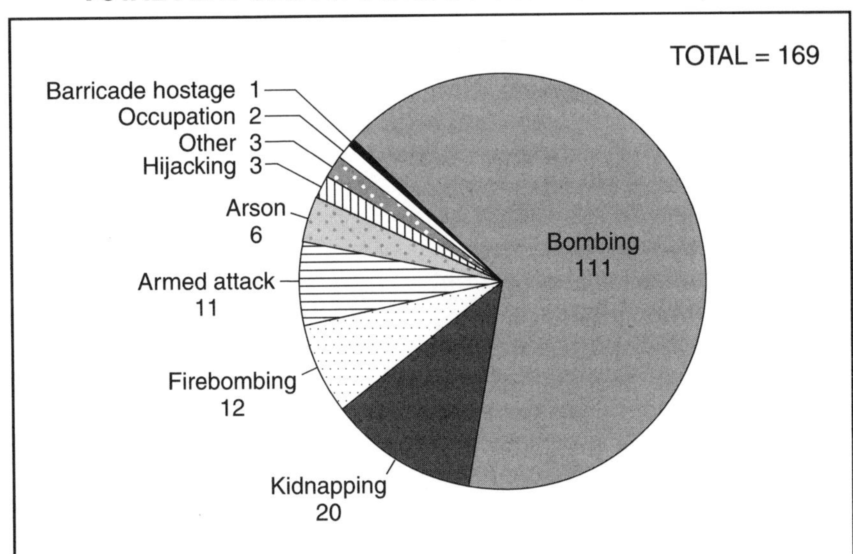

Note: This chart includes attacks against U.S. facilities and attacks in which U.S. citizens suffered casualties.

Source: U.S. Department of State. *Patterns of Global Terrorism 1999.*
URL: http://www.state.gov/www/global/terrorism/1999report/1999index.html.

Who Gets Hurt (1999)

The pie chart "Total Anti–U.S. Attacks by Total U.S. Casualties, 1999" breaks down terrorist victims according to their status. Considerably more U.S. citizens were killed or hurt in 1999 than in 1998, but the total is still relatively low, and it is difficult to draw conclusions from this (thankfully) sparse data. Most U.S. victims in 1999 were businesspeople.

TOTAL ANTI-U.S. ATTACKS BY TOTAL U.S. CASUALTIES, 1999

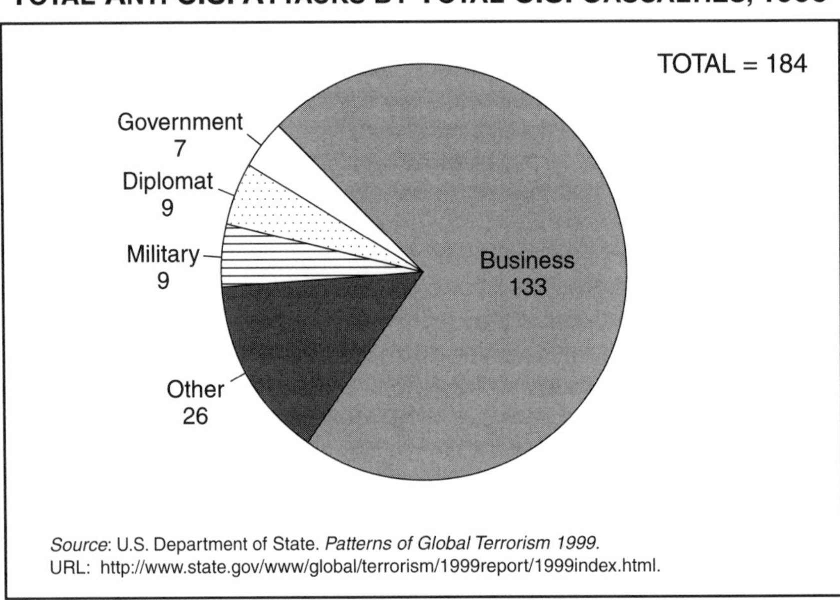

Source: U.S. Department of State. *Patterns of Global Terrorism 1999.*
URL: http://www.state.gov/www/global/terrorism/1999report/1999index.html.

U.S. DOMESTIC TERRORISM

TERRORISM IN THE UNITED STATES, 1990–1997

Statistics on the activities of U.S. domestic terrorist groups are compiled by the Federal Bureau of Investigation (FBI). The chart "Terrorism in the United States, 1990–97" shows the number of incidents, suspected incidents, and incidents prevented, according to the FBI report *Terrorism in the United States 1997*. This report is available online at http://www.fbi.gov/publish/terror/terroris.htm.

TERRORISM IN THE UNITED STATES, 1990–1997

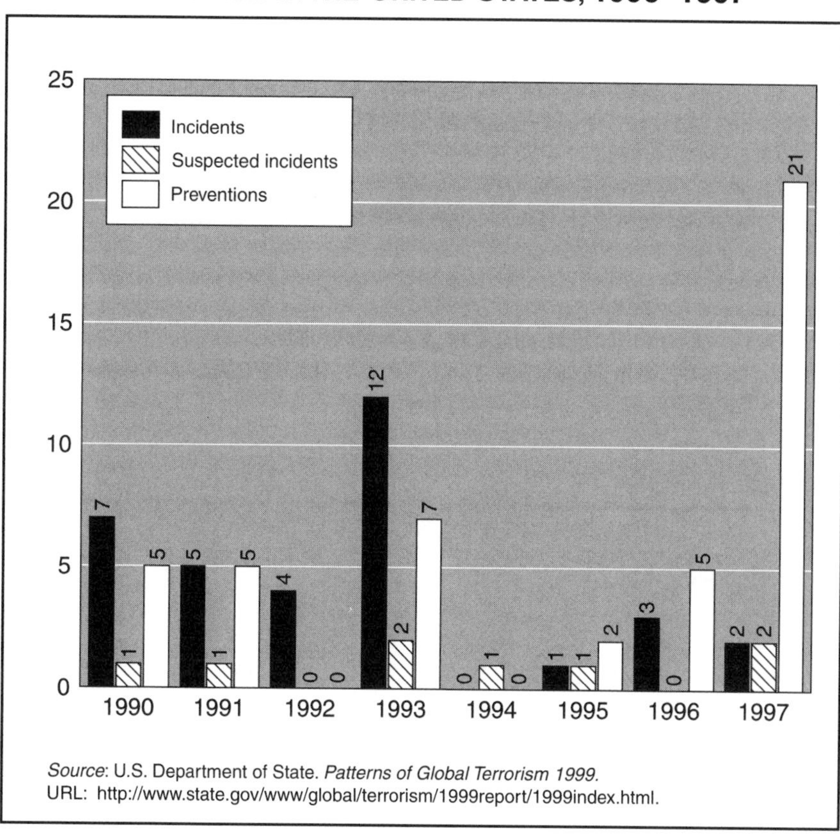

Source: U.S. Department of State. *Patterns of Global Terrorism 1999.*
URL: http://www.state.gov/www/global/terrorism/1999report/1999index.html.

APPENDIX C

STATE DEPARTMENT TERRORISM DESIGNATIONS

FOREIGN TERRORIST ORGANIZATIONS

Designations by Secretary of State Madeleine K. Albright
Released by the Office of the Coordinator for Counterterrorism
October 8, 1999

THE DESIGNATION

Secretary of State Albright today designated 28 organizations as Foreign Terrorist Organizations.

Of these, 27 were redesignations, organizations placed on the list two years ago and remaining on the list. Redesignation is a positive act and represents a decision by the Secretary of State that the organization still meets the criteria specified in law. In the absence of action by the Secretary, the organization would be removed from the list.

Three organizations were dropped from the list because they no longer meet the criteria.

One organization was added to the list because it now meets the criteria.

The Antiterrorism and Effective Death Penalty Act of 1996 authorizes the Secretary of State to make these designations every two years. The Secretary of State may add organizations to the list at any time.

CHANGES

Deletions:
The Manuel Rodriguez Patriotic Front Dissidents (FPMR/D) and the Democratic Front for the Liberation of Palestine (DFLP)* were dropped pri-

marily because of the absence of terrorist activity, as defined by relevant law, by those groups during the past two years. The Khmer Rouge was dropped because it no longer exists as a viable terrorist organization.

Addition:
Al-Qaida, led by Usama bin Ladin, was added because it is responsible for several major terrorist attacks, including the August 1998 bombings of the U.S. embassies in Nairobi, Kenya and Dar Es Salaam, Tanzania.

EFFECTS OF DESIGNATION

Legal

1. It is unlawful for a person in the United States or subject to the jurisdiction of the United States to provide funds or other material support to a designated FTO.
2. Representatives and certain members of a designated FTO, if they are aliens, can be denied visas or excluded from the United States.
3. U.S. financial institutions must block funds of designated FTOs and their agents and report the blockage to the Office of Foreign Assets Control, U.S. Department of the Treasury.

Other Effects

1. Deter donations
2. Increase awareness and knowledge of terrorist organizations

THREE CRITERIA FOR DESIGNATION

1. The organization must be foreign.
2. The organization must engage in terrorist activity as defined in Section 212 (a)(3)(B) of the Immigration and Nationality Act.
3. The organization's activities must threaten the security of U.S. nationals or the national security (national defense, foreign relations, or the economic interests) of the United States.

* The DFLP is still subject to the provisions of an Executive Order signed by President Clinton in January 1995 aimed at terrorist groups that threaten to disrupt the Middle East peace process. The Executive Order prohibits financial transactions with these terrorist groups and blocks their assets in the United States.

FOREIGN TERRORIST ORGANIZATIONS AS OF OCTOBER 8, 1999

(See Narrative descriptions of each organization and a complete listing of their aliases.)

Abu Nidal Organization (ANO)
Abu Sayyaf Group (ASG)
Armed Islamic Group (GIA)
Aum Shinriykyo
Basque Fatherland and Liberty (ETA)
HAMAS (Islamic Resistance Movement)
Harakat ul-Mujahidin (HUM)
Hizballah (Party of God)
Gama'a al-Islamiyya (Islamic Group, IG)
Japanese Red Army (JRA)
al-Jihad
Kach
Kahane Chai
Kurdistan Workers' Party (PKK)
Liberation Tigers of Tamil Elam (LTTE)
Mujahedin-e Khalq Organization (MEK, MKO, NCR, and many others)
National Liberation Army (ELN)
Palestine Islamic Jihad-Shaqaqi Faction (PIJ)
Palestine Liberation Front-Abu Abbas Faction (PLF)
Popular Front for the Liberation of Palestine (PFLP)
Popular Front for the Liberation of Palestine-General Command (PFLP-GC)
al-Qa'ida
Revolutionary Armed Forces of Colombia (FARC)
Revolutionary Organization 17 November (17 November)
Revolutionary People's Liberation Army/Front (DHKP/C)
Revolutionary People's Struggle (ELA)
Shining Path (Sendero Luminoso, SL)
Tupac Amaru Revolutionary Movement (MRTA)

THE PROCESS

Designations Subject to Judicial Review and Congressional Revocation
Under the statute, designations are subject to judicial review. The Secretary of State made her designations following an exhaustive interagency effort. We have kept an administrative record of each recommendation to the Secretary. Because the records would reveal intelligence sources and methods, they are classified.

The designations expire in two years unless renewed. The law also allows groups to be added at any time following a decision by the Secretary, in consultation with the Attorney General and the Secretary of the Treasury. Designations can also be revoked if the Secretary determines that there are grounds for doing so and notifies Congress. Congress can also pass legislation to revoke designations.

BACKGROUND

The law responds to concerns about foreign terrorist organizations raising funds in the United States.

Some terrorist organizations have tried to portray themselves as raising money solely for charitable activities such as clinics or schools. These activities have helped recruit supporters and activists and provided support to terrorists.

Congress was quite aware that terrorist organizations might cloak their activities with professions of good works and addressed the matter squarely:

> *Foreign organizations that engage in terrorist activity are so tainted by their criminal conduct that any contribution to such an organization facilitates that conduct. (Section 301(a)(7)).*

Therefore, any contribution to a designated foreign terrorist organization, regardless of the intended purpose, is prohibited by the statute, unless the contribution is limited to medicine or religious materials.

FREQUENTLY ASKED QUESTIONS

Q: Are any of the designated groups actually raising funds in the United States?

That is always possible, but such an activity would be unlawful.

Q: What if people want to contribute to medical clinics or mosques that may be run by HAMAS or another designated group? How can they provide charitable contributions to, say, Palestinians living in Gaza?

There are numerous ways of contributing to charitable works through private voluntary agencies that are not designated foreign terrorist organizations. Additionally, donations of medicine and religious materials are not prohibited.

Q: Some of these groups seem to have been dormant for some time. Is it appropriate to continue designating them as Foreign Terrorist Organizations?

We note that "engaging in terrorist activities" includes soliciting funds, training, and planning. It is not unusual for groups to remain publicly dormant for long periods while continuing to engage in terrorist activity and then resume terrorist attacks.

We are confident that every organization on the list belongs there. The Secretary's determinations have been tested in court and prevailed, and we believe they would prevail again.

Q: Why isn't the IRA on the list?

There is a strong body of evidence documenting historic IRA involvement in terrorist activity. This evidence precedes the time, two years ago, when we first considered designating the IRA as an FTO.

At that time, the Secretary of State took note of the IRA's unequivocal cease-fire, as well as the subsequent decision by the British government that the cease-fire was "genuine in word and deed." This permitted Sinn Fein to join inclusive, all-party talks in Belfast.

The peace process in Northern Ireland continues, albeit not without obvious difficulties, and we have again determined that the IRA should not be designated at this time. We are, however, concerned over recent indications of increased terrorist activity in Northern Ireland, and we will continue to monitor closely the activities of all paramilitary groups.

Q: What happens if the IRA carries out another act of terrorism, such as killing a police officer or blowing up a police station?

We will not speculate on hypothetical situations. We expect the IRA to adhere to its responsibility to maintain the cease-fire. Obviously, any resumption of violence by the IRA would have a direct impact on the ongoing review.

Q: Are the Administrative records going to be made available to Congress or the public? If not, why not?

Classified summaries of the administrative records were provided to Congress. Each administrative record contains classified information. Some are hundreds of pages long.

Unclassified descriptions of terrorist organizations (including all those designated) appear in the annex of the Department's annual report Patterns of Global Terrorism. We can make copies available. Patterns of Global Terrorism is also available on the State Department's web site.

Q: Since there already was a list of terrorist organizations in Patterns, why not just use the Patterns material?

The designations made under the legislation are based on specific legal criteria, including the requirement for an administrative record. Congressionally mandated administrative records require detailed documentation. This is a much more complicated and time-consuming process than developing the appendix to Patterns.

Q: Why was the MEK designated? They largely target other Iranians. Is this some kind of a grudge match because some of their leaders were involved in the seizure of the U.S. Embassy in Teheran 20 years ago?

We have sufficient grounds for concluding that they are a terrorist organization and continue to engage in terrorist violence. The designation is based on activities much more recent than the takeover of our embassy.

Additionally, directing terrorism against a government or entity with whom we have differences does not exclude an organization from designation as an FTO.

MEK is designated as a Foreign Terrorist Organization because of the acts they commit, not who they act against and not who they are.

Q: There are groups mentioned in Patterns of Global Terrorism that do not appear here. Why is this? Are there foreign policy considerations involved?

This list responds to the requirements of U.S. law, not policy interests.

We are entirely aware that formally designating groups as terrorists invites controversy about those designated and not designated. This list represents our best judgment based on all available information.

Q: How do you plan to disseminate this information to American citizens resident abroad and to U.S. businesses abroad?

While these organizations by definition threaten U.S. nationals or interests or national security, that does not mean we have information that there is going to be an attack in a specific place or at a specific time.

Information about that kind of threats is disseminated in other ways, including Consular Information Sheets, which discuss conditions in individual countries or other mechanisms operated by the Department.

Q: What is the status of the two legal challenges by groups that were designated as FTOs?

On June 25, 1999, the U.S. Court of Appeals for the D.C. Circuit issued a unanimous opinion upholding the Secretary's designation of the LTTE and MEK as Foreign Terrorist Organizations and rejecting various due process and other challenges to the designation statute.

On August 27, the court denied the LTTE and MEK's motions for rehearing and rehearing en banc.

We are still awaiting a decision from the Ninth Circuit in a separate constitutional challenge to the designation statute brought by individuals and groups seeking to make contributions to designated organizations.

APPENDIX D

LEGISLATIVE SUMMARY OF THE ANTITERRORISM AND EFFECTIVE DEATH PENALTY ACT OF 1996

S.735 (Major Legislation)
Public Law: 104–132 (04/24/96)
SPONSOR: Sen Dole (introduced 04/27/95)
SUMMARY:
(REVISED AS OF 04/15/96—Conference report filed in House)
TABLE OF CONTENTS:

- Title V: Nuclear, Biological, and Chemical Weapons Restrictions
- Subtitle A: Nuclear Materials
- Subtitle B: Biological Weapons Restrictions
- Subtitle C: Chemical Weapons Restrictions
- Title VI: Implementation of Plastic Explosives Convention
- Title VII: Criminal Law Modifications to Counter Terrorism
- Subtitle A: Crimes and Penalties
- Subtitle B: Criminal Procedures
- Title VIII: Assistance to Law Enforcement
- Subtitle A: Resources and Security
- Subtitle B: Funding Authorizations for Law Enforcement
- Title IX: Miscellaneous

Antiterrorism and Effective Death Penalty Act of 1996—**Title I: Habeas Corpus Reform**—Amends the Federal judicial code to establish a one-year statute of limitations for habeas corpus actions brought by State prisoners.

(Sec. 102) Specifies that: (1) there shall be no right of appeal from a final order in a habeas corpus proceeding; and (2) unless a circuit justice or judge issues a certificate of appealability, any appeal may not be taken to the court of appeals from the final order in a habeas corpus proceeding in which the detention complained of arises out of process issued by a State or Federal court. Permits such certificate to issue only if the applicant has made a substantial showing of the denial of a constitutional right.

(Sec. 104) Provides that if the applicant has failed to develop the factual basis of a claim in State court proceedings, the Federal court shall not hold an evidentiary hearing on the claim unless: (1) the claim relies on a new rule of constitutional law, made retroactive by the Supreme Court, that was previously unavailable or on a factual predicate that could not have been previously discovered through the exercise of due diligence; and (2) the facts underlying the claim would be sufficient to establish by clear and convincing evidence that, but for constitutional error, no reasonable fact finder would have found the applicant guilty of the underlying offense.

(Sec. 105) Sets forth provisions regarding: (1) the statute of limitations for motions; and (2) limits on second or successive applications.

(Sec. 107) Sets forth special habeas corpus procedures in capital cases. Requires (with exceptions): (1) a district court to render a final determination of an application for habeas corpus brought in a capital case not later than 180 days after the date on which the application is filed; and (2) a court of appeals to hear and render a final determination of any appeal of an order granting or denying such petition within 120 days after the date on which the reply brief is filed and to decide whether to grant a petition or other request for rehearing en banc within 30 days after the date on which the petition for rehearing is filed.

Requires the Administrative Office of United States Courts (Administrative Office) to submit to the Congress an annual report on the compliance by the courts of appeals with the time limitations under this section.

(Sec. 108) Amends the Controlled Substances Act (CSA) to allow the court, upon a finding that investigative, expert, or other services are reasonably necessary for the representation of a defendant in a criminal action in which a defendant is charged with a crime punishable by death and in certain post-conviction proceedings, to authorize the defendant's attorneys to obtain such services and order the payment of fees and expenses. Prohibits any ex parte proceeding, communication, or request (proceeding) from being considered unless a proper showing is made concerning the need for confidentiality. Requires that any such proceeding be transcribed and made a part of the record available for appellate review.

Title II: Justice for Victims—Subtitle A: Mandatory Victim Restitution—Mandatory Victims Restitution Act of 1996—Amends the Federal criminal code to require the court to order restitution of the victim when a convicted defendant is being sentenced for specified offenses (**see** Sec. 204). Authorizes the court to order restitution in certain other cases. Makes specified procedures (**see** Sec. 206) applicable to all orders of restitution.

(Sec. 203) Requires the court to provide, as an explicit condition of a sentence of probation, that the defendant make restitution as ordered, pay the assessment imposed, and notify the court of any material change in his or her economic circumstances that might affect his or her ability to pay restitution, fines, or special assessments.

Repeals certain restrictions on the court's authority to order the making of restitution.

(Sec. 204) Directs the court to order, in addition to any other penalty authorized by law, that the defendant make restitution to the victim of the offense or, if the victim is deceased, to the victim's estate.

Defines "victim" as a person directly and proximately harmed as a result of the commission of an offense for which restitution may be ordered, including any person directly harmed by the defendant's criminal conduct in the course of an offense that involves a scheme, conspiracy, or pattern of criminal activity. Permits a legal guardian or the representative of the victim's estate (other than the defendant), another family member, or any other person appointed as suitable by the court to assume the victim's rights in the case of a victim who is under age 18, incompetent, incapacitated, or deceased.

Sets forth provisions regarding: (1) restitution to persons other than the victim; (2) the form and amount of restitution; and (3) plea agreements not resulting in a conviction.

Requires restitution in all sentencing proceedings for convictions of, or plea agreements relating to charges for, any offense: (1) that is a crime of violence, an offense against property (including fraud), or an offense relating to tampering with consumer products; or (2) in which an identifiable victim has suffered a physical injury or pecuniary loss. Makes exceptions where the number of identifiable victims is so large as to make restitution impracticable or where determining complex issues of fact or the amount of the victim's losses would create an excessive burden on the sentencing process.

(Sec. 205) Authorizes the court, when sentencing a defendant convicted of specified CSA offenses, to order that the defendant make restitution to any victim of such offense. Specifies that a participant in an offense may not be considered a victim of the offense.

Directs the court, in determining whether to order restitution, to consider the amount of the loss sustained by each victim as a result of the offense, the financial resources of the defendant, the financial needs and earning ability of the defendant and the defendant's dependents, and such other factors as the court deems appropriate. Permits the court to decline to order restitution upon determining that the complication and prolongation of the sentencing process resulting from fashioning such an order outweighs the need to provide restitution to any victims.

Sets forth provisions regarding situations in which there is no identifiable victim. Directs that an order of restitution in such case be based on the amount of public harm caused by the offense. Limits the amount of such restitution ordered to the amount of the fine ordered for the offense charged in the case. Directs that such restitution be distributed as follows: 65 percent to the State entity designated to administer crime victim assistance in the State in which the crime occurred and 35 percent to the State entity designated to receive Federal substance abuse block grant funds.

Directs: (1) that certain penalty assessments or fines take precedence over a restitution order; (2) that requests for community restitution be considered in all plea agreements negotiated by the United States; and (3) the United States Sentencing Commission (the Commission) to promulgate guidelines to assist courts in determining the amount of restitution that may be ordered.

Prohibits: (1) the court from making an award if it appears likely that such award would interfere with a forfeiture under the Federal criminal code or the CSA; and (2) any restitution from being ordered under this section until such time as the Commission promulgates its guidelines.

Makes conforming changes to the Violence Against Women Act of 1994 and to telemarketing fraud provisions of the Federal criminal code.

(Sec. 206) Revises procedures for the issuance and enforcement of restitution orders. Directs the court to: (1) order the probation officer to obtain and include in the presentence report, or in a separate report, information sufficient for the court to exercise its discretion in fashioning a restitution order (including a complete accounting of the losses to each victim, any restitution owed pursuant to a plea agreement, and information relating to the economic circumstances of each defendant); and (2) disclose to both the defendant and the attorney for the Government all portions of the report pertaining to such matters. Directs the probation officer to inform the court if the number or identity of victims cannot be reasonably ascertained, or if other circumstances exist that make such requirement impracticable.

Makes specified provisions of the Federal criminal code and Rule 32(c) of the Federal Rules of Criminal Procedure the only rules applicable to proceedings for the issuance and enforcement of restitution orders.

Directs: (1) the attorney for the Government, upon the request of the probation officer but not later than 60 days prior to the date initially set for sentencing and after consulting (to the extent practicable) with all identified victims, to promptly provide the probation officer with a listing of the amounts subject to restitution; and (2) the probation officer, prior to submitting the presentence report, to provide specified notice to identified victims and provide each victim with an affidavit form to submit.

Sets forth provisions regarding: (1) each defendant preparing and filing with the probation officer an affidavit fully describing the defendant's financial resources; (2) the court's authority to require additional documentation or hear testimony; (3) the privacy of any records filed or testimony heard; (4) final determination of the victim's losses and subsequent discovery of further losses; (5) court referral of issues arising in connection with proposed restitution orders to a magistrate judge or special master; and (6) resolution of disputes as to the proper amount or type of restitution.

Directs the court to order restitution to each victim in the full amount of each victim's losses as determined by the court without consideration of the defendant's economic circumstances.

Sets forth further requirements, including provisions regarding the form of payments, situations involving multiple defendants, a prohibition on considering the fact that a victim has received compensation with respect to a loss from insurance or any other source in determining the amount of restitution, notification of material changes in the defendant's economic circumstances, and such adjustment of the payment schedule as the interests of justice require.

Specifies that: (1) a defendant's conviction for an offense involving the act giving rise to a restitution order shall estop the defendant from denying the essential allegations of that offense in any subsequent Federal civil proceeding or State civil proceeding, to the extent consistent with State law, brought by the victim; (2) a restitution order may be enforced by the United States, as specified; and (3) an order of in-kind restitution in the form of services shall be enforced by the probation officer.

Directs the clerk of the court, at the request of a victim named in a restitution order, to issue an abstract of judgment certifying that a judgment has been entered in favor of such victim in the amount specified in the order. Specifies that upon registering, recording, docketing, or indexing such abstract, it shall be a lien on the property of the defendant, subject to specified limitations.

Specifies that a sentence that imposes an order of restitution is a final judgment notwithstanding the fact that such sentence can be subsequently corrected, appealed and modified, amended, or adjusted under specified provisions, or that the defendant may be resentenced.

(Sec. 207) Amends Rule 32(b) of the Federal Rules of Criminal Procedure to require that: (1) a presentence investigation and report, or other report containing information sufficient for the court to enter an order of restitution, be required in any case in which restitution is required to be ordered; and (2) a presentence report contain, in appropriate cases, information sufficient for the court to enter an order of restitution.

Adds restitution to existing provisions governing the imposition of a fine in Federal criminal cases. Directs the court to impose a fine or other monetary penalty only to the extent that such fine or penalty will not impair the ability of the defendant to make restitution required to a victim other than the United States. Sets forth provisions regarding payment schedules, notification to the court of material changes in the defendant's economic circumstances, and default on a restitution fine or payment.

Adds restitution provisions to provisions governing the post sentence administration of fines, including collection. Makes it the responsibility of each victim to notify the Attorney General or the appropriate court entity of any change in the victim's mailing address while restitution is still owed. Directs that the confidentiality of any information relating to a victim be maintained. Sets priorities for the disbursement of money received from a defendant.

Revises provisions regarding civil remedies for satisfaction of an unpaid fine to authorize the United States to enforce a judgment imposing a fine in accordance with the practices and procedures for the enforcement of a civil judgment under Federal or State law. Sets forth provisions regarding: (1) the enforcement of such judgments; (2) termination of liability; (3) liens and the effect of filing notice of a lien; (4) inapplicability of the discharge of debt in bankruptcy proceedings; and (5) applicability of specified provisions to the enforcement of an order of restitution.

Authorizes the court, upon a finding that the defendant is in default on a payment of a fine or restitution, to revoke probation or a term of supervised release, modify the terms or conditions of a probation or a term of supervised release, resentence a defendant, hold the defendant in contempt of court, enter a restraining order or injunction, order the sale of property of the defendant, accept a performance bond, enter or adjust a payment schedule, or take any other action necessary to obtain compliance with the order of a fine or restitution.

Allows any hearing arising out of such default to be conducted by a magistrate judge, subject to de novo review by the court. Requires that proceedings in which the participation of a defendant who is confined in a correctional facility is required or permitted be conducted by telephone, video conference, or other communications technology without removing the prisoner from the facility.

Prohibits incarcerating a defendant solely on the basis of inability to make payments because of indigency.

(Sec. 209) Requires the Attorney General to ensure that: (1) in all plea agreements negotiated by the United States, consideration is given to requesting that the defendant provide full restitution to all the victims; and (2) restitution orders are enforced to the fullest extent of the law.

(Sec. 210) Doubles the special assessments on persons convicted of a felony in Federal cases.

Subtitle B: Jurisdiction for Lawsuits Against Terrorist States—Amends the Federal judicial code to make exceptions to: (1) foreign sovereign immunity for certain cases in which money damages are sought against a foreign government for personal injury or death caused by an act of torture, extra judicial killing, aircraft sabotage, hostage taking, or the provision of material support or resources to terrorists (but sets a ten-year statute of limitation, subject to equitable tolling principles, and directs the court to limit discovery that the Attorney General certifies will interfere with a criminal investigation or prosecution, or a national security operation, related to the incident that gave rise to the cause of action, subject to specified restrictions); and (2) immunity from attachment with respect to a foreign state or an agency or instrumentality of such state.

Subtitle C: Assistance to Victims of Terrorism—Justice for Victims of Terrorism Act of 1996—Amends the Victims of Crime Act of 1984 (VCA) to authorize the Director of the Office of Justice Assistance to make supplemental grants to States: (1) to provide compensation and assistance to State residents who, while outside U.S. territorial boundaries, are victims of a terrorist act or mass violence and are not eligible for compensation under the Omnibus Diplomatic Security and Antiterrorism Act of 1986; and (2) for eligible crime victim compensation and assistance programs to provide emergency relief, including crisis response efforts, assistance, training, and technical assistance, for the benefit of victims of terrorist acts or mass violence occurring within the United States and funding to U.S. Attorney's Offices for use in coordination with State victims compensation and assistance efforts in providing emergency relief.

Revises provisions of such Act to: (1) authorize the Director, if the sums available in the Crime Victims Fund are sufficient to fully provide grants to the States, to retain any portion of the Fund that was deposited during a fiscal year that was in excess of 110 percent of the total amount deposited in the Fund during the preceding fiscal year as an emergency reserve; (2) prohibit such reserve from exceeding $50 million; and (3) permit the emergency reserve to be used for supplemental grants and to supplement the funds available to provide grants to States for compensation and assistance in years in which supplemental grants are needed.

Amends such Act to: (1) permit any amount awarded as part of a grant that remains unspent at the end of a fiscal year in which the grant is made to be expended for the purpose for which the grant is made during the two succeeding fiscal years, at the end of which period any remaining unobligated sums in excess of $500,000 shall be returned to the Treasury (with any remaining unobligated sums in an amount less than $500,000 to be returned to the Fund); and (2) define "base amount" for purposes of crime victim assistance to mean $500,000 and for the territories of the Northern Mariana Islands, Guam, American Samoa, and the Republic of Palau, $200,000, with the latter's share governed by the Compact of Free Association between the United States and the Republic of Palau.

(Sec. 233) Amends the VCA to provide for the compensation of victims of terrorism.

Designates the Federal building at 1314 LeMay Boulevard, Ellsworth Air Force Base, South Dakota, as the Cartney McRaven Child Development Center.

(Sec. 234) Amends the VCA to: (1) prohibit payments to delinquent criminal debtors by State crime victim compensation programs; and (2) exclude victim assistance from income for purposes of determining eligibility for Federal benefits.

(Sec. 235) Directs the trial court in criminal cases where the venue is moved out of State more than 350 miles from the location in which those proceedings originally would have taken place, to order closed circuit televising of the proceedings for viewing by such persons whom the court determines have a compelling interest and who are otherwise unable to view the proceedings by reason of the inconvenience and expense caused by the change of venue. Limits access to such broadcast. Specifies that: (1) the signal so transmitted shall be under the control of the court at all times and shall only be transmitted subject to the terms and conditions imposed by the court; (2) no public broadcast or dissemination shall be made of that signal (and, in the event any tapes are produced in carrying out such provision, such tapes shall be the property of the court and kept under seal); and (3) any violations shall be punishable as contempt of court. Authorizes the Administrative Office to accept donations to enable the courts to carry out such provision.

Title III: International Terrorism Prohibitions—Subtitle A: Prohibition on International Terrorist Fundraising—Amends the Immigration and Nationality Act (INA) to authorize the Secretary of State, in consultation with the Secretary of the Treasury (Secretary) and the Attorney General, to designate an organization as a terrorist organization upon finding that the organization is a foreign organization that engages in terrorist activity and such activity threatens the security of U.S. nationals or U.S. national security.

Sets forth provisions regarding: (1) procedures for such designation, including notification to specified congressional leaders, and the freezing of assets; (2) creation of an administrative record and the handling of classified information; (3) the period of designation; (4) revocation by Act of Congress, revocation based on a change in circumstances, and the effect of revocation; (5) use of the designation in a trial or hearing; (6) judicial review of such designation.

(Sec. 303) Sets penalties for knowingly providing, or attempting or conspiring to provide, material support or resources to a foreign terrorist organization. Requires any financial institution that becomes aware that it has possession of, or control over, any funds in which a foreign terrorist organization or its agent has an interest, to retain possession of or maintain control over such funds and report to the Secretary the existence of such funds, with exceptions. Establishes civil penalties for knowingly failing to comply with such provision.

Sets forth provisions regarding: (1) injunctions; (2) extraterritorial Federal jurisdiction; (3) investigations; and (4) the discovery and handling of classified information in civil proceedings brought by the United States.

Subtitle B: Prohibition on Assistance to Terrorist States—Imposes penalties upon U.S. persons who engage in a financial transaction with a country knowing or having reasonable cause to know that such country has been designated under the Export Administration Act as a country supporting international terrorism, with exceptions.

(Sec. 322) Directs the Administrator of the Federal Aviation Administration to continue in effect the requirement that a foreign air carrier must adopt and use a security program approved by the Administrator. Prohibits the Administrator from approving such a program unless it requires the foreign air carrier in its operations to and from U.S. airports to adhere to the identical security measures that the Administrator requires air carriers serving the same airports to adhere to. Specifies that such requirement shall not be interpreted to limit the ability of the Administrator to impose additional security measures on a foreign air carrier or an air carrier when the Administrator determines that a specific threat warrants such additional measures.

(Sec. 323) Modifies existing provisions setting penalties for providing material support to terrorists, including by: (1) eliminating language that excludes from the definition of "material support or resources" humanitarian assistance to persons not directly involved in violations; and (2) adding language to exclude from such definition medicine or religious materials.

(Sec. 324) Makes findings regarding international terrorism, including that the President should use all necessary means, including covert action and military force, to destroy international infrastructure used by international terrorists.

(Sec. 325) Amends: (1) the Foreign Assistance Act of 1961 to authorize the President to withhold assistance to the governments of countries that aid (including providing military equipment to) terrorist states, with exceptions by presidential waiver when in the national interest; and (2) the International Financial Institutions Act to direct the Secretary to instruct the U.S. executive director of each international financial institution to oppose assistance by such institutions to terrorist states.

(Sec. 328) Revises Foreign Assistance Act provisions regarding antiterrorism assistance to permit arms and ammunition to be provided under such provisions only if they are directly related to antiterrorism assistance. Limits the value of equipment and commodities provided. Repeals a prohibition on using such funds for personnel compensation or benefits.

Makes up to $3 million in any fiscal year available to procure explosives detection devices and other counterterrorism technology and for joint counterterrorism research and development projects on such technology conducted with the North Atlantic Treaty Organization (NATO) and major non-NATO allies under the auspices of the Technical Support Working Group of the Department of State. Sets a $1 million limit on assistance provided to a foreign country for counterterrorism efforts in any fiscal year, subject to specified conditions.

(Sec. 329) Defines "assistance" to mean assistance (excluding international disaster assistance) to or for the benefit of a government of any country that is provided by any means on terms more favorable than generally available in the applicable market.

(Sec. 330) Amends the Arms Export Control Act to prohibit assistance under such Act in a fiscal year to a country that the President determines and certifies to the Congress, by May 15 of the calendar year in which that fiscal year begins, is not cooperating fully with U.S. antiterrorism efforts, subject to presidential waiver if the transaction is essential to U.S. national security interests.

Title IV: Terrorist and Criminal Alien Removal and Exclusion—Subtitle A: Removal of Alien Terrorists—Amends the INA to establish procedures for the removal of alien terrorists.

Directs the Chief Justice of the United States to publicly designate five district court judges from five of the U.S. judicial circuits to constitute a court with jurisdiction to conduct removal proceedings.

Sets forth provisions regarding: (1) terms of such judges; (2) designation of the chief judge of the removal court; and (3) the expeditious and confidential nature of such proceedings.

Authorizes the Attorney General: (1) to seek removal of an alien terrorist by filing an application with the removal court that contains specified information, such as a statement of the facts and circumstances relied on by the Department of Justice (DOJ) to establish probable cause that the alien is a terrorist, that the alien is present in the United States, and that removal under normal immigration procedures would pose a risk to U.S. national security; and (2) to dismiss a removal action under this title at any stage of the proceeding.

Allows a single judge of the removal court, in determining whether to grant an application, to consider, ex parte and in camera, in addition to the information contained in the application: (1) other (including classified) information presented under oath or affirmation; and (2) testimony received in any hearing on the application of which a verbatim record shall be kept.

Sets forth provisions regarding: (1) the approval or denial of an order; and (2) the exclusivity of this title with respect to the rights of the alien regarding removal and expulsion, if an order is issued granting the application.

Directs that, where the application is approved, a removal hearing be conducted as expeditiously as practicable and be open to the public. Sets forth provisions regarding: (1) notice; (2) rights in the hearing, including the right to counsel, to introduce evidence, and (subject to specified limitations) to examine witnesses; (3) subpoenas (but denies aliens access to classified information); (4) discovery; (5) arguments; (6) burden of proof; (7) rules of evidence; (8) determination of deportation; (9) written orders; (10) no right to ancillary relief; (11) appeals; (12) custody and release pending a removal hearing; and (13) custody and release after a removal hearing, including criminal penalty for reentry of alien terrorists and elimination of custody review by habeas corpus.

Subtitle B: Exclusion of Members and Representatives of Terrorist Organizations—Makes being a member or representative of a foreign terrorist organization a basis for exclusion from the United States under the INA.

(Sec. 412) Grants the Secretary of State authority to waive requirements concerning notice of denial of a visa application, or for admission or adjustment of status, in the case of a particular alien or any class or classes of excludable aliens, with exceptions.

(Sec. 413) Denies specified deportation relief for alien terrorists.

(Sec. 414) Deems an alien present in the United States, who has not been admitted after inspection under the INA, to be seeking entry and admission, and subject to examination and exclusion.

Subtitle C: Modification to Asylum Procedures—Prohibits the Attorney General from granting asylum to an alien excludable as a terrorist unless the Attorney General determines that the individual seeking asylum will not be a danger to U.S. security.

(Sec. 422) Authorizes the examining immigration officer, upon determining that an alien seeking entry is excludable under specified provisions (with respect to misrepresentation or insufficient documentation) and does not indicate either an intention to apply for asylum or a fear of persecution, to order the alien excluded from the United States without further hearing or review.

Directs the Attorney General to promulgate regulations to provide for the immediate review by a supervisory asylum office at the port of entry of a determination that an alien does not have a credible fear of persecution.

(Sec. 423) Sets forth provisions regarding limits on judicial review, including preclusion of collateral attacks on the validity of orders of exclusion, special exclusion, or deportation pursuant to this title.

Subtitle D: Criminal Alien Procedural Improvements—Revises the seven-year residency defense against a deportation or exclusion order to permit deportation or exclusion of a permanent resident alien who has been sentenced (currently, imprisoned) to five or more years for an aggravated felony.

(Sec. 432) Permits the Attorney General to authorize an application to a Federal court of competent jurisdiction for, and a judge of such court to grant an order authorizing, disclosure of information contained in the alien's application for adjustment of status to be used: (1) for identification of the alien when there is reason to believe that the alien has been killed or severely incapacitated; (2) for criminal law enforcement purposes against the alien whose application is to be disclosed; or (3) to discover information leading to the location or identity of the alien.

(Sec. 433) Amends the Violent Crime Control and Law Enforcement Act of 1994 to: (1) rename the criminal alien tracking center as the criminal alien identification system; (2) specify that the system shall be used to identify and locate deportable aliens who have committed aggravated felonies; and (3) transfer the system from the Attorney General to the Commissioner of the Immigration and Naturalization Service (INS).

(Sec. 434) Amends the Federal criminal code to: (1) bring certain alien smuggling-related crimes under the purview of the Racketeer Influenced and Corrupt Organizations Act; and (2) authorize wiretaps for alien smuggling investigations.

(Sec. 436) Amends the INA to: (1) expand the criteria for deportation for crimes of moral turpitude; and (2) permit the use of electronic and telephonic media in deportation hearings.

(Sec. 438) Directs the Attorney General and the Commissioner of Immigration and Naturalization to develop an interior (home country) repatriation program.

(Sec. 439) Amends the INA to authorize deportation of nonviolent offenders prior to Federal or State sentence completion.

(Sec. 440) Authorizes State and local law enforcement officials, to the extent permitted by relevant State and local law, to arrest and detain an illegal alien who has previously been convicted of a felony in the United States and who has been deported from or left the United States after such conviction, after obtaining appropriate confirmation from the INS of such individual's status, for such time as may be required for the INS to take that individual into Federal custody for purposes of deporting or removing the alien from the United States.

Directs the Attorney General to cooperate with the States to assure that information in the Attorney General's control, including information in the National Crime Information Center, that would assist State and local law enforcement officials in carrying out such duties is made available to such officials.

(Sec. 441) Revises INA provisions regarding terrorism to provide that any final order of deportation against an alien who is deportable by reason of having committed specified criminal offenses shall not be subject to review by any court. Makes such an order final upon the earlier of a determination by the Board of Immigration Appeals affirming such order or the expiration of the period in which the alien is permitted to seek review of such order by the Board.

Expands the range of offenses for which the Attorney General shall take an alien convicted of a crime into custody upon release (currently, limited to aggravated felonies) for deportation as expeditiously as possible. Repeals provisions under which the Attorney General may release an alien who demonstrates that he or she is not a threat to the community and is likely to appear before any scheduled hearings.

Revises provisions regarding: (1) nonapplicability of requirements that aliens be ineligible for visas and excluded from admission into the United States if such aliens are deportable by reason of having committed specified criminal offenses (currently, limited to those convicted of one or more aggravated felonies and having served at least five years' imprisonment for such felonies); and (2) the definition of "aggravated felony" to expand its scope.

Specifies that when a final order of deportation under administrative process is made against any alien who is deportable by reason of having committed a specified criminal offense, the Attorney General shall have 30 days within which to effect the alien's departure from the United States and shall have sole and unreviewable discretion to waive such provision for aliens who are cooperating with law enforcement authorities or for purposes of national security.

(Sec. 442) Limits collateral attacks on deportation orders.

(Sec. 443) Subjects a conditional permanent resident alien convicted of an aggravated felony to expedited deportation.

(Sec. 444) Sets forth provisions regarding the extradition of aliens who have committed crimes of violence against U.S. nationals. Makes certain Federal criminal code provisions regarding extradition of fugitives applicable to such aliens.

Title V: Nuclear, Biological, and Chemical Weapons Restrictions— Subtitle A: Nuclear Materials—Revises Federal criminal code provisions regarding prohibited transactions involving nuclear materials to cover specified actions involving nuclear byproduct material and actions knowingly causing substantial damage to the environment.

Expands jurisdiction by making such prohibitions applicable where an offender or victim is a U.S. national or a U.S. corporation or other legal entity. Repeals a requirement for jurisdiction that at the time of the offense the nuclear material must have been in use, storage, or transport for peaceful purposes.

Modifies the definition of "nuclear material" to mean material containing any plutonium (currently, with an isotopic concentration not in excess of 80 percent plutonium 238).

(Sec. 503) Directs the Attorney General and the Secretary of Defense to jointly conduct a study and report to the Congress on the number and extent of thefts from military arsenals of firearms, explosives, and other materials that are potentially useful to terrorists.

Subtitle B: Biological Weapons Restrictions—Amends the Federal criminal code to include within the scope of prohibitions regarding biological weapons attempts, threats, and conspiracies to acquire a biological agent, toxin, or delivery system for use as a weapon. Authorizes the United States to obtain an injunction against the threat to engage in prohibited conduct with respect to such prohibitions.

Redefines: (1) "biological agent" to cover certain biological products that may be engineered as a result of biotechnology or certain naturally occurring or bioengineered components of a microorganism, virus, infectious substance, or biological product; (2) "toxin" to include the toxic material of plants, animals, microorganisms, viruses, fungi, or infectious substances, or a recombinant molecule; and (3) "vector" to include certain molecules, including recombinant molecules, or biological products that may be engineered as a result of biotechnology.

Revises provisions regarding the use of weapons of mass destruction to cover threats to use such weapons and the use of any biological agent, toxin, or vector.

Directs the Secretary of Health and Human Services to: (1) establish and maintain a list of each biological agent that has the potential to pose a severe threat to public health and safety; and (2) provide for the establishment and enforcement of safety procedures for the transfer of listed biological agents, safeguards to prevent access to such agents for use in domestic or international terrorism or for any other criminal purpose, the establishment of procedures to protect the public safety in the event of a transfer or potential transfer of a biological agent in violation of the safety procedures or safeguards established, and appropriate availability of biological agents for research, education, and other legitimate purposes.

Subtitle C: Chemical Weapons Restrictions—Amends the Federal criminal code to set penalties with respect to any person who, without lawful authority, uses or attempts or conspires to use a chemical weapon against: (1) a U.S. national while such national is outside the United States; (2) any person within the United States; or (3) any property that is owned, leased, or used by the United States, whether the property is within or outside of the United States.

Directs the President to establish an interagency task force to determine the feasibility and advisability of establishing a facility that recreates both an urban environment and a suburban environment in such a way as to permit the effective testing, training, and evaluation of government personnel who are responsible for responding to the use of chemical and biological weapons in the United States. Expresses the sense of the Congress that such facility, if established, shall be: (1) under the jurisdiction of the Secretary of Defense; and (2) located at a principal facility of the Department of Defense for the testing and evaluation of the use of chemical and biological weapons during any period of armed conflict.

Title VI: Implementation of Plastic Explosives Convention—Prohibits: (1) the manufacture, importation, exportation, shipment, transport, transfer, receipt, or possession of any plastic explosive which does not contain a detection agent, with exceptions; and (2) any person (other than a U.S. agency or the National Guard of any State) possessing any plastic explosive on the effective date of this Act from failing to report to the Secretary the quantity of such explosives possessed, the manufacturer or importer, and any identification marks.

(Sec. 604) Sets forth: (1) penalties for violation of this title; and (2) affirmative defenses.

(Sec. 606) Amends the Tariff Act of 1930 to require the seizure and forfeiture of a plastic explosive which does not contain a detection agent.

Title VII: Criminal Law Modifications to Counter Terrorism—Subtitle A: Crimes and Penalties—Amends the Federal criminal code to increase penalties for: (1) conspiracies involving explosives; (2) specified terrorism crimes, including carrying weapons or explosives on an aircraft; and (3) the use of explosives or arson.

(Sec. 702) Imposes penalties for acts of terrorism transcending national boundaries, including creating a substantial risk of serious bodily injury to another by attempting or conspiring to destroy or damage any structure, conveyance, or other real or personal property within the United States in violation of State or Federal law. Sets forth provisions regarding proof requirements, extraterritorial jurisdiction, the statute of limitations, and detention.

(Sec. 703) Expands a provision regarding destruction or injury of property within special maritime and territorial jurisdiction to cover any structure, conveyance, or other real or personal property.

(Sec. 704) Revises provisions prohibiting injuring property of a foreign government to set penalties for conspiring to kill, kidnap, maim, or injure people in a foreign government.

(Sec. 706) Subjects whoever transfers explosive materials, knowing or having reasonable cause to believe that such materials will be used to commit a crime of violence or a drug trafficking crime, to the same penalties as may be imposed for a first conviction for the use or carrying of an explosive material.

(Sec. 707) Prohibits the possession, or pledge or acceptance as security for a loan, of stolen explosive materials moving in interstate or foreign commerce.

(Sec. 709) Directs the Attorney General to study and report to the Congress concerning: (1) the extent to which there is available to the public material that instructs how to make bombs, destructive devices, and weapons of mass destruction and the extent to which information gained from such material has been used in incidents of domestic and international terrorism; (2) the likelihood that such information may be used in future terrorism incidents; (3) the application of existing Federal laws to such material, any need and utility for additional laws, and an assessment of the extent to which the First Amendment protects such material and its private and commercial distribution.

Subtitle B: Criminal Procedures—Makes penalties imposed upon an individual committing an offense on an aircraft in flight outside the special aircraft jurisdiction of the United States applicable regardless of whether such individual is later found in the United States. Grants jurisdiction over such an offense if: (1) a U.S. national was or would have been on board the aircraft; (2) an offender is a U.S. national; or (3) an offender is found in the United States.

Provides that if the victim of specified offenses is an internationally protected person outside the United States, the United States may exercise jurisdiction if: (1) the victim is a representative, officer, employee, or agent of the United States; (2) an offender is a U.S. national; or (3) an offender is found in the United States.

(Sec. 722) Provides that there is U.S. jurisdiction over specified maritime violence: (1) regardless of whether the activity is prohibited by the State in which it takes place; and (2) committed by a U.S. national or by a stateless person whose habitual residence is in the United States, regardless of whether the activity takes place on a ship flying the flag of a foreign country or outside the United States.

(Sec. 723) Sets penalties for conspiring to commit various terrorism-related offenses.

(Sec. 724) Expands Federal jurisdiction over bomb threats.

(Sec. 725) Modifies prohibitions regarding the use of weapons of mass destruction to include threats to use such weapons and to specify that, to violate such prohibitions, such use must be without lawful authority and the results of such use (or threat) must affect (would have affected) interstate or foreign commerce.

Includes within the definition of "weapon of mass destruction" any weapon designed or intended to cause death or serious bodily injury through the release, dissemination, or impact of toxic or poisonous chemicals or their precursors.

Imposes penalties (including the death penalty, if death results) upon any U.S. national who, without lawful authority and outside the United States, uses, threatens, attempts, or conspires to use a weapon of mass destruction.

(Sec. 726) Adds terrorism offenses to the money laundering statute.

(Sec. 727) Sets penalties for: (1) killing or attempting to kill any U.S. officer engaged in, or on account of, the performance of official duties or any person assisting such an officer or employee; and (2) threatening to assault, kidnap, or murder former Federal officers and employees.

Specifies that Federal criminal code provisions regarding influencing, impeding, or retaliating against a Federal official by threatening or injuring a family member shall not interfere with the investigative authority of the United States Secret Service.

Revises a provision regarding the meaning of the term "deadly or dangerous weapon" in the prohibition against assaulting Federal officers or employees to include a weapon intended to cause death or danger but that fails to do so by reason of a defective component.

(Sec. 728) Includes among the aggravating factors for homicide that the defendant intentionally killed or attempted to kill more than one person in a single criminal episode.

(Sec. 729) Specifies that the time period in which a detention hearing must be held does not include weekends and legal holidays.

(Sec. 730) Directs the Commission to amend the sentencing guidelines so that the adjustment relating to international terrorism only applies to Federal crimes of terrorism.

(Sec. 731) Excludes from the definition of "electronic information" for purposes of wiretap-related definitions electronic funds transfer information stored by a financial institution in a communications system used for the electronic storage and transfer of funds.

(Sec. 732) Directs the Secretary to conduct a study of: (1) the tagging of explosive materials for purposes of detection and identification; (2) the feasibility and practicability of rendering common chemicals used to manufacture explosive materials inert and of imposing controls on certain precursor chemicals used to manufacture explosive materials; and (3) State licensing requirements for the purchase and use of commercial high explosives. Prohibits inclusion of black or smokeless powder among the explosive materials considered within any such study or regulation proposed thereunder. Requires the Secretary, in conducting: (1) such study to consult with Federal, State, and local officials with expertise in the area of chemicals used to manufacture explosive materials; and (2) any portion of such study relating to the regulation and use of fertilizer as a pre-explosive material, explosive material, to consult with and receive input from nonprofit fertilizer research centers.

Sets forth provisions regarding: (1) reporting requirements; (2) hearings; and (3) regulations for the addition of tracer elements to explosive materials manufactured in or imported into the United States under specified circumstances.

Title VIII: Assistance to Law Enforcement—Subtitle A: Resources and Security—Authorizes the Attorney General and the Secretary to support law enforcement training activities in foreign countries, subject to the concurrence of the Secretary of State, for the purpose of improving the effectiveness of the United States in investigating and prosecuting transnational offenses.

(Sec. 802) Expresses the sense of the Congress that each recipient of any sum authorized to be appropriated by this Act should use the money to purchase American-made products.

(Sec. 803) Authorizes the Attorney General and the Secretary to prohibit: (1) any vehicles from parking or standing on any street or roadway adjacent to any building in the District of Columbia used by law enforcement authorities subject to their jurisdiction, that is in whole or in part owned, possessed, or leased to the Federal Government; and (2) any person or entity from conducting business on any property immediately adjacent to any such building.

(Sec. 804) Requires: (1) a provider of wire or electronic communication services or a remote computing service, upon the request of a governmental entity, to take all necessary steps to preserve records and other evidence in its possession pending the issuance of a court order or other process; and (2) that such records be retained for a 90-day period, which shall be extended for an additional 90-day period upon a renewed request by the governmental entity.

(Sec. 805) Directs the Commission to: (1) review and report to the Congress on the deterrent effect of existing guideline levels as they apply to prohibitions against accessing a Federal interest computer without authorization, exceeding authorized access to further a fraud and obtain anything of value, or damaging a computer or program under specified circumstances; and (2) promulgate guidelines that will ensure that individuals convicted of such offenses are incarcerated for not less than six months.

(Sec. 806) Establishes the Commission on the Advancement of Federal Law Enforcement. Sets forth the duties of such Commission, including reviewing, evaluating, and recommending congressional action on: (1) Federal law enforcement priorities for the 21st century, including Federal law enforcement capability to investigate and deter adequately the threat of terrorism facing the United States; (2) the manner in which significant Federal criminal law enforcement operations are conceived, planned, coordinated, and executed; (3) the independent accountability mechanisms that exist, if any, and their efficacy to investigate, address, and correct Federal law enforcement; and (4) the extent to which Federal law enforcement agencies coordinate with State and local law enforcement agencies on operations and programs that directly affect the latter's geographical jurisdiction.

(Sec. 807) Directs the Secretary to: (1) study the use and holding of U.S. currency in foreign countries; and (2) develop useful estimates of the amount of counterfeit U.S. currency that circulates outside the United States each year.

Requires the Secretary to develop an effective international evaluation audit plan. Sets forth provisions regarding: (1) timetables for the submission of a detailed written summary of the plan and the first and subsequent audits; (2) reporting requirements; and (3) a sunset provision.

Directs the Secretary of State to: (1) consider in a timely manner the Secretary's request for the placement of such number of Secret Service agents as the Secretary considers appropriate in posts in overseas embassies; and (2) reach an agreement with the Secretary on such posts as soon as possible, but not later than December 31, 1996.

Directs the Commission to amend the sentencing guidelines to provide an appropriate enhancement of the punishment for a defendant convicted of counterfeiting U.S. currency outside the United States.

(Sec. 808) Directs the Attorney General to: (1) collect data for the calendar year 1990 and each succeeding calendar year thereafter, relating to crimes and incidents of threats and acts of violence against Federal, State, and local government employees and their families in the performance of their lawful duties; (2) establish guidelines for the collection of such data; and (3) publish an annual summary of the data collected, which shall otherwise be used only for research and statistical purposes. Specifies that the Attorney General, the Secretary of State, and the Secret Service are not required to participate in any statistical reporting activity regarding any threats made against any individual for whom that official or the Service is authorized to provide protection.

(Sec. 809) Directs the Secretary to conduct a study and make recommendations concerning: (1) the extent and nature of the deaths and serious injuries of law enforcement officers in the line of duty during the last decade; (2) whether current passive defensive strategies, such as body armor, are adequate to counter the criminal use of firearms against law officers; and (3) the calibers of ammunition that are sold in the greatest quantities, their common uses, the calibers commonly used for civilian defensive or sporting uses that would be affected by any prohibition on non–law enforcement sales of such ammunition if such ammunition is capable of penetrating minimum level bullet resistant vests, and recommendations for increases in body armor capabilities to further protect law enforcement from that threat. Authorizes appropriations.

(Sec. 810) Directs the Attorney General and the Director of the Federal Bureau of Investigation (FBI) to study all applicable laws and guidelines relating to electronic surveillance and the use of pen registers and other trap and trace devices and to report to the Congress: (1) findings and recommendations for the use of electronic surveillance of terrorist or other criminal organizations and for any legal modifications; (2) a summary of instances in which Federal law enforcement authorities may have abused electronic surveillance powers and recommendations (if needed) for constitutional safeguards relating to the use of such powers; and (3) a summary of efforts to use current wiretap authority.

Subtitle B: Funding Authorizations for Law Enforcement—Directs the Attorney General to: (1) enhance the technical support center and tactical operations of the FBI; (2) create an FBI counterterrorism and counterintelligence fund for costs associated with the investigation of terrorism cases; (3) improve the instructional, operational support, and construction of the FBI Academy; (4) construct an FBI laboratory; and (5) increase personnel to support counterterrorism activities. Authorizes the FBI Director to expand the combined DNA Identification System (CODIS) to include Federal crimes and crimes committed in the District of Columbia.

Authorizes the Attorney General to make grants to eligible States to be used by the chief executive officer of the State, in conjunction with units of local government, other States, or any combination thereof, to establish, develop, update, or upgrade: (1) computerized identification systems that are compatible and integrated with the databases of the FBI's National Crime Information Center; (2) the capability to analyze deoxyribonucleic acid in a forensic laboratory in ways that are compatible and integrated with CODIS; and (3) automated fingerprint identification systems that are compatible and integrated with the FBI's Integrated Automated Fingerprint Identification System. Conditions grant eligibility on a State requirement that persons convicted of a felony of a sexual nature provide a specimen for DNA analysis.

Authorizes appropriations for FBI activities to combat terrorism and provides for the allocation of funds among the States.

(Sec. 812) Authorizes appropriations: (1) to help meet the increased needs of the United States Customs Service and INS, including for the detention and removal of alien terrorists; and (2) for the Drug Enforcement Administration (DEA) to fund anti-violence crime initiatives, to fund initiatives to address major violators of Federal anti-drug statutes, and to enhance or replace DEA infrastructure.

(Sec. 815) Authorizes appropriations for DOJ to hire additional Assistant U.S. Attorneys and attorneys within the Criminal Division and to provide for increased security at courthouses and other facilities in which Federal workers are employed. Authorizes the Attorney General to pay rewards and receive from any department or agency funds for the payment of rewards to any individual who assists DOJ in performing its functions.

(Sec. 816) Authorizes appropriations for: (1) Department of the Treasury law enforcement agencies to augment counterterrorism efforts; (2) the Secret Service; (3) the United States Park Police; (4) the Judiciary; and (5) specialized training and equipment to enhance the capability of metropolitan fire and emergency service departments to respond to terrorist attacks.

(Sec. 820) Authorizes appropriations to the National Institute of Justice's Office of Science and Technology to: (1) provide to foreign countries facing an imminent danger of terrorist attack that threatens the U.S. national interest or U.S. nationals assistance in obtaining explosive detection devices and other counterterrorism technology, conducting research and development projects on such technology, and testing and evaluating counterterrorism technologies in those countries; and (2) develop technologies that can be used to combat terrorism, develop standards to ensure the adequacy of products produced and compatibility with relevant national systems, and identify and assess requirements for technologies to assist State and local law enforcement in the national program to combat terrorism.

(Sec. 822) Amends the Omnibus Crime Control and Safe Streets Act of 1968 to authorize the Director of the Bureau of Justice Assistance to make grants under the drug control and system improvement grant program to develop and implement antiterrorism training programs and to procure equipment for use by local law enforcement authorities. Authorizes appropriations.

(Sec. 823) Permits appropriations for activities authorized in this subtitle to be made from the Violent Crime Reduction Trust Fund.

Title IX: Miscellaneous—Declares that all the territorial sea of the United States is part of the United States, is subject to its sovereignty, and, for purposes of Federal criminal jurisdiction, is within its special maritime and territorial jurisdiction. Provides that whoever commits specified crimes on, above, or below any portion of the U.S. territorial sea which would be punishable if committed within the jurisdiction of the State, territory, possession, or district in which the location would be situated if boundaries were extended seaward, shall be guilty of a like offense and subject to a like punishment.

(Sec. 902) Prohibits a Federal, State, or local government agency from using a voter registration card (or other related document) that evidences registration for an election for Federal office as evidence to prove U.S. citizenship.

(Sec. 903) Amends the Federal criminal code to add provisions requiring that information regarding fees for representation in any case be made available to the public.

Revises CSA provisions regarding attorney compensation to direct that appointed counsel be compensated at an hourly rate of not more than $125 for in-court and out-of-court time. Authorizes the Judicial Conference to raise the maximum for hourly payment according to a specified formula. Limits fees and expenses paid for investigative, expert, and other reasonably necessary services authorized to $7,500, with exceptions.

(Sec. 904) Makes the provisions of, and amendments to, this Act severable.

INDEX

Index

Index

Index

Index

Index